REEL ASIAN

REEL ASIAN

ASIAN CANADA ON SCREEN

EDITED BY ELAINE CHANG

First edition

Canadä

Published with the assistance of the Canada Council for the Arts and the Ontario Arts Council. We also acknowledge the Government of Ontario through the Ontario Book Publishing Tax Credit and the Government of Canada through the Book Publishing and Industry Development Program.

Library and Archives Canada Cataloguing in Publication

Reel Asian : Asian Canada on screen / edited by Elaine Chang.

Co-published by the Toronto Reel Asian International Film Festival.
Includes bibliographical references.
ISBN 978-1-55245-192-2

1. Asian Canadian motion picture producers and directors. 2. Asian Canadians in motion pictures. 3. Motion pictures--Canada--History. 4. Independent films--Canada--History and criticism. 5. Experimental films--Canada--History and criticism. I. Chang, Elaine Kyung
PN1993.5.C3R44 2007 791.43089'95071 C2007-905649-0

CONTENTS

8 **ACKNOWLEDGMENTS**

10 **INTRODUCTION: HYPHE-NATION;**
OR, SCREENING 'ASIAN CANADA'
Elaine Chang

24 **OVERVIEW:**
LOOKING BACK AND LOOKING FORWARD
Richard Fung & Midi Onodera

36 **TRACKING SHOTS:**
MAPPING THE ASIAN CANADIAN FILMSCAPE
Alice Shih

48 **EATING CHINESE**
Cheuk Kwan & Lily Cho

64 **STILLS PART I**

72 **RICE BOWL DIARIES**
Kwoi Gin

80 **F-WORDS**
Ann Marie Fleming & Mina Shum

98 **MEMORY, AGAIN**
Khanhthuan Tran, Pamila Matharu & Elaine Chang

112 **VANCOUVER ASIAN:**
WEST COAST FILM CULTURES, ON THE RIM AND AT THE END OF THE LINE
Su-Anne Yeo

126 **THE KING OF MAIN: UNPLUGGED**
Paul Wong & Christine Miguel

134 **'LET YOUR FINGERS DO THE WALKING': REREADING HO TAM'S *THE YELLOW PAGES***
Ho Tam & Alice Ming Wai Jim

146 **STILLS PART II**

158 **MEN AND MONSTERS**
David Eng & Leon Aureus

172 **ALBERTASIA: ASIAN CANADIAN FILMS ON THE PRAIRIES**
Mieko Ouchi

186 **home misses you**
Nobu Adilman & Romeo Candido

198 **SEARCHING FOR THE WHITE-HAIRED GIRL**
Karin Lee & Loretta Todd

210 **LETTERS FROM SEOUL**
Helen Lee & Mike Hoolboom

224 **ADVENTURES IN CELLULOID GOLD MOUNTAIN**
Keith Lock

240 **STILLS PART III**

250 **QUEER HONGCOUVER AND OTHER FICTIONS**
Wayne Yung & Nguyen Tan Hoang

264 **BLACK MAGIC BUDDHISM**
Julia Kwan & Iris Yudai

272 **CINEMATIC IMAG(IN)INGS OF THE JAPANESE CANADIAN INTERNMENT**
Monika Kin Gagnon

284 **CHINATOWN TOMB RAIDER: REFLECTIONS ON KUNG FU FRIDAYS**
Colin Geddes, Jason Anderson & Phil Tsui

298 **LA CHINOISE; OR, 'THE OTHER'**
Mary Stephen

314 **REEL ASIAN, THEN AND NOW**
Anita Lee & Cameron Bailey

322 **SNAPSHOTS**
Nicole Chung

326 **STILLS PART IV**

RESOURCES
335 Contributors
340 Artists' Works
348 Distributor Contact Information
350 Image and Photo Credits

ACKNOWLEDGMENTS

This book is indebted first and foremost to the brilliant work of all the contributors, and was made possible by the generous support of the Canada Council for the Arts. The idea for this collection emerged from plans to celebrate the tenth Anniversary of the Toronto Reel Asian International Film Festival in 2006, and the entire festival staff, advisory board and board of directors must be recognized for their efforts, particularly for their help in nominating prospective contributors. Special thanks go out to Grace Bai, Aram Collier and Deanna Wong for their truly invaluable contributions.

Coach House Books was consummately professional and committed to this project from beginning to end, and I would like to thank Alana Wilcox for her skilled proofreading and Christina Palassio for her excellent judgment and grace under fire. It was a pleasure and privilege to work closely with our designer, Gilbert Li, to whom this book owes its striking good looks, down to the last detail.

I am profoundly grateful to the book's dedicated and multi-talented team of project manager Kevin Lim, copyeditor John Mani and the coordinator of the Resources section Tom Robles. The three of them brought incredible energy, intelligence and their individual and combined skills to different aspects of the production process, and worked long, often strange hours while juggling other jobs and their studies simultaneously.

In addition to their primary responsibilities, Kevin was instrumental in realizing the two photo essays in this anthology, and Tom transcribed the major portion of the recorded conversations included here.

A collection such as this can ultimately only gesture toward the range, diversity and fullness of its subject; its reach invariably exceeds its grasp. Given the limitations of space and schedules, and the simple fact that there are a great many talented Asian Canadian film- and video-makers in the world, many exceptional artists and writers do not appear in this volume. A number of them, along with other friends and fellow travellers, have nonetheless generously lent their time, influence and assistance to this project.

Finally, I would like to express my deep personal appreciation to Michael Capellupo, Betty Julian, Sarah Lightbody and Dot Tuer for their insightful advice and support while I have been working on this book.

Elaine Chang
October 2007

INTRODUCTION

HYPHE-NATION; OR, SCREENING 'ASIAN CANADA'

ELAINE CHANG

Being a one-and-a-half-generation Chinese Canadian, you have one foot in and one foot out and no strong sense of belonging.
—Julia Kwan

It will take a few generations to melt that barrier and, hopefully, that word 'Asian' will drop out of the lexicon and we will be identified as Canadians and not as hyphenated ones.
—Cheuk Kwan

I think a lot about the transitory space that I exist in, the journeyman in me—here, but not here.
—Ho Tam

NOTES ON HYPHENATION

To refer to Asian Canadian film and video as a hyphenated cinema might seem an obvious or unnecessarily controversial move, worrying the existence or non-existence of punctuation marks perhaps a bit like scratching at dissolving stitches after they have already been absorbed by the skin. Debates in Asian North American cultural studies over the significance and appropriate use of the hyphen have undoubtedly suffered from a certain banality—a banality also apparent in the increasingly routine observation that all North Americans are in some sense 'hyphenated.' Yet the crux of the discussion has been and remains germane to those situated in, not in and/or between racial and national entities such as 'Asia' and 'Canada' or 'Asia' and 'America,' and who continue to seek means to articulate the contradictions and negotiations that bind these categories in their unsettled and mutually unsettling dynamics. For its multiple charges, and for simply occupying the gaps between identifiers at once coextensive (or equal), and subordinate and super-ordinate (or unequal), the hyphen still marks a contentious spot on our cultural-political maps; it serves to punctuate an otherwise awkwardly or deceptively empty space.[1] This mediary space or interval—indeed, in the above quotations from Julia Kwan and Ho Tam, it would seem both a time and a place—has been both easy to overlook and prone to co-optation.

Asian American scholars have offered a number of provocative and competing interpretations of the trouble with hyphens. According to literary critic David Leiwei Li, the presence or absence of the hyphen locates the user squarely on one side of a cultural-political divide: 'the hyphenated "Asian-American" is the rendering used by the dominant (white) culture; without the hyphen, "Asian American" is the way Asians describe themselves.'[2] Of interest in this polarizing formulation is the reading of the hyphen as a sign of exclusion, a gesture that enfolds the 'Asian-American' into a mainstream 'American' discourse at the same that it asserts the homogeneity and separateness of a white majority. In David Palumbo-Liu's *Asian/American: Historical Crossings of a Racial Frontier,* the question of inclusion and exclusion is not decided by the terminology's users but rather inheres in the two-term structure itself, in a 'transitivity' of identifications that the author emphatically re-marks with/as a slash:

> The nature of Asian American social subjectivity now vacillates between whiteness and color. Its visibility is of a particular texture and density; its function is always to trace a racial minority's possibilities for assimilation. . . . Asia/America resides *in transit,* as a point of reference on the horizon that is part of *both* a "minority" identity and a "majority" identity. This constant transitivity evinces precisely the malleability and resistance of "America" with regard to racial reformation.[3]

Hyphen or slash? I think what matters may be less the choice to hyphenate or not to hyphenate than the relationship between the signifiers 'Asian' and 'American' that these markings both and/or either reveal and/or conceal: conjuncture and rupture, an exorable pressure to assimilate or the impossibility of assimilation, a permanent suture and/or an impermeable barrier interposed between presumably distinct racial-national formations. The fluctuations of intractability and elasticity in the very language of identification evoke impasse as well as possibility. For cultural critic Kandice Chuh, 'Asian American' is 'a term *in difference from itself*—at once making a claim of achieved subjectivity and referring to the impossibility of that achievement.'[4] According to theorist and filmmaker Trinh T. Minh-ha:

> The predicament of crossing boundaries cannot be merely rejected or accepted. It has to be confronted in its controversies. There is indeed little hope of speaking this simultaneously outside-inside

actuality into existence in simple, polarizing black-and-white terms. The challenge of the hyphenated reality lies in the hyphen itself: the *becoming* Asian-American; the realm in-between, where predetermined rules cannot fully apply.[5]

For the challenges of becoming that it encodes, the hyphen offers a suggestive metaphor for the Asian Canadian screen, the slash perhaps an image in miniature of a 'slanted screen'[6]: an in-between or off-centre representational space devised and projected onto by many of the contributors to this anthology. In these pages, Ann Marie Fleming describes her work's often at once critical and comedic sensibility as 'sideways.' Helen Lee refers to her 'sideways and askance' way of viewing her own experience in the Asian American world. Several of Keith Lock's 'Adventures in Celluloid Gold Mountain' have navigated the interstices of the Canadian film industry, felicitous accidents and the blind spots of institutional racism. As the essays and conversations gathered here demonstrate, the screen slants and cuts more than one way.

ASIA/CANADA: SPLIT SCREENS, AMBIVALENT IMAGES

Philip Rosen has argued that 'The concept of a national cinema is always implicated in a dialectic of nation and anti-nation.'[7] Asia's status as 'anti-nation,' its exclusion from the formation of Canada and its national cinema, is abundantly apparent in a number of founding contradictions. In her essay for this volume, Alice Shih notes that the Canadian Pacific Railway's vital sponsorship of an early national film industry was underwritten, like the railway itself, by thousands of Chinese workers imported as a surplus labour force beginning in 1881. The exploitation of Chinese labour, along with the genocidal clearing of First Nations peoples from the land, is the underside or repressed of the dazzling Canadian landscapes packaged in CPR-commissioned travelogues, commodity spectacles created to entice Anglo-American and European tourists as well as what Christopher E. Gittings has called the 'right/white kind of invader-settlers' to populate the expanding colony.[8] The implications of this racist disavowal reverberate in the contemporary context, relevant to the operation of cinematic images as well as the politics of production, exhibition and reception today.

As Benedict Anderson's classic study contends, the nation is an 'imagined community,' a 'deep, horizontal comradeship'[9] projected across differences and geographical distances. Film as a technology of fantasy[10] certainly helped to engineer early collective imaginings of a 'right/white' Canada from east to west, the 49th Parallel to the Arctic Circle, in dialectical opposition to the various 'anti-nationals' that would threaten its purity and cohesiveness. *Back to God's Country* (David M. Hartford, 1910), starring Nell Shipman, opens with the public humiliation and murder of a Chinese man in a northern saloon, a gesture that, as Gittings suggests, sanctions the white claim to Canada's natural resources from the outset by marking the Asian other's entry into the Gold Rush as avaricious and therefore illegitimate.[11] Before killing Shan Tung, a drunken, burly, hairy French Canadian trapper (itself a demeaning stereotype) slices off the 'Chinaman's' queue, reclaiming it as a trophy and as a prop in a mocking dance that he performs for the amusement of the other saloon patrons. The act conflates cultural castration and the assimilationist imperative, effecting one kind of murder before the Chinese interloper in the Canadian space is then slain.

Yet while it is tempting to read the disturbing opening frames of *Back to God's Country,* or the loathsome entirety of a film like *Secrets of Chinatown* (Fred Newmayer, 1935),[12] as straightforward exercises in racist representation, it can be self-defeating to take these images at face value, to seal them in a falsely unified conception of the stereotype and its power to define and circumscribe the 'other.' As Homi Bhabha suggests, the stereotype is a fetish, a metonymic displacement of an '"impossible" object' that the racist obsessively claims to know: a 'fantasy that dramatizes the impossible desire for a pure, undifferentiated origin.'[13] The trapper's expropriation of Shan Tung's queue to consolidate community is fetishistic and fantastic in this sense, as is the mimicry of 'Chineseness' performed by the lead detective in *Secrets of Chinatown,* Donegal Dawn, executed supposedly to perfection in improbably dark black face, a turban and a very weird accent. The severed hair, the makeup, the untraceable accent: these detachable, dislocated masks of Asian difference are arguably cinematic souvenirs of a *failure* to fathom the other and achieve or retrieve an indivisible, original white Canadian nationhood at the other's expense. The screen from the very beginnings of 'our' film history is split or ambivalent in this key respect.

Detecting such fractures in national or culturally dominant self-imaginings can interrupt and intervene into racist, sexist, homophobic and other pejorative forms of representation. A number of filmmakers in this collection work (and play) with the play between fetishistic images and the objects they refer to and defer. David Eng, Ann Marie Fleming, Richard Fung, Helen Lee, Midi Onodera, Mieko Ouchi, Ho Tam, Paul Wong, Wayne Yung and others have infiltrated stereotypes and other reified images in their art, at times reiterating them with a Butlerian difference,[14] as can be seen in Ho Tam's *Pocahontas: TransWorld Remix* (1998), Wayne Yung's *The Queen's Cantonese* (1998) and Mieko Ouchi's impersonation of Marilyn Monroe in *Shepherd's Pie and Sushi* (1998). Ouchi intriguingly both recalls and defamiliarizes the screen icon by displacing and replacing her signature platinum blonde hair, blue eyes and beauty mark around and onto a recognizably Asian face. The unexpected difference the viewer confronts in this instance of 'race drag' may be complicated, visibly and invisibly, by the fact of the impersonator's bi-racial identity. In this and other works, the split between celluloid or video as opaque surface and as transparency is acknowledged and exacerbated. Midi Onodera's use of split screens and multiple framing often exploits the slippage between the thing and its cinematic materialization, decomposing composition in ways that estrange the aesthetic object and disrupt the visual field. These kinds of breaks and interstitial openings become spaces for possibly reimagining the normative (perceptual, social, cultural) ties that bind what a spectator is seeing to an external referent.

At the same time, images do not only (fail to) reflect back on or displace some unknowable, 'impossible object'; they also act on viewers in the world. As W. J. T. Mitchell has argued, visual images have lives of their own. They want, love and, in some cases, take hostage:

> The stereotype is an especially important case of the living image because it occupies [the] middle ground between fantasy and technical reality, a more complexly intimate zone in which the image is, as it were, painted or laminated directly onto the body of a living being, and inscribed into the perceptual apparatus of a beholder. It forms a mask, or what W. E. B. DuBois called a "veil," that interposes itself between persons. . . . [I]t is the pictures—the stereotypes, the caricatures, the peremptory, prejudicial images that mediate between persons and social groups—that seem to take on a life of their own—and a deadly, dangerous life at that—in the rituals of the racist (or sexist) encounter.

> And it is precisely because the status of these pictures is so slippery and mobile, ranging from phenomenological universals, cognitive templates for categories of otherness, to virulently prejudicial distortions, that their life is so difficult to contain.[15]

The ability of images to shape social reality and their capacity to persist and proliferate as if on their own are engaged by a number of contributors here. Monika Kin Gagnon traces a particular splitting of the national screen over time in the National Film Board's documentary representations of the Japanese Canadian internment, beginning with the cinematic containment strategies employed by the blatantly propagandistic *Of Japanese Descent: An Interim Report* (1945), produced as part of an initially pan-Canadian, 'right/white' nation-building project during John Grierson's tenure as NFB Film Commissioner.[16] David Eng and Leon Aureus discuss the myopia of an industry that seems to offer the same limited yet almost self-propagating repertoire of the same small roles to Asian male actors. Aureus suggests that to cast an Asian actor as an iced-coffee drink-dispensing monster in a convenience store chain's commercial is a non-innocent act, however unintentional; it is an example, perhaps, of what Mitchell describes as the 'lamination' of the monstrous image on an otherwise largely invisible Asian male body.

THE VISIBILITY OF ASIAN CANADIAN VISIBILITY

> *There is, in other words, a visibility of visibility—a visibility that is the condition of possibility for what becomes visible, that may derive a certain intelligibility from the latter but cannot be simply reduced to it.*
> —Rey Chow[17]

To create an anthology that takes Asian Canadian film and video as its subject matter is to make a bid for recognition in a complex and contradictory cultural-political field, in which it is difficult, if not impossible, to see anything or anyone 'as they are.' As discussed above, onscreen images mediate between reality and fantasy, hyphenating them (if you will) in both directions. On the one hand, no film or video—not even the documentary variant, as Monika Kin Gagnon, Karin Lee and Loretta Todd, and Khanhthuan Tran and Pamila Matharu demonstrate—transparently scopes unequivocal, empirical truth. On the other hand, film and video play undeniably significant roles in orchestrating social reality, including the ongoing determination of those who cannot or will not be seen or heard. Attempts to identify, let alone promote, an Asian Canadian cinema as such would thus seem to be both problematic and strategically imperative.

Cultural theorist Rey Chow writes that 'the fetishization of identity as it is currently found in the study of cinematic images . . . tends to proceed with a Janus-faced logic.'[18] Identity-based interventions such as feminist film theory and minority cinema studies have, she contends, confined themselves to the very visual realm onto which they have displaced a much broader political battlefield, limiting their efforts to commending or rebuking images that appear on the stages and screens of a now 'virtual field of global visibility' and a '"Look at me! Look at us!"'[19] culture for their putative authenticity or inauthenticity. 'There are those,' Chow notes, 'who, mistaking simple visual presence for the (entirety of) visibility, will always insist on investing artificial images with an anthropomorphic realism.'[20] In his conversation here with Nguyen Tan Hoang, Wayne Yung calls attention to precisely this mistaken investment in accusations that his videos 'misrepresent' gay Asian experience, to which he has responded by inviting such critics to make their own videos. Yung further describes, in an insightful and hilarious spin on Chow's observation, having recognized that:

> . . . purely 'positive representations' of Asian Canadians were boring, unrealistic, and often counterproductive. (It can become a straitjacket if you're not allowed to show your 'unacceptable' side.) I depicted these attitudes in my videos, especially in *Lotus Sisters* (1996) and *The Queen's Cantonese* (1998), but in such an overblown way that it looks like Vancouver is completely dominated by radically queer Asians, which it certainly isn't. It's more like a 'serving suggestion,' where the glossy photo looks much more appetizing than the real thing, or a fantasy of how I wish Vancouver really was.

Yung's notion of a 'serving suggestion' conjures the wishful magic of the image that Chow rightly argues is suppressed in a great deal of current thinking about cinematic representation. It also points to the forces that enable and disable visibility in a larger, beyond-the-screen sense, to the fact, for example, that Vancouver is not dominated by radically queer Asians: far from it. This is where 'the condition of possibility for something to become visible' must be, if not deduced from onscreen visibility, then thought together with it, coactively and case by case. I think Chow offers a compelling and illuminating analysis of the 'repressive hypothesis' governing much identity-focused work in cinema- and media-related studies and activism. However, I also find that her readings of the sentimental in contemporary Chinese film—'the tenacity, in the midst of global visibility, . . . of residual significatory traces of a different kind of social behavioral order'[21]—are themselves somewhat limited, in that they tend to occlude an important dimension of global visibility: namely, the shifting, particularized material conditions of film/video production and distribution. In a transnational marketplace in which certain commodified forms of Asianness are being increasingly, even voraciously, consumed, it may be important to ask not only what specific types of Asian film dominate the offerings and why—but what else is there to consume? What kinds of works are not being made, or have been made but not seen, and why not? What does becoming visible really, fully mean and entail?

To ask these sorts of questions need not necessarily be to fall back on preconceptions of an enduring and essentialized identity prior to the image's capacity for distortion, to demand more of the 'positive representations' of an ethnic/racial or cultural minority group that Yung quite accurately notes are often boring to watch and straitjacketing to create. It can be to inquire into some of the precise ways and means of showing, telling and seeing that constitute the mechanisms of local and global visibilities. Canada is fairly unique among multi-ethnic, post-industrial societies for its official understanding of difference in terms of 'visible minorities'; attributes such as skin colour, gender and able-bodiedness comprise some allegedly equivalent coordinates of a national grid for identifying (among) citizens—the 'majority,' by contrast and extension, invisible or less visible on this map. Perhaps because vision is both so privileged and so vexed in the Canadian cultural-political framework, it seems neither easy nor altogether useful to extricate questions regarding the cinema or media spectacle and spectatorship from a more far-reaching context of visibility: one that includes employment, entitlement and access to social services, government subsidization of culture and the arts, mobility, voting, buying and other practices of daily life.

The contributors to this collection telescope areas for investigating the visibility of Asian Canadian visibility both on and off the screen. Several of them do so in part by interrogating the label for what it obscures from view: other social locations and the democratizing potential of technological expertise (Onodera); a largely unreflected and culturally specific assumption that 'identity' is private property, anchored in notions of private life that do not translate well outside North America (Yung); mixed-race and hybrid identities (Nobu Adilman, Nicole Chung, Fleming, Ouchi); and the traffic of the 'particular' with the 'universal' (e.g., Romeo Candido, Fleming, Cheuk Kwan, Julia Kwan, Mina Shum). Others, like Richard Fung, Karin Lee and Ho Tam, struggle with the challenging, palpable divide between art and off-screen activism while at the same time practicing their inseparability in their videos and films. As an optic, 'Asian Canadianness' clearly works unevenly across institutional, economic, regional, linguistic, technological, thematic, generic and other specificities, as well as differences by ethnic and national origin, gender and sexuality. Su-Anne Yeo suggests that concentrated movements of capital, talent and product between western Canada, the western US and the Pacific Rim render west coast film cultures distinctive, creating the formative conditions for the diverse work of highly individualized Asian Canadian film and video artists such as Ling Chiu, Karin Lee, Desiree Lim, Michelle Wong and Paul Wong. A number of contributors—including Colin Geddes, Kwoi Gin, Cheuk Kwan and Lily Cho, Mary Stephen, and Wayne Yung and Nguyen Tan Hoang—consider and track displacement, travel and cultural migration within Asian diasporas that far exceed a Canadian frame.

The mediation of 'Asian' and 'Canadian' by historically ambivalent institutions[22] registers in an institutional ambivalence that reads across the span of this anthology. Many artists acknowledge the vital, invaluable support of NFB diversity initiatives, the Canada Council for the Arts, provincial arts councils, the Canadian Broadcasting Corporation and other bodies. Yet at the same time that these organizations are genuinely appreciated and applauded for their constitutive role in developing something like an Asian Canadian film and video culture, it would seem also understood that they have established certain limitations, shaped governing norms of participation in regional and national art-making enterprises, and laid down steps by which members of pre-identified groups can ascend to onscreen visibility. In a way, these artists are thus seen before they are or can be seen on screen, in another Janus-faced operation whereby the support of 'visible minorities' could be said to 'minoritize' them, or render them visible as minorities, again or in the first place.

Contributors to this volume remark similar double-binds in the artist-run centres that have been the crucible for many independent film- and video-makers, and in the smaller, community-based film festivals that have been crucial in nurturing and showcasing their work. Both outside and inside, anti- or extra-institutional and institutionally dependent, ARCs and specialized festivals perform supplementary[23] kinds of work, in that they both expose and compensate for what totalizing structures may lack. Numerous artists and critics here note the pitfalls of an allegedly all-inclusive notion of Canadian multiculturalism that, in practice, often means that the 'centre' remains unchallenged while the 'margins' proliferate, and also help to bolster the power and apparent neutrality and centrality of the centre. It is, for instance, widely, complacently assumed that minority filmmakers have their own small, safe places in which to make and screen their work (see Fung and Onodera, Shih), and that the true sign of arrival and success is the 'maturation' or 'graduation' of a minority artist to a mainstream, one that would appear to be unmarked racially or otherwise if only by virtue of comparisons with the 'niche' production and exhibition channels.

These quandaries number among the challenges faced by an organization like the Toronto Reel Asian International Film Festival, to which this book owes its impetus and its main title. Many of the contributors have come together in recognition of the festival's support of their work, and its influence in both dismantling and forging older and newer imagined communities. Like the many facets of Reel Asian, the pieces and pictures assembled here are variously critical, celebratory, searching, irreverent, reflective, funny, lyrical and visionary; established and emergent artists are represented, and persons and places near and far. At the same time, this anthology does not and cannot presume to offer any overarching or comprehensive portrait of a multiply hyphenated Asian Canadian cinema, and indeed reproduces many of the problems of the categories it both critiques and repeats. 'Asian Canadian' can be a term of resistance, marking a national difference within a notion of shared ethnicity or race (e.g., 'Asian American') or an ethnic/racial difference within a notion of shared nationality (e.g., 'Canadian'). But it can also operate as a term of elision, collapsing other differences while preserving the authority of primary or empiricist designations by race and nation. The virtual omission of South Asian Canada from the purview of this collection may be a case in point, deriving from but by no means justified by Reel Asian's particular genesis, as festival co-founder Anita Lee recounts in her conversation with Cameron Bailey, amidst myriad other Toronto-based festivals in 1996. The terms and the images mobilized here do not invoke, cover or exhaust any Asian Canadian essence or totality; they mediate partially and imperfectly between plural realities and delimited representations. Perhaps this is why the word 'reel' in Reel Asian is so suggestive,[24] and why readers might be inspired by this collection to look, and to envision visibility, both within and beyond its pages.

1. The hyphen's simultaneous demarcation and erasure of a demographically complex space is suggested by the title of Anne Marie Nakagawa's documentary on mixed-race Canadians, entitled *Between: Living in the Hyphen* (2005). The NFB-produced documentary takes issue with the assumption that 'in Canada, diversity often means "one ethnicity + hyphen + Canadian"' (National Film Board of Canada website, http://www.nfb.ca/collection/films/fiche/?id=51629xv=h&lg=en&exp=112204, accessed 2 July 2007).

2. David Leiwei Li, *Imagining the Nation: Asian American Literature and Cultural Consent* (Stanford: Stanford University Press, 1998), 207, n. 12.

3. David Palumbo-Liu, *Asian/American: Historical Crossings of a Racial Frontier* (Stanford: Stanford University Press, 1999), 5.

4. Kandice Chuh, *Imagine Otherwise: On Asian Americanist Critique* (Durham, NC: Duke University Press, 2003), 9.

5. Trinh T. Minh-ha, *When the Moon Waxes Red: Representation, Gender and Cultural Politics* (New York and London: Routledge, 1991), 157.

6. I borrow the expression from the title of Jeff Adachi's 2006 documentary, *The Slanted Screen: Asian Men in Film and Television.*

7. Philip Rosen, 'Nation and Anti-nation: Concepts of National Cinema in the "New" Media Era,' *Diaspora* 5.3 (1996): 375–402, 391; quoted in Christopher E. Gittings, *Canadian National Cinema* (London and New York: Routledge, 2002), 1.

8. Gittings, *Canadian National Cinema,* 8.

9. Benedict Anderson, *Imagined Communities: Reflections on the Origin and Spread of Nationalism* (London and New York: Verso, 2000), 7.

10. See Peter X. Feng's *Identities in Motion: Asian American Film and Video* (Durham, NC: Duke University Press, 2002) for a nuanced, sustained discussion of the distinction between 'reality' and 'fantasy' in film, and the implications of this distinction for readings of race and ethnicity at the level of the cinematic image. It is precisely because film is a 'technology of fantasy' that it is contestable and resistible, that images and identities move in more than one sense and direction.

11. Gittings, *Canadian National Cinema,* 23.

12. This would-be British 'quota-quickie' is steeped in anti-Asian racism, from its representation of eastern religion as the occult to its depiction of drugs, white slavery and what Homi Bhabha

has called the 'duplicitous Asiatic' (*The Location of Culture* [London and New York: Routledge, 1994], 75). Keith Lock's documentary on the fascinating life of a pioneering Chinese Canadian restaurateur, *The Road Chosen: The Lem Wong Story* (1997), incorporates some revealing clips from *Secrets of Chinatown*.

13. Bhabha, *The Location of Culture,* 81.

14. In *Gender Trouble: Feminism and the Subversion of Identity* (New York and London: Routledge, 1999), Judith Butler has theorized parody and impersonation as denaturalizing re-performances of bodily regimes, serving both to reinscribe and to subvert them.

15. W. J. T. Mitchell, *What Do Pictures Want? The Lives and Loves of Images* (Chicago and London: University of Chicago Press, 2005), 295–6 and 297.

16. By Gittings's provocative reading, *Of Japanese Descent* furnishes a striking example of the NFB's original work as an ideological state apparatus, creating a community of properly (white, anglophone) Canadian subjects in part by 'offering spectators the vicious pleasure of consuming stereotypes of its cultural and racial Others' (*Canadian National Cinema,* 75; see esp. 69–75).

17. Rey Chow, *Sentimental Fabulations, Contemporary Chinese Films: Attachment in the Age of Global Visibility* (New York: Columbia University Press, 2007), 11; italics hers.

18. Chow, 12.

19. Chow, 11.

20. Chow, 11.

21. Chow, 22–3. Chow enlists the term *wenqing zhuyi*—'warm sentiment-ism,' connoting moderation and tolerance as well as 'touchy-feely,' more western-style emotionalism—to elaborate a definition of the sentimental that she locates in a number of 'typical situations' in recent Chinese films. These include 'filiality,' 'the preparation, consumption, sharing and/or offering of food' and 'childhood and old age.'

22. As Gittings notes, 'It would take forty-six years before the NFB would shift its institutional structure to fund the representation of racial difference as an identifying co-ordinate of Canadian-ness under the New Initiatives in Film programme of Studio D' (*Canadian National Cinema,* 84).

23. Jacques Derrida's concept of the supplement was first introduced to the anglophone North American academy in his 1966 lecture, 'Structure, Sign and Play in the Discourse of the Human Sciences,' *Writing and Difference,* trans. Alan Bass (Chicago: University of Chicago Press, 1978), 278–93 and 339.

24. Colin Geddes's appearance in this volume might conform more to a 'Reel Asian' than to any 'real Asian' logic, and not only because so many people closely affiliated with the festival enthusiastically suggested his involvement. In his reclamation and recirculation of little-known and forgotten Asian genre cinema, he has made a distinctive mark on the Asian Canadian screen.

OVERVIEW: LOOKING BACK AND LOOKING FORWARD

RICHARD FUNG & MIDI ONODERA

Richard Fung, still from *Dirty Laundry* (1996).

Over the course of a few weeks, in between crazy deadlines, looming projects and personal obligations, Toronto-based artists Richard Fung and Midi Onodera sat down to have an extended email conversation. Although the two have known each other for over twenty years, this was a rare opportunity for them to come together, if not in person then through print, to discuss concerns about their work, their creative practice and some of the pressures they've encountered in their careers.

MIDI ONODERA: Unofficially, I began making films back in 1979 when I was still in high school. I was fortunate enough to attend a film studies class where we screened a variety of different films—from NFB documentaries to old gems such as *The Cabinet of Dr. Caligari* (1920), a groundbreaking German Expressionist film by Robert Wiene. At the end of the term we could choose to make a super 8 film or write an essay. Naturally, I chose to make a film. From the moment I picked up the camera, I never looked back. The desire to make films struck me as something that was both creatively challenging and empowering. I can't say that my early work reflects any political awareness in terms of gender or race, and back then it hadn't yet consciously occurred to me that I might be a lesbian. I would have to say that it wasn't until I spent time at OCAD in the Experimental department that I began to view the world with a finer lens. When did you start making videos and why? Did you approach your work from a political position or was it motivated by the passion of working with moving images?

RICHARD FUNG: Like you, I studied at the Ontario College of Art, OCA before it acquired the D for Design. I majored in what was called Photoelectric Arts, the precursor to Integrated Media, the area I now teach in. After leaving school, I got a job as a community video animator at Lawrence Heights, a public housing area in Toronto that was getting bad press. My job was to train people in the community to produce their own images, which were then aired on the community TV channel. I later got a degree in cinema studies and was very interested in the language of the moving image, but even so it took me a long time to 'own' the word 'artist'; I saw my work as primarily social and political. So I think we were starting from different places. By the time I interviewed you for my first independent video, *Orientations: Lesbian and Gay Asians* (1984), you'd already made short experimental films. Those works, as I remember them, didn't have identity markers. In fact, in the video you talked about a primary affinity with punk and artistic communities. I was in the midst of organizing lesbian and gay Asians, so in a sense, I was at the centre of that identity project, but I always felt outside essentialized categories. Growing up in Trinidad during the Black Power era gave me a different perspective on what it meant to be Chinese or Asian. And in the '70s when I came out, I was often the only person of colour at queer events.

In your landmark short, *Ten Cents a Dance (Parallax)* (1986), you and Anna Gronau feature in an interracial lesbian flirtation scene set in a Japanese restaurant. Is this the first time you dealt with ethnicity and queer sexuality together? What led up to that decision?

MO: When I decided to make *Ten Cents A Dance (Parallax),* I originally never intended to do a piece that was specifically lesbian/gay/interracial; the scenes that finally ended up on the screen were conceived through a collaborative process with the non-actors involved. It wasn't until after the film was shot, and I was dealing with various post-production censorship issues, that it became apparent that perhaps the characters and the subject of a one-night stand might be controversial within a mainstream context. Then, when the film started to be screened at various festivals, the political impact of the work hit me. As you will recall, the gay and lesbian film circuit was in its infancy and it felt like we were all just beginning to find our footing—or perhaps it was just me. I remember when you approached me to be in *Orientations,* I honestly hadn't really publicly acknowledged what it meant or means to be an Asian lesbian.

Your work was/is very empowering on a personal and community level. It opened discussion on identity and made 'visible' the invisibility of being a gay or lesbian Asian. I actually never knew your academic background in detail, so it makes perfect sense that you were approaching video with a completely different agenda. I am very interested in hearing your thoughts and perhaps a bit about how you approached *Orientations: Lesbian and Gay Asians.* I don't think it was a particularly open interview. I recall being a bit suspicious of what I considered to be 'serious' politics. I think I was just too involved in exploring my artistic process and trying to do something interesting with the moving image. Although I officially came out during my years at OCA, the lesbian/feminist awakening was difficult. Back then, as you probably recall, some of the L/F communities were rather anti-men, gay or straight. There was an intensity about the time that was never easy to figure out, and I always felt as if I was being tested—about what I thought and how I saw my work.

Was there one thing/incident/memory that motivated you to focus on work that was coming from a more 'community-based' perspective? And then, why did it take you a long time to 'own' the word 'artist'? What kinds of controversial markers of identity did it bring up for you and for your audience? Do you think that these points are relevant today, to a younger generation?

RF: I don't believe there was one thing. I actually came out as gay before I had any sort of relationship with a man—that might tell you something. I was also influenced in my introduction to video by my studies with Sylvia Spring, who had recently finished the first feature fiction film directed by a Canadian woman since Nell Shipman: *Madeleine Is* (1971). She taught for one year at OCA and had us document the University of Toronto library workers' strike. She taught us 'guerrilla television,' and so my use of the medium was influenced by the various social movements of that time. It was this orientation that held me back from identifying my practice as 'artistic,' even though my second tape, *Chinese Characters* (1986), was clearly an art tape and not a social-issues documentary. My distance from the term was heartfelt, and not a political or judgmental stance—I admired my artist friends, I just didn't think it was me. I think I began to use the term for myself because it began to seem pretentious not to after having received arts grants and such. After a residency at the Banff Centre in the early '90s I became fascinated by the process of visual artists and have learned a lot from them.

If I think of younger queer Asian film- and video-makers today—younger than us, anyway—I see quite a range of approaches. Some, like Wayne Yung, who is now based in Germany, are still engaging the politics of race and sexuality head on, but with an aesthetic precision, technical polish and an approach to identity as contingency that is quite different from the '80s. Others, like Mishann Lau, are also making reference to race, culture and sexuality, but the pleasure of watching a film like *Shaolin Sisters* (2004) is as much about clever writing as it is about the 'politics.' Folks like Alison Kobayashi and Ho Tam seem very much in that productive, overlapping zone between media and visual arts.

I'm interested in your own training, because you really took the technical aspect seriously. There is an attention to the art of filmmaking that characterized your work from the start. Weren't you in the professional union?

MO: I guess I came out, as well, before I was involved with another woman; hmm. As we are discussing the issues of coming out and making work, it of course makes sense that we are talking about how our identities are formed and how we perceive ourselves—rather than how others observe us through their filter of the physical body or more specifically through the indicators of race, gender, age, etc. I think that's why I gravitated toward the identity of an artist rather than one that seemed to me an external or 'assumed' identity. Of course I know that I am a woman working primarily in a male domain, and perhaps that's why I became so caught up in the technical side. I felt and still feel that as an artist (there I go again), I need to understand the tools of my craft so that I can not only use them as they were designed to be used, but also 'break the rules' and 'be inventive.'

I was tired of men telling me what I could and could not do; I was fed up with their stereotypical notions that a woman couldn't understand the tech side of film/video-making.

When I work with people, I look at the skills they bring to the table, and now automatically expect that they will respect me in the same way. Perhaps this is a sign of getting old, but when you've been working with moving images for almost thirty years, it does something to the way you operate in the world. When I think of younger artists/filmmakers today, I want to mentor and am interested in young women. There is still such a small number of women authoring media work. When I speak with some of my academic friends, I am always amazed to hear the same stories that I heard back when I was young. They tell me that young women are still intimidated by technology. They are afraid of making mistakes (in front of their male colleagues), looking foolish (in front of their male colleagues), etc. This is a terrible disappointment to me since I think technology is getting easier and more accessible everyday. But this kind of techno-insecurity seems to stem from the larger global issue of women's identities in the twenty-first century. Young women don't seem to own what it means to be a feminist; I've heard that to some, the word 'feminist' equals 'bitch' (and not in a good, reappropriated meaning of the word). Whatever happened to equal pay for equal work? Whatever happened to the reproductive rights of women? One only has to look toward the blatant erosion of the basic right to choose in the US. Perhaps Canada, with its current Conservative government, is the next to act. Being supportive of young women film/video-makers is important for the next generation—without these women taking control over the technology, how many personal stories or good stories will not be told? Even for those women who have been making work for years and who now have families—both children and aging parents to look after—the creative path always seems to be the road less taken. We are called upon to be the caregivers and asked to give up our time to nurture others. But I know that I am ranting; perhaps I'm being a bitch, or perhaps I'm just an old feminist.

As an educator, what are you seeing in your classes? How does identity create or locate itself in the next generation? I know that you've mentioned some Asian queer artists, but does the work that is produced by queer Asians *still have to have* queer and/or Asian content? Do you think that we're still at that point in the debate, or has technology moved us into another direction of identity politics? I don't mean in the sense of technological determinism, I am merely wondering if technology has truly allowed us to reach audiences in another way, or if we are still speaking to 'the converted,' a specialized audience yet perhaps in a more worldwide (www.) way?

RF: Funny you should mention the gender disparity. I don't know if it's always intimidation, but you're right that fewer female than male students become geeks or have a techno aesthetic. Though there are exceptions, my female students often shine at a conceptual level; male students can get stuck in trying to reproduce the genres they like. In teaching I stress 'appropriate technology.' I try to give students a sense of technical choices: some projects need to be slick and some should be down and dirty.

Many young women in my classes are impatient with any implication that they may be oppressed as women; they see themselves as having choices and being in different circumstances from feminist writers. Women students are often hostile when reading Laura Mulvey's work on the male gaze,[1] for example, and talk about the ways that men's bodies are objectified today. I recognize the ways that their consciousness is in fact different from pre-feminist women, but as someone who came of age in the '70s, when style was so politicized, I am struck by the spirited resurgence of looks-based femininity.

It's not that common that my students produce work that arises from their identities or social locations, even though I show videos and films by queer artists, racially and culturally diverse artists, Aboriginal artists and disabled artists. I go for the gamut. I think it may not be seen as cool or creative enough, especially at the lower levels. When I do get these projects, I emphasize that the success of the work is in the specific story they choose to tell and in their storytelling, broadly speaking.

For myself, I haven't been making work on either queer or Asian themes. My most recent single channel piece is a doc on contemporary art in Trinidad, and my current installation project is on a Palestinian Canadian. What I find, though, is that the queer and Asian distribution and exhibition circuits are so developed that it becomes harder to circulate work that does not fit into these slots. It is hard to place it. Have you found this to be true?

MO: I think what I am hearing from your comments is the feeling that we're somehow being restricted by our past identity constructions. By this I mean that the younger generation is naturally turning away from the previous one. Young women today don't think there is any need to be concerned with gender equality because they believe they are equal. But some may not have reached a point in their work careers where they may face the glass ceiling that women of my generation encountered.

The same thing goes for work created today that seems to be located in identity politics. Our generation was focused on this kind of work in the '80s and '90s as a response to the absence of voices. So, naturally, the younger generation has also turned away from this kind of work. I agree that it's not enough nowadays to produce work that focuses solely on 'coming-out stories'—referring to race, gender or sexuality. But if we move on from there, then what is it that defines Asian or queer work? Are we once again addressing the cultural/racial/gender/sexual orientation of the maker? How has identity shifted, and how does it locate itself in the work that we choose to do now?

I feel that the queer and Asian exhibition and distribution networks have become institutionalized and restrictive. There seems to be little support or interest in work that doesn't, as you say, 'fit into these slots.' In some cases, I had a larger and more diverse audience for my work when the 'alternative' distribution/festival culture was just beginning to be developed more than twenty years ago. Now it seems that as I choose to expand the subject matter of my work, it gets more difficult to locate the audiences who might be interested.

As I speak to other women film/video-makers, we all see the same thing happening on the international film festival circuit. There seem to be fewer women programmers in the alternative/independent film circuit. And then within a mainstream context, there are fewer women and fewer people of colour in programming positions, and given the number of alternative festivals there are out there, it is sometimes easier to believe that works by queers and people of colour will be taken up at 'specialty' festivals rather than included in a mainstream context. In other words, although the number of works by queers and people of colour continue to grow, the titles and perhaps their makers are still ghettoized by the mainstream. Now we have our own screening places, so no need to come knocking on our door.

Within the mainstream festival circuit, the emphasis is on male-centred drama and quirky oddball 'family' dramas. When I finished *I have no memory of my direction* (2005), which is a 77-minute 'experimental' video, it became obvious to me that the work didn't fit within any kind of current framework, alternative or mainstream. It was rejected by so many festivals that had previously showcased my work that it was quite shocking. I understand that there are different format concerns when dealing with a long-form piece, and that there are never enough programming slots, so the majority of work that gets programmed is short films/videos.

I think in reaction to this experience, I again turned to technology. In late 2005, I began a project to make 365 short 'movies': one per day. This year-long project focused mainly on using toy camera technology. Recently I've felt dragged down by distribution and exhibition concerns, so by shooting with toys I rediscovered a playfulness that I had forgotten. The thirty-second to one-minute shorts were an incredible creative challenge since I tried not to repeat myself but always tried to look for something different. They were all designed for the small format of an iPod or online viewing. For a while I was posting them online—free to whomever wanted to see them. But recently a distributor has purchased 160 titles, so I've pulled down the website. I will, however, be posting the other 205 films on my site and will probably end up doing another 160 to replace the purchased titles, just to have 365 available online.

In part, I see that the web still has enormous untapped potential for reaching audiences. Once again, it has become an alternative distribution path—but aesthetically, works online or produced for an iPod or cellphone are very different from the large movie theatre experience. For me, it's not so much about producing work that fits within a convention; rather, I am interested in work that pushes me to see and read the world in a different way. It's making work that of course is informed by my politics and aesthetics, but not dictated by it. Your current work is not specifically queer or Asian—where do you place it in the context of your own personal creative development, and then within the larger exhibition/distribution structure?

RF: I have been thinking of the arc of your career, in fact, from films with few markers of identity to ruminations in different genres on sexuality, gender and ethnicity. I was struck that *I have no memory of my direction*

Midi Onodera, still from *Basement Girl* (2000).

(2005) develops ideas begun with *Made in Japan* (1985) twenty years earlier, both I guess riffing on Chris Marker's *Sans Soleil* (1983). It seems to me that your work moves in spirals, ever forward but simultaneously circling back to reconsider previously visited territory.

I think I also move in spirals. I keep coming back to two elements that haunt me: (1) Trinidad, the country of my birth, and (2) my extended family. Whenever I think I'm done with them, something that has been tickling my mind suddenly presents itself as a possible project. These are about the past, though, and I'm interested in confronting the present. I want to make work on Toronto, where I live now. It is intimidating as it's too familiar, too messy; it's hard to get the distance.

You've done experimental, documentary, drama and hybrid forms. You've worked in film, video and now web-based digital media. What holds it together for you? Do you have a driving central interest?

MO: Looking over your body of work, I think your thoughts about the connections between the past and current pieces are quite accurate. Like you, I think that it's not necessarily the genre or the format that ties everything together, but rather the content and the exploration of the familiar themes that keeps resurfacing in our work. I think taking on Toronto as a

Richard Fung, still from *Sea in the Blood* (2000).

subject is interesting, and as you say, it will be difficult to find that distance. However, I trust that by delving into the city, you may find you have a clearer picture of yourself and your relationship to the place you now call home.

1. Laura Mulvey, *Visual and Other Pleasures* (Bloomington: Indiana University Press, 1989).

TRACKING SHOTS

MAPPING THE ASIAN CANADIAN FILMSCAPE

ALICE SHIH

The Cinematographe, an early film camera-projector, was reported to have been invented by the Lumière brothers in 1895. The world gradually caught on and Canada is said to have had its first film screening as early as 1896. However, early Canadian productions were few and insignificant, compared to our neighbour south of the border. These early Canadian commissioned films were made mostly by Americans or the English, as they were considered 'expert' in this new technology. Perhaps inadvertently, the Canadian Pacific Railway became instrumental in the advent of Asian Canadian filmmaking. Most of the pioneering films produced in the late nineteenth century were travelogues showcasing the distinctive Canadian landscape in an effort to entice tourists, and were commissioned by the CPR. Chinese labourers were brought in by the CPR to help build the railroad in 1881, more than twenty years after the first wave of Chinese that arrived in Canada with the Gold Rush in British Columbia around 1858.

It is perhaps a grim historical irony that Asian Canadian filmmaking owes its existence, in part, to the CPR, which both stimulated Chinese immigration in its exploitation of imported workers and produced the first Canadian films. From the Chinese Exclusion laws to the Japanese internment, and over waves of Korean, Filipino, Vietnamese and Hong Kong Chinese migration from the 1950s to the '90s, the history of Asian immigration and settlement in Canada is complex, multiple and rife with discriminatory legislation and practice. The long-term effects of past discrimination as well as the myriad facets of the immigrant experience, past and present, are richly represented in the work of Asian Canadian film- and video-makers. One of the issues this essay means to address is the lengthy, approximately seventy-year gap between the introduction of film in Canada and the first examples of Asian Canadian filmmaking. Another is the question of how to ensure the continued production, dissemination and visibility of Asian Canadian film/video and Asian film/video in Canada in an era of shrinking resources coupled with unprecedented access to this work.

TRACKING SHOT 1: HISTORY

Despite the fact that the Chinese settled both in Canada and in the US at roughly the same time, Asian American film predates any Canadian counterpart by many years. The first Chinese American director on record is a woman named Marion Wong. She made *The Curse of Quon Gwon: When the Far East Mingles with the West* in 1916. According to the San Francisco International Asian American Film Festival, *Curse*, a love story, featured Wong and many of her family members as individuals placed under a curse by a Chinese god because of their westernization. After its completion, the film did not find distribution and disappeared, never having met an audience.

Distinguished Chinese American personnel who worked in the film industry came on the scene much earlier than our Canadian counterparts as well. Cinematographer James Wong Howe and his cousin, the charismatic but ill-fated actress Anna May Wong, were both being recognized for their talent in the 1920s. However, it wasn't until 1954 that James Wong Howe got to direct his first movie, *Go, Man, Go!* Howe became the first Asian American director to work within the Hollywood system; Japanese American silent star Sussue Hayakawa had previously gone his own route, independent of the studio system. Around 1918, he established his own production company, Haworth Pictures, to write, produce and later direct Asian-themed films starring himself and his wife, Tsuru Aoki. His films are largely portrayals of the immigrant's yearning to assimilate into a society free of racial discrimination. His films fell out of popularity in 1922 with the rise of anti-Asian sentiment during the post-WWI economic slump.

Films with Asian content helmed by non-Asians were also made much earlier in the US than Canada, like D.W. Griffith's *Broken Blossoms* in 1919, with Caucasian actors in Oriental drag so as to avoid the slightest hint of miscegenation. 'Chinatown fiction,' a genre reinforcing 'chink' stereotypes as vicious, immoral and deceitful, was also produced at the time, which eventually led to the popular *Fu Manchu* series for a few decades. Canadians also tried their hand at this genre with the British 'quota film,' *Secrets of Chinatown*, in 1935, where Chinese were portrayed as criminals who practiced exotic witchcraft to cast spells on Caucasians. Approximately twenty years later, Asians were given a new image in Hollywood mainstream representation: that of the exotic lover. Miyoshi Umeki, playing Red Buttons's love interest, proudly took home the best supporting actress Oscar in 1957 for *Sayonara*, the first-ever nomination and win for an Asian performer. In 1960, Eurasian Nancy Kwan's portrayal of an Asian prostitute with an undying love for her Caucasian lover in

The World of Suzie Wong further reinforced the stereotype of the submissive and sensual Asian woman, a compliant alternative to the modern North American woman. James Shigeta established himself as the only Asian romantic leading man in the late 1950s. Canadian director David Secter followed suit in 1966 with *The Offering*, a romantic love story about a visiting Chinese dancer and a Caucasian stagehand.

Asian-themed films made by non-Asians performed a certain kind of political and ideological function. By the late 1950s, North Americans had developed a sympathetic view of the Chinese, who were supposed to be suffering mightily under Communist rule. The Japanese needed to be guided away from imperialism, and other Asian countries were so backward that all of them needed to be rescued by the West. These films by non-Asians tended to have Caucasian heroes who emerged as the Asians' 'great white saviours,' to whom the benighted Asians would be forever indebted and grateful.

Having established a presence in Canada for more than a century, it was not until the late '60s and early '70s that Asian Canadians finally ventured into filmmaking. Some were visual experimentalists while others were social and political activists who worked in documentaries; most of them were unknown to the general cinema-going public. The best known of these pioneers were future Governor General Adrienne Clarkson and Jesse Nishihata, both of whom worked on TV documentaries not intended for theatrical release.

There was not much of an indie film scene forty years ago, but more independent productions started to appear sporadically in the mid-'70s. The first Asian Canadian experimental feature, *Everything Everywhere Again Alive* (1975) was made by Keith Lock, who started making films in 1969, when he was seventeen. Keith's student film, *Flights of Frenzy*, won the Best Super 8 Award at the UNESCO Tenth Muse International in Amsterdam. Apart from being one of the first Asian Canadian filmmakers, Lock also contributed to the burgeoning film community as a founding member of the Toronto Filmmakers' Co-op in 1969, which eventually became the Liaison of Independent Filmmakers of Toronto (LIFT). In 1973, pioneering Vancouver-based video artist Paul Wong helped found a non-profit, artist-run video production, exhibition and distribution centre, Satellite Video Exchange Society, since renamed Video In (VI). Following Wong's inspirational example, an active supporter of VI is Wayne Yung, a member of the next generation of Asian Canadian media artists.

The '70s produced many blossoming experimental artists with the arrival of the avant-garde film and video scenes in Toronto, Montreal and Vancouver. For these artists, film was not merely a vehicle for conveying narrative but a visually expressive medium in its own right. This opening up of greater opportunities and applications for the medium inspired some Asian artists to conduct their aesthetic experiments on film and video. In mainstream cinemas, however, Asians were invisible on the Canadian screen, with the exception of Bruce Lee flicks and other imported martial arts films. Awareness of Asian Canadians was as yet not a part of the dominant national consciousness.

In 1977, after working for years at the CBC, Jesse Nishihata independently produced *The Inquiry Film: A Report on the Mackenzie Pipeline Inquiry*, which went on to win a 1977 Canadian Film Award (the future Genies) for best documentary over sixty minutes. The Canadian tax-shelter law, with its introduction of the Capital Cost Allowance in the late '70s to early '80s, stimulated massive Canadian productions, but only a few Asian Canadians benefited from it.

The '80s were the planting and germinating period for Asian Canadian filmmaking. All four major areas of filmmaking—experimental, animation, documentary and drama—witnessed the emergence of Asian Canadian talent. Documentaries and animation works were well developed, thanks in part to years of nurturing by the CBC and NFB. Experimental works, particularly in video, were embraced by Canada's burgeoning arts scenes. However, there was still no Asian representation on the dramatic screen with the exception of humiliating stereotypes. Some North American talents found it alienating, as they saw no positive Asian screen images and finally decided to make some changes. Filmmakers like Wayne Wang in the US started to thematize minority voices, stories and communities, in close conjunction with the consciousness-raising and identity-politics movements that had begun in the 1960s. The inspirational extended run of *Chan is Missing* (1982) helped raise Asian consciousness in Canada and showed Asian Canadians that the mainstream market was ready for diversity on screen. Asian Canadian dramas started to emerge. These films were usually made by struggling first-generation Asian immigrants, or roots-searching second- and third-generation Asians. Other second- and third-generation Asian filmmakers who had completely assimilated into mainstream society produced works that did not present any visible Asian content at all. Stories that went beyond such dominant concerns as racial discriminaton, immigration and issues of identity to explore other problems and themes gradually emerged.

The Asian Canadian population by the 1980s was a diverse mix. As discussed previously, offspring of the first wave of Asians were third- or even fourth-generation Asian Canadian. With government immigration policy welcoming Asians in the '80s, there were also 'fresh-off-the-boat' immigrants who were still struggling to fit in. Important immigrant filmmakers included Richard Fung, who came to Canada from Trinidad, Jeannette Loakman from England, and Ho Tam and Kal Ng from Hong Kong. Their experiences were poles apart and their vastly different concerns and priorities are reflected in the diversity of their stories.

Diversity exists even within the same generation. Art has never been a popular career choice among Asian Canadians. Many immigrant parents, themselves with little to fall back on, perceive the arts as an economically unstable proposition from which their children should be discouraged. It has taken guts and determination for Asian Canadian filmmakers to subsist and persist. Some of them demonstrated an inclination toward filmmaking very early on in life, like Mina Shum and Ann Marie Fleming, but others stumbled into the director's chair by accident, in many cases against their parents' wishes. Julia Kwan wanted to be a writer, but, uncomfortable letting others fiddle with her words, has also ended up a director. Richard Fung is a social activist turned director. Khanhthuan Tran went to art school to study painting and came out a filmmaker. Their different paths are one index of difference and diversity within one generation of filmmakers. Yet their stories are always personally significant, uniquely Canadian with an Asian flavour, and never genre pieces. These films are not always easy for an audience to appreciate without pre-existing exposure to or experience of an immigrant community; perhaps less successful in Asia, these films have found their audience and success in the Asian diaspora.

Although each of these filmmakers excels in one particular film form, many Asian Canadians have crossed generic lines to experiment in different filmmaking media and disciplines. Ann Marie Fleming has produced an impressive body of work and garnered awards in areas as diverse as personal documentaries, experimental films, animation and dramas. Keith Lock has gradually moved from experimental work into dramas and documentaries.

Midi Onodera, initially an experimental filmmaker, at one point developed an interest in drama. Richard Fung started out as a documentary media activist and ventured successfully into personal and experimental films and videos. Their works have never been commercial, with most pieces self-funded through grants or family members. With film and video co-ops springing up across the nation, they have been able to work independently on small budgets, but limits have also been imposed on the length of their productions as well as their access to audiences.

The West Coast art scene was shaping up in the 1980s with emerging visual artists-turned-filmmakers like Fumiko Kiyooka, Linda Ohama and Emily Carr Institute of Art and Design graduate Ann Marie Fleming, who in 1990 made the first Asian Canadian dramatic feature, *New Shoes.* Other directors followed. Keith Lock made his first dramatic feature, *Small Pleasures,* in 1993. In 1994, Mina Shum wrote and directed *Double Happiness* and Midi Onodera directed *Skin Deep.* By choice, most of these works were somewhat marginalized because of very strong Asian content and the very specific audience each director had in mind. Theatrical releases of these Asian Canadian films were limited to particular communities and repertory theatres, never receiving strong nationwide distribution. But they explored universal themes, and some sophisticated mainstream movie-lovers started to notice them at film festivals: at the time, the only real option for exhibition. The favourable critical response to most of this clutch of dramatic features increased the visibility of Asian Canadian films, inspiring the next generation of filmmakers. They started to emerge with their own works: directors like Helen Lee, Larissa Fan, Julia Kwan, Nicole Chung, Romeo Candido, Jane Kim, Nobu Adilman, Min Sook Lee, Cheuk Kwan and Sook Yin Lee. Dylan Akio Smith, director of the award-winning short, *Man Feel Pain* (2004), has openly cited Ann Marie Fleming's influence on him.

TRACKING SHOT 2: FESTIVALS PAST, PRESENT AND FUTURE

Increased Asian Canadian independent productions did not garner more screen time as major film festivals continued to be dominated by mainstream cinema with limited Asian representation on screen. Noticing this growing gap between Asian filmmakers and their audience, the Vancouver Asian Film Festival (VAFF) and Toronto Reel Asian International Film Festival (TRAIFF) emerged concurrently in 1997; 2006 marked the tenth anniversary of both festivals. It was also the inaugural year of the Calgary ImaginAsian Film Festival. Their mandate is to showcase films with an Asian connection, particularly North American Asian filmmakers.

There were film festivals that showcased Asian films as early as the Festival International du Cinéma Chinois de Montréal, founded by Tammy Cheung between 1987 and 1992; Asian Canadian films, however, were not their focus. The West Coast can boast being the first in the nation to launch an Asian North American focused film festival; the Chinese Film and Video Festival was started by Lorraine Chan and Karin Lee through the Chinese Cultural Centre of Vancouver, and ran from 1994 to 1996. In the inaugural year, the main focus was on Chinese Canadian and Chinese American films. By the second year, the board of directors expanded to include film industry professionals and film critics, and a special focus on Taiwanese films was presented, including works by Hou Hsiao Hsien. In the third year, apart from focusing on Chinese Canadian works, a series on Hong Kong films brought superstars like Leslie Cheung and Michelle Yeoh to attend the Vancouver festival. The festival ended in 1996 with the departure of a major administrator/programmer.

Chinese film aficionados were mourning the loss of their beloved Chinese Film and Video Festival, so Barbara Lee founded VAFF in 1997. 'I was researching Asian film festivals to submit my films to and was so disappointed that Vancouver didn't have one that I started it.'[1] Concurrently, Anita Lee and Andrew Sun, co-founders of TRAIFF, came up with the idea of a festival after attending the San Francisco International Asian American Film Festival and realizing what the city of Toronto lacked. Lee and Sun applied for a grant of $5,000 from the Canada Council; TRAIFF has since showcased Asian filmmakers for ten consecutive years. In November 2006, it rolled out its red carpet for the North American premiere of *After This Our Exile*, a feature shot in Malaysia by Hong Kong's Patrick Tam, which has since garnered best picture honours at both the Golden Horse Awards (Taiwanese Oscars) and the Hong Kong Film Awards (Hong Kong Oscars). It was a record-breaking year for TRAIFF with a twenty per cent increase in attendance.

Calgary is the new kid on the festival block. The first ever Calgary ImaginAsian Film Festival was born in May 2006 as part of Asian Heritage Month. The festival has been renamed the Calgary Pan Asian Film Festival (CPAFF) to increase the visibility of its founding organization, the

Calgary Pan Asian Cinema Society, a not-for-profit film society headed by Ben Tsui.

First-time or emerging Asian filmmakers who had always been shut out of major film festivals were finally exhibited in venues like these. Veteran filmmakers also had a chance to show their more personal works in between major projects. Asian Canadian filmmakers with remarkable bodies of work have been granted special attention; for example, Mary Stephen, who has worked with Eric Rohmer extensively as an editor, was the subject of the TRAIFF's Artist Spotlight in 2002. Showcasing films from Asian countries provides opportunities for cultural and artistic exchange, recognizing and inspiring creativity from diverse places and artists. These festivals also provide a one-stop shopping opportunity for an audience interested in Asian-content films, to which they did not have much access before.

It seems like filmmaking is easier for Asian Canadians now with the arrival of digital video technology, which can lower the cost of filmmaking significantly, but the funding budgets for independent films have also declined. Like the struggling Asian Canadian filmmakers, Canadian Asian film festivals are also finding themselves facing challenges, especially in recent years. With the increasing popularity of worldwide online DVD shopping and internet video downloading, audiences these days are not as reliant on film festivals to access Asian films. Some Asian film lovers who already know how to obtain film and video work online might choose to buy a DVD instead of coming to the festival, unless there are other incentives, such as the chance to meet the stars of the film. The festivals have had to constantly reinvent themselves to stimulate audience growth. TRAIFF, for example, launched a new free database service, www.rafilms.ca, in 2006 to serve the Asian Canadian film community year round.

Another way of attracting an audience is by premiering the works of established Asian filmmakers, but this has become a challenge as well. The Asian festivals have, to some extent, become the victims of their own success, as they may no longer have the chance to premiere or even program emergent Asian Canadian filmmakers' works after they have 'graduated' to major film festivals. Programming the best in the Asian Canadian film community, which is very much the intention of these festivals, has become virtually impossible. Films like *Long Life, Happiness and Prosperity* by Mina Shum and *Eve and the Firehorse* by Julia Kwan were not programmed at TRAIFF, as they premiered at the Toronto International Film Festival (TIFF) two months earlier, and would not have drawn much audience interest a second time around. Competition among other Toronto-based film festivals of similar size is also intense, as the city has over sixty community film festivals a year that serve audiences with diverse interests. Films made by Asian Canadian filmmakers may have content that other film festivals—such as gay and lesbian, experimental, documentary, short film and other festivals—are also pursuing.

Shortage of funding is another challenge. Government grants are becoming less reliable as budgets for the arts continue to shrink while the number of applicants rises. A film festival needs to grow to justify funding, as well as to attract corporate sponsorship. One way to increase audience attendance and industry participation is to fly in high-profile stars and important Asian film producers, but this is an extremely expensive strategy. Asian film festivals of TRAIFF's scale find it particularly hard to meet this demand. This essential growth component cannot materialize without the support of sponsors who share the festivals' visions.

Appropriate marketing and publicity costs have to be budgeted for as well, as media attention is needed to reach an audience. Positive press is crucial for screening attendance, and in turn for a festival's survival. Critics' tastes and audience interests would thus have an influence on future programming decisions.

Although the support structures for Asian Canadian filmmaking have improved greatly, and more opportunities for artists are available, the process of funding and making works here is still highly challenging, as reflected in the limited number of produced works by both established and emerging filmmakers. The US has turned out more Asian American films comparatively, but the market share of these films is still insignificant as compared with that of the vast American film industry as a whole. Asian film festivals continue to work hard to nurture and grow the community. VAFF introduced the Mighty Asian Moviemaking Marathon (MAMM), a one-week filmmaking competition for young filmmakers in the community, and TRAIFF has launched a first-ever Reel Asian Industry Series, providing networking access for Asian Canadian professionals and connecting emerging filmmakers with established funders and broadcasters.

Asian Canadian film festivals are vital to the healthy development of the Asian Canadian filmmaking scene, as well as to highlighting and increasing Asian representation on Canadian screens. The festivals have also been instrumental in breaking Asian stereotypes and other restrictions on Asian artists and performers, very much an ongoing issue in the North American context. There have been seventy-nine years of Academy Awards, during which only six nominations have gone to Asian actors, all in the supporting category. Ang Lee became the first Asian to win the best director Oscar in 2005. Although Julia Kwan garnered the Claude Jutra Award in 1997, no Asian has ever won a Genie for best direction in Canada. It seems that Asian North American talents are better recognized at foreign film festivals than they are at 'home.'

Canada celebrates diversity, yet Asian-content film at the Toronto International Film Festival constitutes less than ten per cent of the total program, far fewer than films from Europe or the United States. Asian Canadian filmmakers and film festivals have to work together strategically to generate more exposure and recognition in the years to come. It may be a good time to celebrate much hard-won success, but a great deal more work for Asian Canadian filmmakers, festival organizers and industry professionals lies ahead.

1. Barbara Lee, email to the author, 27 November 2006.

EATING CHINESE

RECORDED, EXCERPTED

CHEUK KWAN & LILY CHO

From 2000 to 2003, Cheuk Kwan and his cinematographer, Kwoi Gin, scoured the world for good eats and intriguing stories from the Chinese diaspora. The films that comprise Chinese Restaurants *explore issues of migration, family, history and identity through the lens of Chinese restaurants from Haifa, Israel, to Outlook, Saskatchewan. Lily Cho, who wrote her doctoral dissertation on the cultural politics of Chinese restaurants in the Canadian Prairies, focuses on diaspora, postcoloniality, food culture, citizenship and affect in her research. Cho and Kwan spent a sunny morning talking about food, film and much more.*

LILY CHO: Tell me, why are you interested in Chinese restaurants?

CHEUK KWAN: I've always loved to travel and I would always walk into a Chinese kitchen and say, 'Hey, I'm Chinese. Give me some real Chinese food, not what you have on your menu.'

LC: That's something that I wanted to ask you about because there's a very consistent declaration in your films that there were places that were serving more authentic Chinese food, more real Chinese food, than others. I've always been suspicious about the idea that there might be an authentic cuisine. But you feel beautifully unproblematic about it. When you were in Brazil in this amazing restaurant, you were saying, 'This is really real, and this is really good.' What is real Chinese food to you?

CK: In my definition, it's anything that is true to the region where it came from. For example, I grew up eating Cantonese food in Hong Kong and Singapore, so I consider what's there real food.

LC: So what does it taste like? What are the signs?

CK: For Cantonese food, it's got the purity of taste and the fresh ingredients. And, of course, the way you pair the ingredients together is very different: you don't have the sweet 'n' sour, and those yucky, pink, heavy sauces.

LC: But I love those sauces! (*Laughs.*)

CK: Sweet and sour is Cantonese, but in Hong Kong the sauce is made with real tomato paste, real Chinese vinegar and nutritious rock sugar. Not the ketchup, red food dye kind you get in North America.

LC: And how does it matter to you, the realness of the food?

CK: I guess it's what I am used to.

LC: Even though the dishes may be changing all the time?

CK: Yes, because there is now a lot of fusion and new wave Cantonese food in Hong Kong. Colette, my chef in Mauritius, works her wonderful fusion magic in her Indo-Hakka-Creole cuisine. Her food is authentic and from that island.

LC: You have such a clear idea about what real Chinese food is and what authentic Chinese food is. And that really interested me because you knew right away. You stepped into a kitchen in one of your films and you saw how everything was being prepared. You knew right away. How did you come to develop this quite clear and very consistent idea around the authentic?

CK: Travelling around, I learned to deconstruct the Chinese food that I get. I got to be a kind of connoisseur of each type of cooking. It's not that I don't like chop suey, I think they all have their place, but...

LC: But you just said you don't like them...

CK: (*Laughs.*) But if I'm going to spend the money, I'd rather have authentic Chinese food.

LC: Do you think that leads to notions of ethnic purity that might be complicated as well? I mean, do you think there's a relationship between food and ethnicity?

CK: There's a relationship, but not the ethnic purity you mentioned. To me it's more about the essence of art, or the essence of cuisine.

LC: If you're going to talk about an essence or purity to, let's say, an artistic process, it seems to me that that risks reconsecrating a kind of ethnic nationalism. And I think one of the moves right now that I find interesting, in terms of the rise of China globally, is this incredibly romantic and nostalgic recuperation of pre-Communist Chinese culture and its greatness. I'm not saying it wasn't great, but there's a form of amnesia happening in terms of feudalism and class privilege. I speak of this naively, but it seems to me that this came at the expense of some impressive forms of oppression internally. So I wonder when we talk about a purity of art or essence to a cultural production, I worry that we produce that oppression.

CK: I don't think that you can argue that purity of food is equivalent to ethnocentrism or internal oppression. To me, French *haute cuisine* borders on nationalism and is in many ways a class privilege. Unlike the French, the Chinese were never elitists in cooking, unless we are talking imperial banquets, which are now extinct anyway. Chinese, like the Italians, have always had this egalitarian and communal approach to food. If you watch my films you'll see that I'm trying to defuse this issue of ethnocentrism.

LC: Well, especially because I think your films do both things. They take up, really beautifully, the ways that assimilation transforms and challenges all of these notions of authenticity and purity. But I think there are these moments where you sit down to a dish and you say, 'My taste buds are so happy because I can taste the ginger and the fish.' (*Both laugh.*) And it's almost as if you're doing two things there: there are two moods.

CK: I was in Mombasa, Kenya and I happened to eat at this wonderful Hong Kong restaurant where black chefs were stir-frying with papayas and watermelon. So it was an entirely different experience of eating Chinese food. After that meal, I walked across the street to the Museum of Lost Treasures. Inside was a permanent exhibition of Ming Dynasty ceramics recovered from sunken Chinese junks off the east coast of Africa. The exhibit also tells of how Chinese junks influenced an entire generation of African boat design. That afternoon I made up my mind: I was going to make a film to deal with the spreading of Chinese culture and people around the world, using Chinese restaurants as a motif.

LC: There's something about Chinese restaurants...

CK: It's an icon of the Chinese diaspora.

LC: It's such a strange thing, don't you think? In my research, for example, what really struck me, and especially in the Prairies, often the first restaurants in any town were the Chinese restaurants, and given the racist culture of Canada at the turn of the century, and given the political climate, it still boggles my mind that the first instances of the public serving of food occurred within the context of, not just with Chinese cooks, but a Chinese restaurant. And there's something very peculiar to me about that.

CK: Because eating is a very cultural thing for the Chinese. In a Chinese family, the whole social thing is about food, you know, family dinners like in Ang Lee's *Eat, Drink, Man, Woman.*

LC: But also about a father disciplining his daughters, or trying to...

CK: That's also part of the authoritarian family culture, and eating is incorporated into that culture. So it was very easy for Chinese immigrants to say, 'Hey, this is something that's very important to us, and has also commercially and economically allowed us to survive.' And that's why you find Chinese cafés everywhere in the Prairies.

LC: But we're talking about hundreds or thousands of people who start restaurants with absolutely no experience in the kitchen, no experience cooking, which I think, around the world, is one of the most difficult businesses to run successfully. So I wonder about what it is about this kind of work that makes Chinese diasporic culture so ubiquitous.

CK: First of all, you have to look at the social economics of it. Running a restaurant is the easiest and the most natural way for new Chinese immigrants to get started in the society. You don't need the language, you have a demand for your product, the restaurant gives you a social base in the new country, and, as I always tell people, you don't need to know how to cook well because you can fool a lot of people a lot of times with Chinese food. The last point is very true because people would not know how to judge your product or service, unlike being a doctor or an engineer. So Chinese food becomes very popular and is, in a sense, a market-driven global consumer product.

LC: Are we all dupes of global consumerism?

CK: Well, you get bombarded with advertising every day: about technology, about services that you don't need.

LC: (*Laughs.*) So Chinese food was simply at the forefront of this system? You didn't know that you needed sweet 'n' sour chicken . . . (*Laughs.*)

CK: You create a demand, you create desire for a whole generation of people who say, 'Hey, I want my sweet 'n' sour pork and chicken balls.' When I made *Chinese Restaurants*, I had another thing in mind. I wanted to show the Chinese that they're not as ethnically and culturally pure as they think they are. The Chinese can be very ethnocentric, of course, but they also absorbed all kinds of foreign cultures without realizing it. For five thousand years, sitting as Middle Kingdom, they really had a lot of contact with the rest of the world. Through Zheng He's fifteenth-century voyages to the Indian Ocean, for example. That's a full sixty years before Vasco da Gama rounded the Cape of Good Hope. Those voyages brought giraffes to the Imperial Court.

LC: Zheng He had enormous influence in Southeast Asia.

CK: That's right. In the Tang Dynasty, Islam came in through the Silk Road and through Quanzhou, a very multicultural and international trading port in the southern coast of China. One of the 'lost' Jewish tribes also settled in China on their way to the India/Burma border. I dealt with all these in my films. The point is all these imports had enormous impact on the Chinese culture.

LC: And what we know as Chinese food today.

CK: Right. In fact, going back to my other point, there's no pure Chinese food other than what you grew up with and that you know as authentic.

If you look at any dim sum menu, you'll see the egg tarts. Egg tarts came from Portugal. And they became the Cantonese egg tarts. And I made a big deal out of that in my Brazil South story.

LC: And they looked so good. I've never seen egg tarts look that good. I loved the egg tarts. So it seems to me that you're suggesting a kind of realness to Chinese food that is deeply subjective.

CK: Chefs and writers will tell you food is all about memory. And memory, by definition, is subjective. So all food is, in one way or another, defined by time and space. If you grew up in Hong Kong in the '80s tasting all this Western-concept food that your mother incorporated into her kitchen, you'll come to me and say, 'Oh, that's authentic Chinese food.' With egg tarts, the purists will say, 'Well, that's not Chinese food.' Well, these, to me, are real Chinese real food because that's what I grew up with. So in that sense, there's a lot of relativism in defining what is pure Chinese food.

LC: I think that comes out very nicely in your films because you ask a lot of questions about the construction of the dishes. In asking people to talk about how they have constructed these dishes, you seem to be asking them to deconstruct their own sense of cultural ethnicity in some ways. So I was wondering if you could speak to this whole concept about incorporating deeply diasporic memory in cooking Chinese food.

CK: It's a cliché, but food is a metaphor for life. And fusion food is a metaphor for immigrant assimilation. My argument is that the first generation always knows where they came from, but once you get past that, you become more assimilated, like through interracial marriages. And the so-called pure Chinese food gets assimilated, just like a generation is assimilated.

LC: In the films, you make a real point of following the next generation. And sometimes it's not easy. In the opening Israel segment, it became really clear to me that you made a real effort to talk to the next generation. Was that part of your conscious choice in terms of talking about assimilation?

CK: Yeah, because you cannot talk about a diasporic community without dealing with its future or what will happen to it. I've gone through a whole cycle of community activism in the late '70s and early '80s within the Chinese Canadian communities; I understand full well what it means to be Chinese and what it means to be Chinese Canadian. Or, to take it one step further, what it means to be Canadian, period. In Fred Wah's *Diamond Grill*,[1] he spent a whole chapter talking about his name and how people could not associate him—Wah is only one-eighth Chinese—with a Chinese name like Wah. This problem would not happen to him if he was Italian. People would not blink if they saw an almost-white person with an Italian name. But they do a double take when they see an almost-white person with a Chinese name.

LC: So we can't get away from that stigma...

CK: That's right. Asian names and Asian faces still carry that stigma that says, 'Maybe you're not Canadian.' It will take a few generations to melt that barrier and, hopefully, that word 'Asian' will drop out of the lexicon and we will be identified as Canadians and not as hyphenated ones.

LC: There is an argument in some Asian American critical circles against understanding some of these issues in terms of generations. Lisa Lowe, for me, would be one of the primary proponents.[2] She argues that focusing on generational issues, especially the kind of progressive narrative of one generation to the next, risks obscuring the relationships that work horizontally across the community—not just Pan-Asian, but even the non-familial kinds of relations. In almost every part of your films there was a very clear indication on the part of the people who ran the restaurants that they did not want their children to take up their business. It was long hours, hard work, and they didn't want their kids to be doing it. And yet many of those restaurants won't just die when these people retire. They might just get passed on to someone else in the village, another new immigrant. And so I wonder if that can be understood as a different kind of passing on.

CK: Yes, it's another kind of passing the torch. You'll find that, very interestingly, a lot of retiring owners will go back to their villages and offer to bring in someone to take over the restaurant.

LC: Do you think that changes or expands or actually just maintains a sense of family, which is not necessarily about blood, but about a different kind of genealogy?

CK: Yes, that's right. And that's where kinship and brotherhood come in. I know for one that I do that.

LC: I noticed in the films that you always introduce yourself by your surname and by your village. You really work that connection shamelessly.

CK: I do, I do. Shamelessly!

LC: See, my name's Cho and I don't have a big village network and I'm jealous. It's like I can't go anywhere: they all think I'm Korean. So, lucky you, Mr. Kwan!

CK: Well, I have General Kwan from the Three Kingdoms period to thank for that. Everywhere I go, I would see these ubiquitous Kwan temples where he is worshipped as a god for his loyalty and integrity.

LC: Exactly. You've got some major history.

CK: I take advantage of that. I would walk into a restaurant and parlay this kinship and brotherhood business to its fullest, ingratiating myself into the goodwill and friendship of the restaurant owner. And there's something about the Chinese people in general that treasures this kind of blood connection.

LC: And again, let me push you on this a little bit, because I noticed that when you said 'brotherhood,' you hesitated, and so . . . The way gender plays itself in your films is interesting. There are a few key exceptions where the women are the real cooks. The kitchens are spaces managed mostly by men. And this notion of brotherhood seems less easily translatable in terms of sisterhood and I don't know why. But maybe I'm not reading that right.

CK: When I use 'brotherhood,' I mean both genders. I have a lot of feminist friends and I'm very conscious that I need to have a good number of women subjects.

LC: That's true. You have four of them: in Mauritius, South Africa, Turkey and Madagascar.

CK: And if you count the two equally strong partner/wife halves from inside the Arctic Circle and from São Paulo, we have five. Five out of fifteen is not a bad ratio, especially for restaurant work.

LC: Why do you think that is?

CK: I don't think it's specifically a Chinese thing. It's the restaurant business.

LC: But in terms of the way the perception of family and kinship plays out in those instances—that *guanxi* [connection] business, I feel it's different for women.

CK: Well, this notion that Southeast Asian Chinese businessmen shaking hands is as good as a contract comes from the whole kinship thing. But, of course, unfortunately, most of these businesses are still run by men.

LC: Was it hard for you to find women proprietors?

CK: No, and I made sure that I had enough representation. I usually find them more interesting than men anyway, especially Hakka women.

LC: Hakka women are impressive.

CK: They're a very maternal society, so it's no surprise that many of my women chefs are Hakka.

LC: And you didn't expect to make a food film when you started.

CK: No.

LC: We say 'food film' as if we've discovered a genre, but it's actually not...

CK: If you look at any of these films, it's not about food as much as it is about art, family and, of course, love.

LC: And *Tampopo* is about this amazing love story.

CK: Exactly!

LC: And I guess this raises another interesting question for me, and that is at what point does food...I mean it's both in the background and the foreground in a curious kind of way in your films. And you navigate that in a number of ways. But I don't think you could say that your documentaries are about Chinese restaurants. And you can't say they're about Chinese diaspora entirely. I think that would be not quite right.

CK: It's got food so that it gets into the Food Network craze. But it's also socio-political, historical, anthropological and current events. I'm not an academic. I can't go deep into history.

LC: But you did. I mean there are huge historical sections.

CK: History informs us and we cannot get away from it. But sometimes for the Chinese, they get overly historical. I mean, every time we have to go back five thousand years to dynasties and emperors, and I say, 'Oh, give me a break!'

LC: But what I find very moving about your films is that you recuperate huge sections of Chinese immigrant history that many communities want to forget or move past, and most explicit for me is the history of indentured labour, and the kind of peasant history or underground history, which, I think, you draw out again and again in your films.

CK: My South African episode dealt with the whole whitewashing of apartheid history by the Chinese South African community. Part of the community didn't want me to make the film. They asked the restaurant owner not to open up to me. So I spent five days just waiting around for her to open up.

LC: How did they try to stop you?

CK: The first time I went to see her, she would call her friends up and say, 'Oh, come and meet this filmmaker from Canada.' And when they found out what I wanted to do, they convinced her not to give me an interview.

LC: What were their objections?

CK: They didn't want to talk about apartheid. The issue really split the Chinese community. Part of the community wanted to stand by and resist alongside with the blacks and the 'coloureds'—there's a photograph of Chinese men standing with Gandhi in a protest march, in solidarity. But the other side would say, 'Let's not rock the boat, let's take whatever crumbs the whites give us, at least we'll survive.' That was very apparent when I started talking to the community. I wanted to dig up that part of the community history, the good and the bad.

LC: And you also did that with this incredible story on Havana's Chinatown...

CK: People tell me that that's the saddest segment in my series. They couldn't bear to watch it a second time. It's all about indentured labourers replacing slaves in Cuban sugarcane plantations. There's a Cantonese expression, *mai ju jai*, you know: selling little piglets. These piglets went to Australia for the gold mines, to Canada for the railroad and to Peru for the guano mines. It was the poverty in nineteenth-century China that drove a lot of the Chinese men overseas.

LC: And also the Chinese government was too weak to protect its overseas workers.

CK: Exactly.

LC: Part of my own work has been to really ask contemporary Chinese diaspora theorists to think seriously about indentured labourers as a formative episode in all the triumphalism of the new global China and transnationalism. It's so easy to forget that there was this other diaspora that paved their way for most of what we have now in terms of diasporic communities.

CK: And they don't acknowledge that.

LC: No, and there's this enormous focus on the merchant class. But the merchant class wouldn't have been there if there hadn't been an indentured community in the first place. And it seems to me that your films quietly assert the importance of that history in a number of ways, and it's incredible that you manage to tell that story in a number of ways and recuperate that history within that context.

CK: It's about preserving the collective memory.

LC: So what was the biggest surprise for you when you finished the film, in terms of where you thought you would begin and where you ended up?

CK: I became a Chinese food expert. (*Both laugh.*)

LC: You weren't one to begin with?

CK: No, no. I was just someone who liked to travel and eat.

LC: Could have fooled me . . .

CK: The *New York Times* Food section came out with this big article on hyphenated Chinese food and featured my series. So I instantly became an expert, getting calls from as far away as the *Prague Post* to talk about Peruvian Chinese food, of all things. But I'm especially proud that *Chinese Restaurants* is now in the pantheon of food films, together with such films as *Babette's Feast* and *Like Water for Chocolate.* Atlanta's High

Museum of Art ran a Food in Film program two summers ago. The University of British Columbia has a course on food and literature, and my series is on the reading list.

LC: Congratulations on a tremendous achievement. Your films document a history of Chinese diasporic migration that has been overlooked. Tell me, what is your favourite Chinese food dish?

CK: Like I said in my Norway episode, steamed fish with ginger and scallion!

LC: It sounds delicious.

1. Fred Wah, *Diamond Grill* (Edmonton: NeWest, 1996).
2. Lisa Lowe, *Immigrant Acts: On Asian American Cultural Politics* (Durham, NC: Duke University Press, 1996).

STILLS

PART I

Midi Onodera, still from *Down the Garden Path* (2006).

Midi Onodera, still from *Skin Deep* (1995).

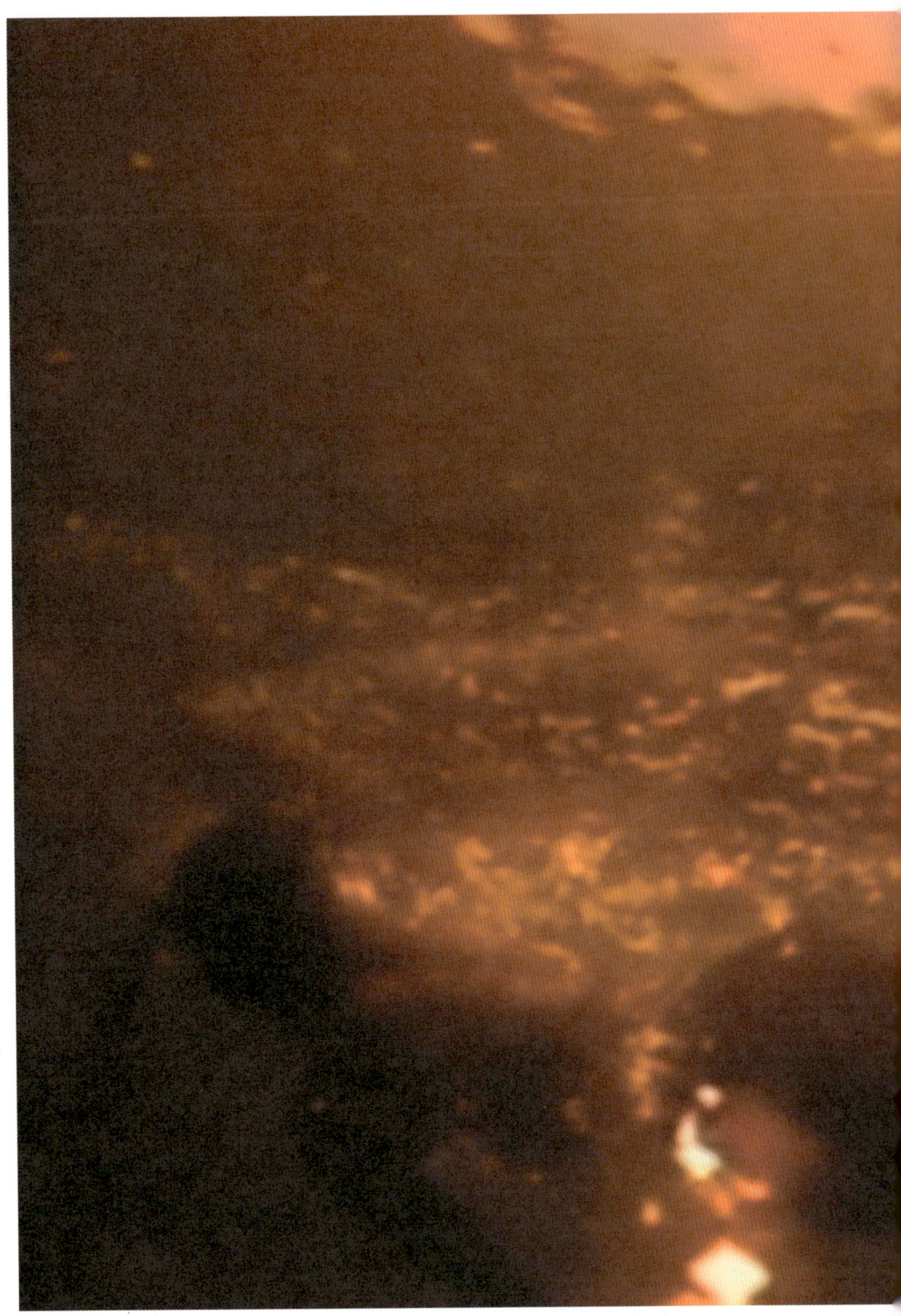

Richard Fung, still from *Sea in the Blood* (2000).

Richard Fung, still from *Dirty Laundry* (1996).

Kwoi Gin, still from *Three Continents*, dir. Cheuk Kwan (2004).

RICE BOWL DIARIES

KWOI GIN

began as just another 20-hour flight...into a lifetime of lost identity...with all that I hated about displacement and exile coming back to haunt me more deeply with each passing time zone and magnified more terrifyingly through the bottom of each duty-free whiskey glass.

two cameras, thirteen countries, more mileage than Che's motorcycle could rev up, copious amounts and endless varieties of comida china, chifas and soupe chinoise,

an extended global family and five years later...
my ethnic and cultural boundaries are transcended
beyond my imagination.

SUR
BAR SUR
UNION BAR

this odyssey became the glue that solidified my experiences and now I'm making peace with the notion of living on the margins without borders & ready to stake claims to a 'paradise' with decent Chinese food that crosses boundaries of colour, race & nationhood...

peace & rice.
banana kowboy

COMES HOME
CAUGHT!
Hits BOTTOM
with parents

GOES BACK
to TAI
CHI MASTER
He's →she gets
weird vibe
dissappeared

TAI CHI
Master is
mysterious
KILLED
IN LIBRARY

SAME +
PALAIS in
HOME EC.
T's describing
love Amy throws
cake mix, gets
it on herself.

S + PALAIS AR
grossed out by
the kiss – they
finally get it
Dump him.

PING + COOK

F-WORDS

RECORDED, EXCERPTED

ANN MARIE FLEMING & MINA SHUM

Award-winning filmmakers Ann Marie Fleming and Mina Shum met as students in 1989 and have been sharing stories, experiences and laughter ever since. The following conversation, recorded in Vancouver on May 10, 2007, evokes many of their discussions over the years. Reflecting on a series of F-words (without swearing), Fleming and Shum allow the reader inside their enduring friendship.

MINA SHUM: Today's conversation will be an overview of the many many conversations we've had over the years using the theme of F-words.

ANN MARIE FLEMING: I'm not swearing on paper.

MS: Family, friends, film, food and the future.

AMF: Always directing.

MS: Structure will set you free. (*Both laugh.*)

AMF: Let's start with family. Not the fact you have one, but that this is a recurring theme in both of our works, yes?

MS: Yes. Do you think it's because we weren't loved enough as children?

AMF: Definitely! But what would be enough? (*Both laugh.*) Exactly.

MS: It's not that I wasn't loved enough, it's just I had problems with the way of loving.

AMF: Yes. Chinese style, and I am the product of two colonials. Repression is a good thing.

MS: I have a different experience. Both my parents are Chinese, but one came from farmer stock and one came from fallen aristocracy. Do you think it's a class thing or a gender thing?

AMF: Yes.

MS: Or do you think it's all our fault because we wanted a different life than our parents envisioned for us?

AMF: Yes. (*Both laugh.*) Everything's cool now, though, right?

MS: Yes. (*More laughter.*)

AMF: Seriously, why are we constantly returning to themes of family? I think it has something to do with art practice in general, where you start from the autobiographical, and a large part of your younger life at least, is family. What do you think about that?

MS: I agree.

AMF: And why do we continue? Personally, my family has some great stories that nobody even wants to talk about. A lot of my work, subtextually, is about what is not acknowledged. What cannot be seen but must be asked about or searched out. Histories: something that family members are often not able to interpret since we all see each other through our own needs and boxes . . . mother, daughter, sister, etc.

MS: I completely agree. I could say exactly the same thing about my own work and where I'm coming from. But our work is so different. I work in a very structured, narrative form, and in three-act (or four- or five-act) structure narratives, one of the reasons family is such a perfect dynamic for stories is that there is always the question of what does each character want and what do they need, so when you create any character onscreen there is always this duality, which is how we live in a family. It's like the public and private selves.

AMF: It's how we always live. Also, I would disagree that our approaches are so different (which means they probably are *really* different), in that I think I work in three- (or four- or five-) act narrative structure too, except it is outside the mainstream, somehow. Why is that?

MS: What you want and what you need are two different things.

AMF: Not always.

MS: No, but in my work, it is.

AMF: Aha! That's the difference!

MS: This way, a character may want you to phone them, but what they need is absolution of guilt. Does that make sense?

AMF: Perfectly, and working with actors, they force you to make those delineations clearly or they can't do their work. I work in other forms besides dramatic and I think I am more ambiguous with intentions and imperatives. I guess that's an obvious difference in our personalities, too! You're easier to read. You're very direct.

MS: Where you're direct-ish! (*Both laugh.*)

AMF: That's right! Back to families . . . I'm not so upfront about using them for dramatic conflict as you are. Oh, and we both have humour in our work, but really different kinds.

MS: That's how you survive a family.

AMF: *Absolument!* And, I gotta say that humour has come in handy for both of us.

MS: Is it partly because we're immigrants?

AMF: You came here as a baby!

MS: But my parents didn't. And we're not white . . .

AMF: I look white . . .

MS: I mean, being outsiders, we have to have a sense of humour about society in general.

AMF: Because we don't totally fit into it?

MS: Yeah.

AMF: I think that is the role/fate of an artist, generally. We are outsiders.

MS: But what about the people who make super-serious stuff with no humour?

AMF: I don't call them at 8:30 in the morning like I call my mother. But seriously, that's not necessarily an immigrant thing, humour. Think about it.

MS: It's part defence. I remember, in the schoolyard, conversations that went: 'You Chinaman, blah blah blah,' and I'd turn around and say, 'Oh yeah, you're just jealous.' Cue rimshot.

AMF: You sound like my mother, except that's how she really thinks.

MS: I thought someone was going to hit me.

AMF: Funny, I use humour so people don't want to hit me. Also, I think it allows you to say things that are difficult and it doesn't always push people away. Kind of like the court jester in Shakespeare, the fool, except I'm a little more deadpan.

MS: I remember, in *Picture Perfect*—my first short, about a man obsessed with pornography and the effects of media on his personal life—I used humour and the silent-movie motif to tell the tale and ask who is culpable. Kind of uncomfortable stuff. Yet, many men told me after they screened the film that it didn't make them question themselves until the next day because it was so funny. Which is exactly what I hoped for, that kind of resonance.

AMF: Well, my work is sideways. It speaks of specific experiences (often women's experiences) and makes them accessible in a more general way. For example, *You Take Care Now,* which is about being raped and run over. Fun! A lot of men—because of the parallel I'm making in the film with a non-sexual, non-gendered violent event, the car accident—could actually relate more to what a woman might experience as a victim of sexual violence. And I do it through non-judgmental humour. The specific is the universal.

MS: In *Picture Perfect,* I'm dealing with a specific event, more directly, with my boyfriend at the time being a porno addict and me discovering it. And I ended up casting him in the lead.

AMF: Yes, interesting choice. Do you know what?

MS: What?

AMF: This is actually the first time in eighteen years we've ever discussed our filmmaking with each other.

MS: It's true. I guess because we're close friends, all this stuff is implied.

AMF: I also think we don't ever want our filmmaker opinions to get in the way of our friendship, no?

MS: No, I respect the way you work, and am inspired by the way you work, and like that it's different. So, I don't want to know too much.

AMF: So, we're a mutual admiration society?

MS: Yes.

AMF: Okay, well, let's talk about friendship then. Isn't that next on your list?

MS: Yes. But I'm open to restructuring.

AMF: Of course you are. You work with producers. (*Both laugh.*)

MS: Does our work talk about friendship?

AMF: Relationships, always. Yours: family, lovers...

MS: ...friends. In *Double Happiness* there are two friends struggling with the same issues in completely different ways.

AMF: But that's not the main storyline.

MS: No. But I did want to touch upon how friends deal differently with the same problems.

AMF: In *New Shoes,* the documentary, I present the story of my friend, and in the feature, *New Shoes,* I explore the nature of my voyeurism through the central character's obsession with her friend's history, even though the friend herself is a little ambivalent about having it told, and the manner of its telling. In *The French Guy,* my latest dramatic feature film, Elizabeth Murray (played by Babz Chula... the *real* Elizabeth Murray being an actual friend of mine who gave me the germ of the idea for the film in the first place) accidentally kills and eviscerates her best friend. Oops, what am I saying? Life is complicated!

MS: Her sister eats him.

AMF: It's a terrible mistake. These things happen. I'm thinking more about the importance of my friends in supporting my work. Because my work is fairly solitary and the process, as you know, is intense. You need to be able to bounce ideas off people and also to get out of your head space. I am lucky to have a lot of old friends and I'm always up for new ones.

MS: For me, friends who are outside of the art-making/movie-making world are so important. It's nice to find out what the problems a vice-principal of a high school has, as opposed to what my problems are.

AMF: That's part of why I came back to Vancouver. Because my friends did different things. Now, they all work in film. What happened?

MS: It makes it rather convenient when you need a crew.

AMF: I can't afford them.

MS: For instance, when Ileana Pietrobruno, our mutual friend and filmmaker, needed a crew, I jumped in as a first AD to help her out...

AMF: For one day.

MS: Still, I hauled gear. I lied to the police...

AMF: Stop right there—you don't want to incriminate yourself. (*Both laugh.*) Okay, I've worked with Ileana as my editor a few times. It's great. I love working with her.

MS: Do you think it's specifically because she's a woman and a filmmaker, and she's funny and an optimist? Her practice is completely different from both of ours.

AMF: I think it's because she's a good editor. She listens well. She doesn't impose her own aesthetics on your work.

MS: No, no, I don't want to talk about why we want to work with her. I want to talk about why we are all friends!

AMF: Oh, yes! Funny is good! I like that we can all be so different, have such strong opinions, and not be threatened by each other. I love that. But it's true, too. We are different, but if we are helping each other out on our projects, we kind of leave the ego at the door. Is that true?

MS: Mm hmm. When you come to one of my screenings, you're thinking...

AMF: 'What is Mina trying to achieve here?'

MS: Right. Just like when I come to one of your screenings, I'm not thinking, 'I would have done this differently.' I'm actually thinking,

'What is the world that Ann Marie has created for us and is she satisfying her desires in what she is trying to achieve?'

AMF: Oh, Mina, if only I was satisfying my desires more often! (*Both laugh.*)

MS: So, film.

AMF: Yes.

MS: Do you remember . . . one of my highlights of bonding with you was going to see *Speed*, the Keanu Reeves/Sandra Bullock one?

AMF: Oh!

MS: And both of us going 'Keanu, Keanu' in cartoon high-pitched voices.

AMF: No, I have no memory of that.

MS: I guess that's what friends are for.

AMF: It was your interior fantasy.

MS: I was in the middle of a Canada Council–funded film and so were you, and I thought it was so funny that we were both watching a Hollywood film.

AMF: You were in the middle of *Double Happiness*. I was making a trilogy of short animated films with Ontario Arts Council money.

MS: Yes. You *hate* all films.

AMF: That's a rumour. Some people say I hate everything. Like, how true is that?

MS: But more often than not, you'll see a film and I'll think it's uplifting and you'll think it's totally depressing.

AMF: I'm just deeper, Mina. (*Both laugh.*) Seriously, we often have pretty different takes on films. In fact, if you recommend a film, I probably won't go. You are so consistent. It's great.

MS: And if you hate a film, I'll probably go see it.

AMF: Exactly! I'm very passionate and articulate about why I dislike something. I'm always paying attention. Also, I don't always go to see a film because I want to like it. I want to be provoked. I want an experience. Sometimes, I just want *Speed,* or what I was hoping *Speed* was going to be. Personally, I had some issues with that franchise.

MS: My favourite types of films are ones that I think about the next day. I hate the films where I leave the theatre and I can't remember it—which is a lot of the films out there.

AMF: Ohmigod! I was really sick a couple of months ago. I rented a dozen films. I can remember one, *Jesus Camp,* and it's not for edifying reasons.

MS: Now that I have a baby, my mother comes and babysits once a week so I can see a film on the big screen. Sometimes there are no films I want to see in the theatres. I'd rather go to an art gallery or eat french fries.

AMF: But that's fantastic! I am much more inspired by things *not* cinema for my work. I go to cinema completely as an observer. I don't do my research that way, and I never tear a film up while I'm watching it, in terms of craft.

MS: Me neither. My first role is as an audience member. I just want to be enlightened and entertained.

AMF: But you'll go check out movies for specific reasons when you're working on a theme or genre.

MS: Are you talking about our failed screening of *Take the Lead,* that Antonio Banderas dance film?

AMF: Hey, what's not to like? I mean, if you are working on a teen girl character, or a movie in general, you'll check out what's out there, both in terms of how it's made and how it's received, no?

MS: But my first role is as an audience member, to see how I feel about it. Then I know if the film is working.

AMF: Absolutely, but your incentive to get in that seat is as an interested observer, whereas I love teen flicks, period.

MS: I love dance movies.

AMF: I *love* dance movies. In fact, I took up the tango. Yes, I will definitely put that in a film someday.

MS: Funny that I also dance. But this is a reversal in our personalities. You do the precise disciplined dance. I do something called 'boing boing,' which is a free expression, modern form. I'm supposed to be the one obsessed with structure.

AMF: Well, I'm trying discipline on for size. It's interesting, everything I have issues with, all in one art form.

MS: With men in the lead.

AMF: Yes, I could go on for pages about that, but it really is a creative experience. You make it with someone else, and each song is a little story you create together, which is completely different from my writing practice. You, on the other hand, enjoy writing with a partner and dancing with yourself.

MS: Actually, I dance with many people, but the feel is of a community. Because you are not dancing with one person. You are dancing with everyone in the room. For instance, one of the exercises we do is run across the room, at each other, as fast as we can for an entire song. And that's completely different from writing alone or with a partner.

AMF: Interesting, because tango is so intimate and couple-y, but it is really an interior dance. You dance it with yourself. I do the community thing when I give my dinner parties, which brings us to another 'F' word, 'food.'

MS: But dinner parties are not with anonymous communities. I don't know everyone I dance with. And you don't either in your tango. And isn't the anonymity part of the connection we feel—that we come from all walks of life, but at least we can dance together?

AMF: That's beautiful, Mina, but I'm trying to segue to our next subject, 'food.' I absolutely agree about the community aspect, of working with 'strangers.'

MS: Dancing is not work.

AMF: Well, I'm thinking of other things we do in the community. Volunteerism, charity work in and out of the film community, etc. But even though the characters change over time, we do these dances in specific spaces and we begin to recognize the strangers around us. Interestingly, you boing and I tango in the same space.

MS: Yes.

AMF: Can we work that into another metaphor?

MS: Not without a lot of heavy lifting.

AMF: And I have boinged, myself. But I don't like the releasing noises of some of the more exuberant participants. A tango is much more repressed.

MS: Oh, mellow out.

AMF: Know thyself. (*Both laugh.*) I have had strange men grab me closely. It's not always what I want. I'm pushing through many boundaries of my own. (*Both laugh.*)

(*Mina leaves and comes back with a bowl of raw almonds.*)

AMF: Now can we talk about food?

MS: I wake up thinking about . . . no, I go to *bed* thinking about what I'm going to eat the next day. Is that my Chinese heritage?

AMF: Absolutely. I love Cantonese cuisine. I love all cuisine. Ironically, I have such a sensitive stomach. I truly believe my filmmaking is like cooking, and cooking is totally creative and expressive. It relaxes me. It excites me. There's nothing I like more than planning a dinner party. What I'm going to cook and who's going to eat it. I can see it, smell it and taste it. I'm thinking of a Stilton and pear soufflé right now. You know the one, with the sugared bottom, which you probably didn't even notice. Chinese put sugar in everything.

MS: That's where you show your heritage.

AMF: Not that the soufflé is traditional Asian cuisine. Didn't you tell me I was the inspiration for you having dinner parties?

MS: Yes.

AMF: And celebrating your birthday?

MS: Exactly.

AMF: I love celebrating. It's that acknowledgment thing. You might be one of the few people who know I'm a closet optimist.

MS: I love cooking as well. It's creative and always a discovery. I have an ongoing restaurant in my mind. If I cook something particularly unique or I deem worthy, I think, 'This is one for the restaurant.'

AMF: Me too, but I also think of the menu design. The decor. The clientele. Do I serve lunch? Is soup too messy? The personalities in the kitchen. How hard it is to find good management, and then I think about being tied down to one thing. Poof. No restaurant.

MS: Where I will never open my imaginary restaurant because I have worked in the service industry and I know how hard running a restaurant is. It's too much work.

AMF: Right. And we as filmmakers say that. Didn't you win a trip to Paris as Employee of the Month?

MS: London. I was Best Hostess.

AMF: And what fine establishment did you work at, Mina?

MS: McDonald's.

AMF: You learn a lot about production...

MS: Yes. I've been accused, in my films, of shooting the point of view of food, which I take as a great compliment.

AMF: I am thinking of the Lazy Susan scene in *Double Happiness.*

MS: I also do a dim sum cart perspective in *Long Life, Happiness, and Prosperity.*

AMF: Does Sandra Oh continue to enjoy that angle of shooting?

MS: She's the one who accused me of being obsessed with the POV of food.

AMF: Ah!

MS: And I did do an installation called *You Are What You Eat,* which had nothing to do with food.

AMF: I have that very phrase in *Automatic Writing,* where I am doing one of those little fortune games with the ghost of my great-great-grandfather. 'You are what you eat!' it reads. The ghost doesn't find it very funny. I have people eating, drinking, in kitchens, in most of my film work from my animated *So Far So...* (drawn in 1988, finished in 1992) to *New Shoes* (both films) to *The Day My Grandfather Spied on Vladimir Ashkenazy,* an experimental video.

MS: In *The French Guy,* it ends with a dinner party, which is made up of real people who go to your dinner parties.

AMF: I know! Self-reflexive or what? As I said, I love a dinner party. That was a dream fantasy sequence. Beef Wellington gone wrong. *Really* wrong.

MS: I was really glad to *not* be invited to that party.

AMF: Yes! You could have had another cameo! The intestines were veggie haggis. No animals were killed in the making of that film.

MS: We tried to kill a duck in *Long Life,* mostly for comedic effect.

AMF: You and your partner, Brent, are vegetarian, aren't you?

MS: He is, all the time. Me, most of the time.

AMF: You're Cantonese—you can't be a one-hundred percent vegetarian.

MS: Especially when my good friend Ann Marie likes to go for chicken feet every so often.

AMF: So, I don't eat dairy! I didn't realize chicken feet were so tempting.

MS: I remember last year we had to actually call a moratorium on chicken feet, we were eating so much.

AMF: Yes, too much of a good thing. Also, I tend to get cravings for chicken feet every time the avian flu comes on the news. Why is that? I don't even like chicken.

MS: At McDonald's, they call that suggestive selling. (*Both laugh.*)

AMF: I'm very susceptible to the media. I have to be very careful what I watch.

MS: That's the theme of my next installation: *Knowing Me, Knowing You*... (*singing*) Uh huuuuuuh... (*Both laugh.*)

AMF: Now, we haven't really talked much about our actual work. More about our process.

MS: Good.

AMF: Exactly. But why don't we wrap this up by talking about what we're working on now, hopes, dreams, that kind of stuff? Kind of a snapshot of spring 2007?

MS: Ohmigod. You have to go first.

AMF: Well, sit down. I am publishing a graphic novel based on *The Magical Life of Long Tack Sam* that'll be out this fall. I am working on an acupuncture-themed silent animated film that will be scored and played with the Victoria Symphony Orchestra next January at the Victoria Independent Film Festival. I am working on a film adaptation for the NFB of a beautiful illustrated memoir, *I Was a Child of Holocaust Survivors*, by Bernice Eisenstein.[1] I don't know if that will happen or not, but it's a big challenge for me to work with some other artist's material. I'm working on a big sweeping drama-type script about my great-grandfather, Long Tack Sam, called *Shanghai Follies*, I've got a gender-bending contemporary *Hamlet* up my sleeve called *Society*; there's a short drama about cutting down trees for a Vancouver-themed anthology; and an idea for a cellphone series with dogs. I'm also keeping an online comic blog and am thinking of reviving my long-lost stand-up career, and a few other little things. I forget what. Oh! And the tango. It's actually a big part of my life right now. Et toi?

MS: Hmm. Well, I am writing my next feature film with Dennis Foon right now (he co-wrote *Long Life* with me). I don't really want to describe it today, 'cause I'm so in the middle of it, but let me say it's really really

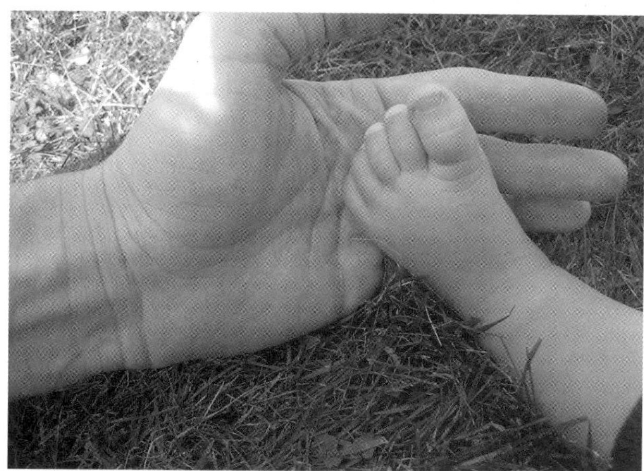

Mina Shum, personal photograph (2007).

exciting and great, and it has a sequel built in. The film centres around a fifteen-year-old Chinese girl and is set in Vancouver, and it has kung fu! I have another feature in the works based on a memoir called *Inner City Girl* by Sabrina Bernardo[2] and I echo your blood, sweat and tears when taking on someone else's material. It's my first time. I'm also developing a couple of series ideas for television, and I've applied for a grant to make my next installation, *Knowing Me, Knowing You.* Plus my life is more chaotic these days 'cause of Tai, my eight-month-old dream come true. I just want to keep making my own work and have a life. And of course, I fit this all in between phone calls, emails and dim sum with you.

AMF: Well, aren't we busy girls? As a new mother, you may win, though. See now, wasn't that easy? Once again, we're working splendidly together. Now, is it time for lunch?

MS: I bet you I know what we'll eat.

1. Bernice Eisenstein, *I Was a Child of Holocaust Survivors* (Toronto: McClelland & Stewart, 2006).
2. Sabrina Bernardo, *Inner City Girl* (Toronto: Harper Collins, 2008).

MEMORY, AGAIN

RECORDED, EXCERPTED

KHANHTHUAN TRAN, PAMILA MATHARU
& ELAINE CHANG

Acclaimed young film- and video-makers Khanhthuan Tran and Pamila Matharu push and cross multiple boundaries in their respective works. Tran's Vietnam, 1997 *(2004) and Matharu's* Fracture *(2003) are award-winning shorts that straddle the divide between experimental and documentary forms, reconfiguring autobiographical material in poetic and searching new considerations of identity, place and the enigmas of departure and return. The two sat down with anthology editor Elaine Chang to view each other's work, and to discuss past, current and future directions in their careers.*

ELAINE CHANG: I'm wondering if we could start with some basics: where you were born, how you came to Canada, steps along the way.

PAMILA MATHARU: I was born in Birmingham, England, and before that, my parents had immigrated from India to England. We came to Canada in 1976, when I was... Oh sorry, it's a little bit unclear but it's either '76 or '78, between '76 and '78. I know I was four or five, so it must have been around '78. And we immigrated to what was Toronto's Indian/Punjabi melting pot at the time, Rexdale.

KHANHTHUAN TRAN: My family came here in, I think, 1980, give or take. In 1979 I think we left Vietnam, and if I remember correctly we stayed in the Philippines for a while waiting for someone to sponsor us over, so I think it was 1980 that we got sponsored by a church group in Nova Scotia and I was about three when we came here. I grew up in Dartmouth, Nova Scotia, a small town, went to school there, and now I am in Toronto.

EC: It's interesting that both of you have just said, 'I can't remember if this was '79 or '80 or '76.' In both of your works, memory has its own kind of temporality. It's not driven by actual, historical years and dates. Khanhthuan, in the text that precedes *Vietnam, 1997,* you say something like 'These are moments *in* Vietnam.' I think both of you deal with the spatial location of memory. Can you talk about this?

KT: I guess this is going on record, but I can say that the film *Vietnam, 1997* is actually not 1997, it's 1998, and I used '97 because I liked those numbers better. (*Elaine laughs.*) For some reason, and I know it sounds weird, but when I thought about the date, I was like, 'I'm sure we went back in 1997,' and I made the video and I thought the numbers worked so well: '1, 9, 9, 7.' And I showed it to my parents and they go, 'You realize we went in '98.' But I thought, 'I am not going to change it now. I like those numbers.' I know there is truth in documentaries; I was making a documentary, but to be quite honest, there are lots of lies in my documentary. Not lies, but they're white lies. I mean, yes, it's my memory, and that is most important, how I remember stuff. How we remember things is the truth. Memories always change and you just try to re-associate them with a time frame that you are in now, and I think that's what the date 1997 does. It doesn't have to be plain, spot-on truth.

PM: I think Anne Michaels, in her book *Fugitive Pieces,*[1] said memory is like a water stain on history. That's the way I think of memorializing, particularly with my art. Funnily enough, I look at memories like stains. Or like remnants of a watermark left on paper or something like that. You know what I mean? Sometimes I wonder: how many memories can we actually hold? When am I gonna bust open with all this stuff? So I have to make art to somehow archive these things; I don't know if my brain can hold them that long.

When I made *Fracture,* it was 2002, and a year after 9/11. On 9/11 I had a slip-and-fall accident that gave me a head concussion. And around that time I wanted to make *Fracture,* because I was starting to lose my memory of my father. It was such a severe injury... I didn't break anything, but I had to force myself to just remember his face. I would fall into tears because I was starting to lose that image and my doctor said, 'Just relax, this is going to take time, of course you can't forget.' But that visual was fading from my mind, so it was like having a traumatic experience revisit my life and kind of wiping the slate clean of that traumatic experience, you know?

EC: Would you be comfortable describing the traumatic experience? You don't have to.

PM: Sure. Well, that near-death fall in 2001 brought me back to my last traumatic experience, when I lost my father to suicide. I think there was a point when I tried to consider what I found, or what was important to me as an artist, and this was something that I needed to do; I had to get it out of my system. If I was going to start losing my memory—at the time, my long-term memory was being affected quite a bit—I had to preserve it in some way. And being an artist, of course I needed to do it through art. I went through all the super 8 tapes we had at home. I had already archived and transferred them because, you know, technology had made it possible to do these things. I said, 'Mom, we should do this, this is our family archive.' When my parents came to Canada in the late '70s, they had a super 8 camera, much like other families, and they documented whatever they could. Once I had compiled all these films on tape, what seemed to me like so much time ended up being only thirty-one or thirty-two minutes, from the mid-'70s to the mid-'80s. I couldn't believe it, and I still sometimes hold this tape and think, 'These are my first memories of Canada in thirty-one, thirty-two minutes.' So there is a lot of deep personal connection to *Fracture*, but it's okay, an audience doesn't have to know this. It's just something I had to do.

KT: I really like what Pamila is saying about archiving your memories. And we can do it with video. We and other artists use this medium to remember our memories. I made a video called *Welcome to Dartmouth*, and that's actually the city I'm from and it's about the time I was there and the place. I guess as an artist I always consider time and place. *Welcome to Dartmouth* is about this girl who's lonely the whole time, it's just her by herself. And I made a documentary called *48 Hours on the Street* in Ottawa, where I spent forty-eight hours living on the street one January. I don't know, for some reason all my titles revolve around time. When I look back at these videos now I go, 'Oh my God, there is me in Ottawa, there is me in Dartmouth, there is me in Vietnam,' you know? The video, the animation I just showed you...

EC: *Good Luck Counting Sheep* (2007)?

KT: Yeah. If you noticed, it's set in 1998.

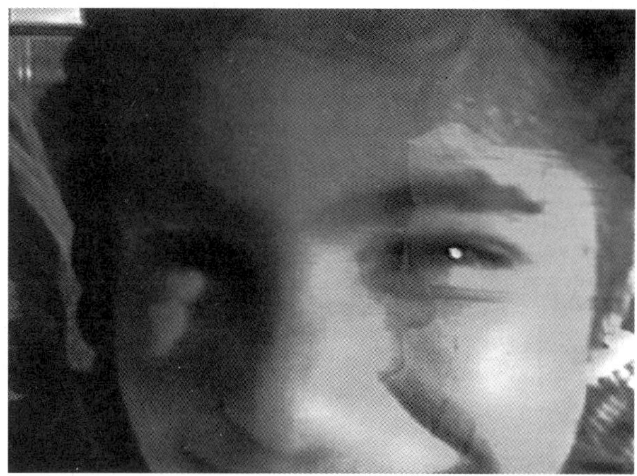

Pamila Matharu, still from *Fracture* (2003).

PM: Yes.

KT: My *Welcome to Dartmouth* piece is 1999, *48 Hours on the Street* is 2000. I think my next work may be 2001. I'll try to remember what happened in 2001. Chronologically: I make work that way. It's kind of an inside thing for me that I find really interesting.

EC: You both disguise and transfigure personal material in your art, and in so doing it's you and it's not you, it's yours and not yours anymore. One thing that strikes me, watching your work together, is that Pamila, you act in your own films, and Khanhthuan, you don't, except for the little 'Bio,' which is not biographical at all. You mentioned that *Welcome to Dartmouth* is a personal work, but that it features a non-Asian girl. So it would seem you have all these surrogates in your work, which to me is really interesting. Pamila, I love how in *Fracture* you alternate between images of you looking at yourself in the mirror and footage of you as a little girl from your family's super 8 films. There seems to be an attempt to connect yourself to yourself through these images . . .

PM: Yeah, I think I look at it like an artist looks at self-portraiture. And of course there's nothing new in that, video self-portraits have been done, but I'm trying to look at it in a different light and from a different angle always. Also testing my own limits. I'm always shitting bricks when I am ready to be in front of the camera. I'm very afraid, but there is a part of me that wants to do it. I have to push myself within. By the time I did *Stains* (2005; and in progress), I was feeling a little bit more comfortable, but still I had times where . . . It's always scary because you're spending the time, money and energy to be in your work and you want it to be good, right? You're going to be your best and your worst critic.

Stains is going to be about looking at suicide from a survivor's point of view. Of course, when I say it's from the survivor's point of view it's my point of view. For a long time this was something I couldn't talk about. I know that we've become open to talking about the subject matter, but I wasn't ready. For some reason, when it comes to my art practice, I'm more than willing to open up to it. But in my life, you know, it's a different story. It boggles my brother's mind that I can put our family shit up on the screen (I'm quoting him right now).

KT: When I come to a new work, I am always trying to challenge myself with a new idea. As you saw, *Vietnam, 1997* is a documentary; I tried to challenge myself with the documentary form. *Good Luck Counting Sheep* is an animation; I tried to challenge myself with what animation is. In terms of the autobiographical and me leaving myself out, that was definitely what I wanted to do in *Vietnam, 1997*. I love video art in its narcisissm, in its pointing-the-camera-at-yourself type of deal. But when I was doing *Vietnam, 1997*, I kind of shied away from those documentaries that use narrative, a voice-over narrator. I don't know if you guys realize this, but it took me a year to edit it.

EC: Well, it's beautifully edited.

PM: It's gorgeous!

KT: Some documentaries try to be a truth medium, but there is not a lot of truth in them, it's very author-based, you know? I was like, 'All I wanna show you is the images, the moments, or what the video camera captured and that's it.' I didn't really want to add anything, so I took away as much text as possible while still telling a narrative. And I decided to make *Vietnam, 1997* because I went to a John Porter screening. He's a super 8 artist and he was having this presentation, showing his super 8 movies and making comments, 'Oh, this is me and my mom. This is . . .' And I was like, 'Oh, I can take out this narrative, and just write in, 'my mom,' 'my uncle,' and that's all people need to know when they're looking at my images; they don't need to know any story other than the fact that these are my images and these are the people in them. And as for taking myself out . . . I love Werner Herzog, but Herzog is in all his documentaries, those are Herzog documentaries, it's not only a documentary about the Grizzly Man, you know what I'm saying? You love Herzog because it's Herzog, you love the way he speaks and I tried to get away from that . . . If that makes sense at all.

EC: In some of your other work, where you also do not appear, there are some very depersonalized people doing things, in some cases committing extremely violent acts. In *Flash* (1998), there's that frightening, anonymous masked attacker, and then there are the gunmen in *Good Luck Counting Sheep* who are also wearing masks over their faces. Where does that come from, this sort of . . .very unexpected jolt of violence?

KT: Yeah, I've used the same theme or gun moment again and that's kind of why I wanted to show it to you guys. When I made *Flash,* I thought violence is one of those key sellers that gets your audience into it, and I just thought that it worked in that context, but . . . You know, *Flash* is very old, it's a student work, it doesn't justify its violence at all. When I look at it I find it totally . . .

PM: I was thinking Roland Barthes . . .

KT: . . . too lyrical, too . . .

PM: . . . Simulacra: I was thinking about all this theory looking at it, actually . . .

KT: . . . I find it too, too . . . It's like it's a flash of life, it flashes, it's like too much of that same metaphor going over and over again. Where I find . . . I don't know, it's funny, *Good Luck* was actually written in 1998, so maybe it's about in the same time frame that I was thinking about these Hollywood movies and how you put action in. And what's key action? It's a gun, and then the story revolves around the gun moment, but you have to build up to it. My work is very narrative. I try to keep it that way.

EC: To pick up what Pamila was saying about simulacra . . . It's interesting, the interplay between *Flash*, which you describe as sort of art school and rough, and then this new animated video in which you re-simulate what you call the 'gun moment,' and the simulacrum of that simulacrum. (*Khanhthuan laughs.*) As an animator you're re-simulating all this stuff, whether it's *Beverly Hills, 90210* or the polar bears who are also already simulacra of actual polar bears in the Coke commercial—oops, the 'cola' commercial. To go back to what you were saying about action and violence and narrative, Dolly is fascinating because . . . Is she 'real' or not? In this video, you kill the clone off, in animated form, and that leaves the audience with a challenging question. If you want to say that this is not a real sheep, then is the blood she sheds not 'real' either, should we not feel really bad about that? Is this not a real, you know, sheep murder, a sheepicide, whatever that would be called? Were you playing on all of these layers?

KT: I was totally playing, and you have to watch it again; it's really short, but there's . . . You realize that all the characters, it's all found footage.

PM: Yeah, I wanted to ask you about that.

KT: Tom Cruise is in the movie . . . Like *Vietnam, 1997*, it's a bunch of pieces and I'm an editor, I just put a bunch of pieces all together, and it's about repeating ideas and, well, if you've got these real actors going up against a real Dolly, is that, does that make it a real death? How many times can you repeat something before we lose interest? I don't know if you got that first bit of dialogue, but *90210* comes up, and then the dialogue goes: 'Dylan's back, that's stupid.' If you know that in the eighth season of *90210*—the eighth season!—they bring back Dylan McKay . . . I'm playing with this idea, like how many times are we gonna keep on doing things before it just doesn't matter anymore?

PM: I was just thinking that you are playing with TV, man... You are playing in TV-land! 'Oh yeah, I remember that!' It brought me back to the time where we were sitting there saying, 'Oh my God, Dylan's back,' you know?

KT: Yeah, 'cause I had that moment too.

EC: Well, anyway...

PM: Yeah, I guess it wasn't your thing, was it? You were on to *thirtysomething* then.

EC: Yeah, but I wasn't thirty-something yet, let me just say. (*All laugh.*) Can you two talk a bit about your experiences working in both visual art and film and video?

PM: When I was starting out, there weren't many artists of colour in this city, and of course we gathered for... at the time, it was Desh Pardesh and Fresh Arts that I was introduced to. I got some interesting advice early on. I was going to York University and spending most of my time learning about the Toronto scene. A senior visual artist had told me, 'Girl, get it, get out there! You're gonna have a tough time, and you gotta get busy'—meaning: learn the ropes, learn the system. So it wasn't something that I naturally fell into, it was something I had to fight to be included in.

KT: You made an interesting comment while your video *Haphazard* (2003) was playing. I wrote it down 'cause it's something that I reflect upon too. You said something about video having no boundaries, unlike visual art...

PM: Yeah, I think that when I started to familiarize myself with the Toronto film and video community and the people involved, it just felt so much more welcoming in terms of the genres that were out there. Yes, there's documentary, and, well, it's not just voice-over, and yes you can include drama, and yes you can make it very diverse, and yes you can incorporate all these other forms of art. It just blew my mind because it was different from what I learned and what I was experiencing working in the visual art sector. In film and video, I felt like there was so much more freedom to have a voice, to have an identity, and to feel very affirmative about it.

KT: I went to art school to study painting, and I was very very into painting. I mean, it's still my one true love, but after studying for two years—and I guess NSCAD (Nova Scotia College of Art and Design) at the time was really known for its painting program—I had to take an elective, and I took video, video production or video foundation, and I totally agree with you. All of a sudden I didn't have to conform to these . . . I don't know how I explain it to people, but it was like there was so much art history that you had to tackle before you could do a painting that I never felt mature enough, I didn't know enough about the medium itself to tackle it.

PM: And Western art history? That's what we're taught, right?

KT: Uh huh, and then I get into video, and all of a sudden you can do whatever you want: here's a camera, enjoy it! Here's some technical stuff, but make whatever you want. And, I mean, we talk about identity and identity is about doing whatever you want, I guess. Whatever you're making is your identity, your piece, right? It was so freeing, and that's when I switched over and started making videos.

PM: That's such an interesting way to frame identity. Identity is whatever you want to make of it, whereas in the context of visual art you learn that it's your skin colour, or your ethnicity, or your sexuality, or your . . . It's so limiting and I hated all these little compartments and labels. Why does identity have to be just confined to my sexuality or the fact that I'm a brown woman?

KT: Maybe it's my growing up in the Maritimes because, I mean, I never really thought about myself as Asian, but I never thought about myself as white. If anything—it's like the only biographical part in my bio—I call myself an Atlantic Canadian. I call myself a Maritimer all the time 'cause that's how I identify myself. *Welcome to Dartmouth* is about . . . I'm a Dartmouthian, that's my identity.

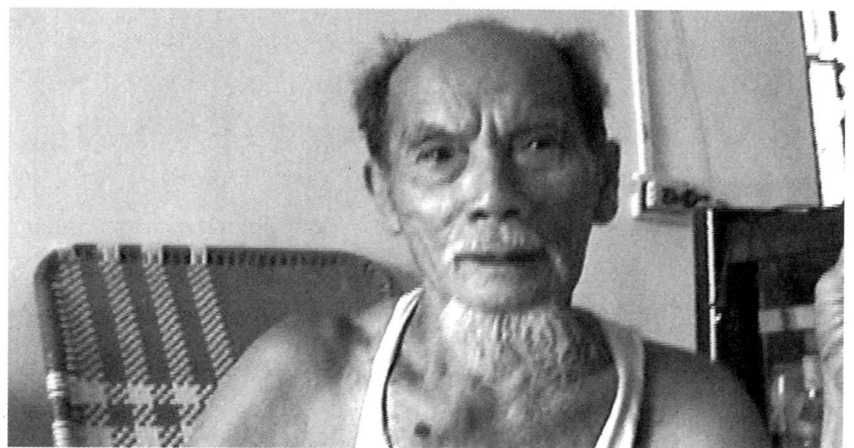

Khanhthuan Tran, still from *Vietnam, 1997* (2004).

PM: It's funny having been born in England. When my brother and I were children it was the flag and the Queen and 'The Queen's English'! But I recently went back for my brother's wedding—he lives there now—and I just detested everything about British culture; I couldn't believe I loved everything British when I was a kid. I wanted to run back to Toronto so fast! I felt like I knew that I was Canadian, because what is Canadian, anyway? It's true, we're so connected to our places and I guess Dartmouth is the place for you, right?

KT: Yeah. You know what I think works in *Vietnam, 1997*? I think it's a reflection of Canadian or North American society. When I was editing it, I tried to put in the things that make our... I don't know, I showed that dog... It's like, you'll see those movies where the dog barks at the mailman, except in Vietnam it's the dog barking at the person, the motorcycle going across the street, which is the same moment, I just tried to show. It's like I'm not Viet... oww, that sounds so bad. I'm not from Vietnam anymore really. I'm Vietnamese, I know that, but all I could show was how much Vietnam reminds me of Canada, and those are the moments where I try to show something universal. I guess that's what I'm saying. And I think if people like *Vietnam, 1997* it's not because they're seeing Vietnam, but because they're seeing similarities between Vietnam and Canada.

PM: Well, it's interesting. If your grandmother was in Canada, in Toronto, would you observe the same customs and traditions that you did for her birthday in Vietnam?

KT: Yeah.

PM: Memories, respect, honour, traditions: these are things that we carry with us culturally, right? And if you went to the most metropolitan city in the world, you'd still do the same thing. It's part of who you are.

KT: Yeah.

EC: So when you're thinking about Asian Canadianness or Vietnamese or South Asian Canadianness, it's not like you can point to proportions of each or the other, and maybe you feel these things most when you're on the move? The portability of identity is something video art might facilitate, in that you bring a camera, and . . . Yeah, we're not seeing an empirically accurate portrait of Vietnam in 1997 which is actually 1998. (*All laugh.*) We're seeing these glimpses of the life of a family through one particular person's eyes, and there too you're not exhausting the truth of the Trans. So your 'Canadianized' eye will rove to a dog or a kid who is trying to hide from the camera.

KT: Exactly, because I'm trying to find those moments that I, as a cameraman, am thinking, oh this is familiar, I'll look at this. I don't know, I probably have footage of us eating, but I didn't show things like Vietnamese food. (*All laugh.*) I didn't show us eating pho as if it were, you know, our cultural identity. I didn't want to do those things.

PM: I call those the clichés of culture. The music, food and fashion. (*All laugh.*) But you're right. You took a totally different approach

EC: And Pamila, your work also lacks those things. You don't make a statement about fracture or dislocation. These experiences inform your work; they might be there in the aesthetic or other elements, but they're not there in a straightforwardly documentary or journalistic way, and definitely not in a 'these are the ways of my people' anthropological way.

PM: Yeah. I think this is why I like to say I'm an experimental artist, because I want to break the moulds of the documentary canon. 'This is the master way, this is what you do.' Well, no: who's saying that? I think it was Carrie Mae Weems, an African American photographer, who said that the photographic greyscale was based on white skin.[2] So who's to say that this or that is what is correct in photography or film or video? Who's to say a video can't be a film or a film can't be a video?

EC: So what's up next for each of you?

PM: I want to continue making shorts. I feel like I want to be a lot more familiar with my craft because I've taken a different route, learning it on my own, do-it-yourself—a bit of an anarchist approach to learning filmmaking. Sometimes it's like beating my head against a brick wall but it's something I want to do. It goes back to my idea of process-based arts. Learning is also process-based for me.

KT: I'm writing my next video, and hopefully it's going to be a feature. Whether it's going to be an animated feature, I don't know. I've got this idea that I'm... again, it's about time and space. I'm writing something, but it sounds so artsy when I say it's about time and space. It's not...

EC: Do you want to describe it or would you rather not?

KT: No, 'cause who knows? Maybe when I'm done writing it, it will be about Dolly the Sheep again or something. (*All laugh.*) No.

1. Anne Michaels, *Fugitive Pieces* (Toronto: McClelland & Stewart, 1996).
2. Referenced in bell hooks, *Art on My Mind: Visual Politics* (New York: New Press, 1995), 91–2.

VANCOUVER ASIAN

WEST COAST FILM CULTURES,
ON THE RIM AND AT THE END OF THE LINE

SU-ANNE YEO

In a recent essay commemorating the twentieth anniversary of the Western Front,[1] Richard Fung, quoting author Vera Frenkel, observed, 'Vancouver is not a place at all, but an excuse.' 'British Columbia,' he went on, 'endures as a state of mind, defined as much by its cultural reputation summed up in the phrase, 'West Coast,' as by the notoriously beautiful geography of mountain, mists, and ocean.'[2] Vancouver's symbolic role as the country's 'western outpost,' or more recently as a 'bridge to the Pacific Rim,' is deeply implicated in the historical and contemporary experiences of Asian Canadians, particularly Chinese Canadians and Japanese Canadians, but other groups as well.

Various factors have conspired to create a West Coast film culture that is eclectic, elusive, sometimes collaborative and frequently contradictory. These factors include a pattern of controlled migration from East Asia, particularly Southern China and Hong Kong; geographic distance from the country's cultural institutions; proximity to the US Hollywood system; and a history of countercultural movements and grassroots campaigns.

In this essay, I will offer some initial observations about the way in which the work of Asian Canadian film and video artists on the West Coast, especially since the 1990s, has both reflected and helped to constitute a sense of Asian Canadian identity and a particular set of artistic and social concerns.

MIGRATION

Chinese migration to Canada began with the discovery of gold in San Francisco and then British Columbia in 1858. In the late 1800s, as many as 17,000 Chinese workers, many fleeing war and famine, travelled from Guangdong Province to the Fraser Valley (via the US in many cases) to help construct the Canadian Pacific Railway.[3] Immediately following the CPR's completion, the Canadian government placed a head tax of $50, then $100, then $500 on Chinese immigrants, and it banned Chinese immigration altogether from 1923 to 1946 through the Chinese Exclusion Act. Many Chinese Canadian immigrants moved east to Calgary, Montreal and Toronto in the early twentieth century, in search of employment and respite from widespread anti-Asian sentiment, or the perceived threat of a 'yellow peril,' on the West Coast.

In the early twentieth century, Japanese Canadian communities were primarily clustered along the BC coast, with many residents in *nihonmachi* or Japantown on Powell Street, Vancouver, or in the fishing community of Steveston.[4] These settlements were radically disrupted with the outbreak of World War II. In 1942, 22,000 Japanese Canadians, now branded as 'enemy aliens' by an Order-in-Council passed by the Canadian government under the War Measures Act, were stripped of their possessions and incarcerated in internment camps in the BC interior and Ontario, or sent to work on sugar beet farms on the Prairies. Those unwilling to live in the camps faced deportation to Japan. At the end of the war, Japanese Canadians were given the choice to 'return' to Japan, although many had never lived there, or to relocate to communities east of the Canadian Rockies. The freedom to live anywhere in Canada, including BC, was not reinstated to Japanese Canadians until 1949.[5]

Shared resistance on the part of Chinese Canadian and Japanese Canadian communities dates back to the turn of the century. On September 7, 1907, several thousand members of the Asiatic Exclusion League, a San Francisco-based labour organization whose mandate was to stop Asian migration to North America, rioted in Vancouver's Chinatown. Japanese Canadians had been alerted to the mob's existence and fought back when the Asiatic Exclusion League moved on to Japantown.

CULTURAL INSTITUTIONS

Historically, Asian Canadians and visible minorities in Canada have been expected to document rather than fictionalize their lives. I will suggest here that this tendency to invite or prescribe participation in certain film forms or genres (for example, ethnography), and to limit or deny participation in others (for example, the musical), constitutes a form of institutionalized racism that is rooted in Canada's colonial and colonialist past.

In her 1994 essay for *Take One* magazine, 'Coming Attractions: A Brief History of Canada's Nether-Cinema,' Helen Lee wrote that Canada's status as a former British colony has led to a three-part studio system comprising the National Film Board of Canada (NFB), the Canadian Broadcasting Corporation (CBC) and Telefilm Canada, plus the provincial film commissions.[6] She argues that the legacy of John Grierson, the so-called 'father' of the British documentary film movement and the first commissioner of the National Film Commission, the precursor of the NFB, has been a national film culture focused primarily on documentary realism, public education and cultural 'uplift'—what the film theorist Bill Nichols refers to as a 'discourse of sobriety'[7]—rather than narrative melodrama (or any other cinematic mode), popular entertainment or mass tastes.

This discourse of sobriety is evident in a number of Asian Canadian documentaries created within the state-mandated studio system. Perhaps the paradigmatic example of the Chinese Canadian pioneer experience is *In the Shadow of Gold Mountain* (dir. Karin Cho, 2005). Produced by the NFB and broadcast on the CBC, the film tells the story of the first Chinese migrants to Canada and their treatment by the federal and provincial governments in the late nineteenth and early twentieth century, as well as their will to survive. Although the film is directed by a Montreal-based filmmaker, it is certainly pertinent in the context of West Coast filmmaking because of its extended use of Vancouver's Chinatown as a setting and its profile of several Vancouver-based community leaders.

Using archival footage, subject interviews and occasional first-person narration, *In the Shadow of Gold Mountain* relates the individual and collective struggle of Chinese Canadians to make a life in Canada. This is despite the xenophobia and discrimination (in forms such as the Head Tax and Chinese Exclusion) that were legally institutionalized and socially rife at the time. The film's sense of 'justice denied' is predicated on its depiction of Chinese Canadians as worthy national subjects, their worth evident in their willingness to labour on the construction of the CPR, enlist in the armed forces during World War II, and celebrate multiculturalism; and on the removal of immigration restrictions based on national origin during Canada's centenary celebrations in 1967.[8]

The distribution and exhibition of *In the Shadow of Gold Mountain* through special community screenings across Canada (Montreal, Ottawa, Toronto, Winnipeg, Calgary and Vancouver) in 2005 helped to draw attention to this so-called 'dark chapter' or isolated incident in Canadian history. It also helped mobilize community and public support for Head Tax Redress. On June 26, 2006, the Canadian government officially apologized for the head tax and Chinese Exclusion, and promised to compensate surviving head tax payers (CCNC). This hard-won decision speaks in part to the Redress movement's capacity to convey, at a symbolic level, the importance of Chinese Canadians to the Canadian national project.

Produced by the NFB and broadcast in both Canada and Japan, *Obachan's Garden* (dir. Linda Ohama, 2001) relates the story of Asayo

Murakami, the filmmaker's 103-year-old grandmother who arrived in Steveston, BC, in 1924 as a 'picture bride.' The documentary constructs Murakami's life against a backdrop of events such as the great Kanto earthquake, the Japanese Canadian internment and the bombing of Hiroshima at the end of World War II. Although it is in this sense 'historical,' the film resists the unproblematic division between memory and history, subjective experience and objective reality by fusing dramatic re-enactment with interviews, dream sequences with archival footage, and music with startling visual motifs.[9]

Vancouver's distance from the cultural institutions of Toronto and Montreal is a double-edged sword. On the one hand, the West Coast's isolation has resulted in a less developed cultural infrastructure for new and already existing work. On the other hand, it has lessened the pressure on filmmakers to conform to documentary conventions, thus helping to support (at least in some circles) a more thematically risky and formally experimental approach. The work of Ann Marie Fleming, whose films combine autobiography, family history and social commentary in playful and unexpected ways, is exemplary here. Defying the rules of form or genre, she experiments with animation, avant-garde aesthetics, documentary and narrative, often within a single film. Many of her recent projects, for example *The Magical Life of Long Tack Sam* (2003), explore the stranger-than-fiction lives of her relatives who hail from around the world.

HOLLYWOOD NORTH

In other circumstances, geographic isolation has also increased pressure on filmmakers to adhere to narrative conventions. In his recent book about the feature film industry in BC, Mike Gasher notes that the province's distance from Toronto and Montreal impeded its integration into the national cinema of feature filmmaking in the late 1960s, just as BC's proximity to Los Angeles facilitated its integration into the Hollywood system in the 1970s, when that industry was decentralizing its production.[10] This has led to the creation of a film industry on the West Coast that is primarily dependent upon foreign service production—so-called 'runaway productions' account for two-thirds of total film production in the province—and that looks upon the cinema less as a form of artistic expression than as a means of creating and sustaining jobs.[11]

Recently, the concentration of commercial film and television production in and around Vancouver has given rise to a constellation of working actors of Asian descent based on the West Coast.[12] These include Grace Park, who plays Lt. Sharon 'Boomer' Valerii in the science fiction television series *Battlestar Galactica,* and Edmond Wong, formerly seen in *Stargate Atlantis.* Often living and working in Vancouver but travelling frequently to Los Angeles and various parts of East and Southeast Asia, these transnational performers resist easy categorization as 'Asian Canadian.' The CBC miniseries *Dragon Boys* (2007), about Asian organized crime in Richmond, BC, featured several such transnational performers, including Byron Mann, who was born in Hong Kong and educated in the US; Steph Song, who was born in Malaysia and educated in Australia; and the highly respected Asian American actor Tzi Ma.

According to Gasher, however, while runaway productions tend to efface their West Coast location—he calls the film industry a 'dis-placed cinema'—a few BC independent productions have drawn attention to their Vancouver home. These include the landmark Asian Canadian narrative feature, *Double Happiness* (dir. Mina Shum, 1994), winner of the Berlin Film Festival First Feature Award, and the critically acclaimed Canada–Hong Kong co-production, *Eve and the Fire Horse* (dir. Julia Kwan, 2005), winner of the Special Jury Prize at the Sundance Film Festival. Writing in 1994, Helen Lee lamented that no women of colour had as yet benefited from institutions such as the Canadian Film Centre.[13] The production since then of a number of narrative features by Asian Canadian women is the result of a periodic West-East-West movement of filmmakers from Vancouver to Toronto and back again.

A romantic and 'family comedy,' *Double Happiness* burst onto the scene in the early 1990s with its snappy dialogue, cultural in-jokes and brilliant casting of a then-unknown Korean Canadian actress named Sandra Oh.[14] The acquisition of the film by Fox Searchlight in the US and its subsequent distribution across North America created a whole new audience of Asian Canadian, Asian American and non-Asian filmgoers eager to see imaginative, rather than documentary, renderings of their personal experiences and everyday lives. More than a decade later, *Eve and the Fire Horse* would move audiences with its sensitive depiction of the repression of the female creative impulse, its ghostly allusions and its poetic visual style. The casting of Chinese actor

Vivian Wu and Hong Kong actor Lester Chit Man Chan is noteworthy as well.

In the late 1980s, tens of thousands of Hong Kong immigrants, many facing political and economic uncertainty as a result of the impending handover of Hong Kong from Britain to the People's Republic of China in 1997, were invited to invest in Canada. To facilitate their entry into the country, the Canadian government launched the Business Immigration Program (BIP) in 1986, offering expedited Canadian citizenship to those immigrants with a minimum personal net worth of half a million dollars CND.[15] Hong Kong immigration to BC reached an annual peak of 16,000 in 1994.[16] Just as Chinese labour helped transform Canada into a nation by linking Eastern Canada and the West through the CPR, Chinese capital has helped transform Vancouver into a 'world-class city' by developing its urban infrastructure, particularly its residential and commercial real estate sectors, for both local and overseas (American and East Asian) interests.

Although it would be tempting to characterize the BIP as simply another head tax, I believe that this overlooks important changes between the late nineteenth century and the present day. Whereas the early migrants and 'old pioneers' were mostly of working-class origin and laboured in Chinese laundries, grocery stores and restaurants, many of the most recent migrants under the BIP have come from upper-middle-class backgrounds. The status of these recent migrants is inseparable from the advent of globalization, the rise of Asian capitalism and the development of the four 'Asian Tigers': Hong Kong, Taiwan, South Korea and Singapore. China has since joined the economic-powerhouse list. If the representative symbols of the older generation were the railway and the Chinese restaurateur, the symbols of the newer generation are the condominium and the consultant/entrepreneur.

NEW DIRECTIONS?

The twenty-first century in Vancouver has seen the emergence of new cultural spaces, alongside new urban spaces, for Asian Canadian expression. These have opened up within established cultural institutions as well as outside the state-mandated studio system. Very recently, public agencies such as the NFB have launched new initiatives to increase 'culturally diverse' production. These include the NFB's Reel Diversity competition, which began in Ontario in 1998 and became a national initiative in 2002. Reel Diversity documentary films from the West Coast have included *A Tribe of One* (dir. Eunhee Cha, 2003), a profile of Rhonda Larrabee, the Leader of the Qayqayt First Nation, who grew up believing she was half French and half Chinese; *Why Thee Wed?* (dir. Cal Garingan, 2005), an exploration of the impact of same-sex marriage legislation in BC on six different couples; and *Between the Laughter* (dir. Barbara K. Lee, 2006), a profile of Stephen O'Keefe, a stand-up comedian and former lawyer who is also deaf.

Responding to local programming cuts and the lack of ethnic-minority media production within the public sector, private companies such as CHUM-TV have begun their own 'cultural diversity' initiatives as well. Since 2002, Citytv Vancouver's 'CineCity: Vancouver's Stories' initiative has supported a number of short narrative films, including *Billy Buckwheat and Madame White Snake* (dir. Michelle Wong, 2004), a story of a young girl who discovers Chinese opera through her grandmother; *Once a Fish* (dir. Ling Chiu, 2005) a story of a young woman who mourns her father's passing in an unusual way; and *Out for Bubble Tea* (dir. Desiree Lim, 2005), a story about May, Kim and Ling, three Chinese immigrants from Hong Kong who meet to share gossip and trade advice at their local Bubble Tea house. Cheeky rather than earnest, and upbeat rather than sober, these productions speak back to the 'high seriousness' of the Canadian documentary tradition.

The narrative, rather than documentary, aesthetic of these short and mid-length films has provided important opportunities for the development of local Asian Canadian creative talent, including writers, directors and performers. It has also helped develop local Asian Canadian audiences who have gathered for script readings and previews of works-in-progress in galleries, studios and cafés. These writers, directors and performers are increasingly drawn from local Asian Canadian arts organizations outside of the film and video sector, such as the Vancouver Asian Canadian Theatre, an ethnic theatre company established in 2000 to 'represent the hyphenated Asian on stage in a contemporary setting,' and the award-winning and wildly popular Asian Canadian sketch comedy troupe Assaulted Fish.

Many recent films and videos address questions of gender and sexuality and, in particular, queer identities. Produced by Holiday Pictures and broadcast as part of Citytv Vancouver's anthology series, 'Stories About Love,' *Floored by Love* (dir. Desiree Lim, 2005) is a 'family comedy' about two families in present-day Vancouver: Cara and Janet, a cross-cultural lesbian couple grappling with the prospect of same-sex marriage, and a Jewish/African American couple whose blended family is under strain from their teenage son Jesse's desire to join his gay biological father in New York. Rather than attempting to 'fix' stable forms of identity, the film draws attention to the fluidity of boundaries—familial, ethnic, sexual and geographic—that characterize modern and especially West Coast urban life.

As the first prime-time television drama in Canada to address queer issues among visible-minority communities, *Floored by Love* pushes the envelope in several ways. Cara and Janet's relationship reworks the generic conventions of the romantic comedy—boy gets girl, boy loses girl, boy gets girl back—along the lines of queer and diasporic politics. Cara is Chinese Canadian, but her Southeast Asian background is reflected in her mother's Malaysian accent and in her lover's attempts to cook *char quay teow*. Janet, whose work as a flight attendant renders her emblematic of a certain transnational mobility, is Japanese Canadian, but she does not display her ethnic or sexual identity in the same way. Much of the humour of the film results from its satirical take on ethnic and gender stereotypes as they are negotiated within the family context.

Competition films such as those from Reel Diversity and CineCity frequently screen at the Vancouver Asian Film Festival. Just as Asian Canadian workers were relegated to 'ethnic enclaves' such as Chinatown or Japantown in the middle half of the last century, many Asian Canadian filmmakers remain confined to community film festivals because of the culturally specific nature of their work.

COUNTERCULTURE

The artist-run-centre movement in Vancouver was born out of sense of revolt against a number of cultural practices in the late 1960s and 1970s, including institutionalized (visual) art, commercial television and independent film. It was also animated by political activism, especially feminism, and a desire to see mediated society radically transformed. In her book *Making Video 'In'*, Jennifer Abbott observes that artist-run centres such as Video In[17] were attempts to create utopian spaces in which ordinary people could live and create in alternative ways: 'The early Video In preceded the theatre-like exhibition space. The centre currently runs with couches and television monitors on coffee tables. It was a homey space which welcomed people in out of the Vancouver rain.'[18]

According to Abbott, the most obvious example of the tension between alternative video and institutionalized art was the cancellation by the Vancouver Art Gallery (VAG) of Paul Wong's video installation *Confused: Sexual Views* in 1984. Comprised of video interviews with twenty-seven participants, many of them bisexual, the installation was rejected on the basis that it was 'not art.' In retaliation, Wong sued the VAG, becoming the first artist to sue an art institution in Canada (he lost), and went on to exhibit *Confused* at a number of other venues, including the Chinese Cultural Centre in Vancouver,[19] instead. The cancellation and lawsuit drew national and international attention from the art press, but also beyond.

The year 1990 saw the launch of the groundbreaking exhibition and publication *Yellow Peril: Reconsidered.* Produced by On Edge,[20] the artist-run centre established by Wong in 1985, *Yellow Peril* featured photography, film and video by twenty-five Asian Canadian artists, the first such exhibition of its kind. In 1990–1991, the exhibition embarked on a tour to artist-run centres in Halifax (Eye Level), Montreal (Oboro Prim), Ottawa (Galerie Saw Video), Toronto (V-Tape), Winnipeg (Plug-In Inc.) and Vancouver (Artspeak Gallery).[21] Crucially, *Yellow Peril* engaged Asian Canadian audiences on issues of memory, history and cultural identity, not only on the basis of 'race' but on gender and sexuality, and class, as well.

Galvanized by *Yellow Peril,* various cultural groups organized a succession of alternative media-arts exhibitions during the 1990s, including *Self Not Whole: Cultural Identity & Chinese-Canadian Artists in Vancouver* in 1991;[22] *Racy Sexy: Race, Culture, Sexuality* in 1993;[23] and *Hong Kong: City at the End of the World* in 1998.[24] In contrast to the Asian American media arts centres in the US that are animated by the identity politics of ethnic difference and are focused primarily on film and video,[25] and the artist-run centres in Toronto that are animated by the cultural politics of artistic self-determination and focused primarily on video art, artist-run activity in Vancouver has long been inter-ethnic and multidisciplinary.

As such, West Coast artist-run culture is often preoccupied with issues of gender and sexuality as they are implicated with 'race,' and tends to encompass the fields of visual culture, film and video, performance, and literary arts. Filmmakers, video artists and activists such as Karin Lee work at the intersections of journalism, issues-based documentary and experimental media art, as well as at the point of contact between the local and the global. Films such as *Made in China: The Story of Adopted Children from China* (2000), produced by Holiday Pictures, point the way towards new ways of representing and thinking about Canada, Asia and the world.

CONCLUSION

Asian Canadian film and video on the West Coast resist unified or cohesive categorization. I would suggest that the lack of standardization across the highly individualized artists and their works is a result of the grassroots, rather than institutionalized, mode of cinematic and video production. Vancouver is a site of numerous arrivals and departures to and from the Pacific Northwest and California, the rest of Canada and, increasingly, East, South and Southeast Asia.

In a year in which many community groups on the West Coast have chosen to mark the anniversaries of the city's anti-Asian riots of 1907, the repeal of the Chinese Exclusion Act in 1947, the enactment of the Immigration Act of 1967 and the Hong Kong handover in 1997, there is an opportunity to look critically at how these events have fundamentally altered Asian Canadian communities and cultural practices. We need an artistic practice and a cultural criticism that are socially and politically engaged, with the acknowledgement that 'politics' has changed irrevocably. We need not only to commemorate the national past, but also to engage with local and global concerns in the present and possibilities for the future.

1. Established in 1973, the Western Front is an artist-run centre in Vancouver that promotes an experimental and innovative approach to artistic practice, with a strong emphasis on new technologies. The centre is housed in a turn-of-the-century wooden building that features a gallery, concert hall, dance hall and production studios for electronic and print media.

2. Richard Fung, 'Finding Yourself at the Western Front,' in *External Network: Videos from the Western Front Archives, 1973–2001,* ed. Maija Martin (Vancouver: The Western Front, 2003), 55.

3. Wing Chung Ng, *The Chinese in Vancouver, 1945–80: The Pursuit of Identity and Power* (Vancouver: University of British Columbia Press, 1999), 10.

4. National Association of Japanese Canadians, 'WWII Experience,' (2005). http://www.najc.ca/thenandnow/experience2e.php (accessed 25 April, 2007).

5. NAJC.

6. Helen Lee, 'Coming Attractions: A Brief History of Canada's Nether-Cinema,' *Take One* (Summer 1994): 3–11, 6.

7. Bill Nichols, *Representing Reality: Issues and Concepts in Documentary* (Bloomington: Indiana University Press, 1994).

8. For a critique of this type of narrative in the context of the Japanese Canadian movement for redress, see Kirsten Emiko McAllister, 'Narrating Japanese Canadians In and Out of the Canadian Nation: A Critique of Realist Forms of Representation,' *Canadian Journal of Communication,* 24.1 (1999): 79–103.

9. For an account of the trend toward autobiographical documentary in the 1990s, see Michael Renov, *The Subject of Documentary* (Minneapolis: University of Minnesota Press, 2004).

10. Mike Gasher, *Hollywood North: The Feature Film Industry in British Columbia* (Vancouver: University of British Columbia Press, 2002), 20.

11. Gasher, 5.

12. For a cursory overview of the so-called 'Asianization of Hollywood,' see Christina Klein, 'The Asia Factor in Global Hollywood,' YaleGlobalOnline (March 25 2003). http://yaleglobal.yale.edu/display.article?id=1242.

13. Lee, 11.

14. *Double Happiness* has been the object of a number of film analyses, although not from the perspective of Asian Canadian film history. See, for example, Kass Banning, 'Playing in the Light: Canadianizing Race and Nation,' in *Gendering the Nation: Canadian Women's Cinema,* eds. Kay Armitage et al. (Toronto: University of Toronto Press, 1991), 291–310.

15. Katharyne Mitchell, *Crossing the Neoliberal Line: Pacific Rim Migration and the Metropolis* (Philadelphia: Temple University Press, 2004), 58.

16. Mitchell, 59.

17. Established in 1973, Video In, or the Satellite Video Exchange Society, is an artist-run centre committed to democratizing media and creating spaces for new forms of art and alternative lifestyles. Video In is housed in a purpose-built facility immersed in the production, distribution, exhibition and archiving of independent video and experimental media arts.

18. Jennifer Abbott, 'Contested Relations: Playing Back Video In,' in *Making Video 'In': The Contested Ground of Alternative Video on the West Coast,* ed. Jennifer Abbott (Vancouver: Video In Studios, 2000), 14.

19. Established in 1973, the Chinese Cultural Centre of Greater Vancouver has hosted several landmark Chinese Canadian visual art exhibitions. See Karin Lee, 'Chinese-Chinese—Canadian-Canadian,' in *Self Not Whole: Cultural Identity & Chinese-Canadian Artists in Vancouver,* ed. Henry Tsang (Vancouver: The Chinese Cultural Centre of Vancouver, 1991), 24–9.

20. On Edge operates on a project-to-project basis with no fixed facilities. It is committed to producing, presenting and promoting art marginalized by its political, social or artistic form or content. It focuses on cross-cultural work that challenges ideas and attitudes about what constitutes art.

21. Paul Wong, *Yellow Peril: Reconsidered* (Vancouver: On the Cutting Edge Productions, 1990), 4.

22. Henry Tsang, ed., *Self Not Whole: Cultural Identity & Chinese-Canadian Artists in Vancouver* (Vancouver: The Chinese Cultural Centre of Vancouver, 1991).

23. Remick Ho et al., eds., *Racy Sexy: Race, Culture, Sexuality* (Vancouver: The Chinese Cultural Centre of Vancouver, 1993).

24. Scott Toguri McFarlane and Henry Tsang, eds., *City at the End of Time: Hong Kong 1997* (Vancouver: The Pomelo Project, 1998).

25. For a historical analysis of the Asian American media arts centres, see Stephen Gong, 'A History in Progress: Asian American Media Arts Centres, 1970–1990,' in *Screening Asian Americans*, ed. Peter X. Feng (New Brunswick, NJ: Rutgers University Press, 2002), 101–10.

THE KING OF MAIN: UNPLUGGED

PAUL WONG & CHRISTINE MIGUEL

Earlier in his distinguished career, multidisciplinary artist Paul Wong marked his territory in the art world by reclaiming emerging technologies in film and video. I sent him an email just before I embarked on a cross-Canada drive in late May 2007. I asked if he would be available to have a conversation with me in person when I arrived in Vancouver. His reply email consisted of a one-sentence response: 'My schedule is open.'
—C. M.

One of the trail-blazing pioneers of video art, Paul Wong was an artist before his time. In the 1970s, video had newly become accessible to anyone and everyone. He often walked around with cameras, both photo and video, capturing the world around him. Now, some thirty years later, in the digital age of instant gratification, at a moment when one's entire life can be webcammed with ease, Wong has unplugged himself from his computer. He has been unplugged for the last year and a half.

'Basically, I think my short circuits were full—they were jammed fucking full of the information age. I just needed to unplug, and it was so freeing to delete the first eight hundred emails without looking at them last year,' he exclaims, in a house located near Vancouver's Kits (Kitsilano) Beach. 'I love the fact that you drove nine days to interview me—that is so snail mail—that's beyond snail mail, that's like going back to the CPR.'

'Pony Express,' I correct him. 'And what a warm welcome to see you at the end of my journey.'

Admittedly, one of the reasons I drove from my home in Toronto to Vancouver was to help out a friend who was packing her life into the trunk of her car and moving it to BC. It was a happy coincidence that I was actually planning to visit the city the same time she was planning to arrive. It also was one of those things that I wanted to be able to do in my lifetime—to drive across Canada, podcasting all the way. But I found myself both tired and inarticulate, unable to express my experiences of the journey apart from digital photos taken on the road from inside the car.

Wong had already gone through this in another manner some twenty-five years back. In '82, he visited China for the first time with his mother. He received a Canada Council grant and had an idea of what he wanted to capture based on stereotypes supported by both mainstream Canadian culture and his own mother. But when he arrived, he couldn't see the project unfolding as he'd planned.

'I was in culture shock,' he continues. 'I had been away from the Wong family for a long time just doing my own thing, so it was amazing for us to reconnect in China where we finally saw each other's idiosyncracies and realized who we each were in relation to everything else. I had always accepted that what my mother was espousing was Chinese—and she always used to say it was—when in fact what I saw was . . . no, that's just you, Mom. That has nothing to do with being Chinese.'

Wong had always used the video camera as a mirror, recording anything and everything around. 'My subject matter was whatever hopped out of bed.'

He immediately runs to a section of the house to show me a series of photos from *Murder Research* (1977), an exhibition of photographs of a homicide crime scene taken from his apartment window.

Often he turned the camera around and onto himself as the subject. His classic piece, which put him on the public stage, was *60 Unit: Bruise* (1976). Pre-AIDS, the video was intended as a blood-brother ritual. Sixty units of blood were carefully taken from his friend Kenneth Fletcher's arm and then carefully injected into Wong's back, resulting in a purple bruise.

'That was when I was given access to a colour camera that the Canada Council owned and shipped around the country, and one of the spaces booked it here. I had access to it for three to four days and whammed a whole bunch of things that would only work in colour,' he recalled. 'And that was the tape that survived that era and it only works in colour. Now in the post-pandemic AIDS drug-injection thing, it's a classic piece of work that keeps reverberating every couple of years.'

In 1978, he released *in ten sity*, a performance/video installation piece where Wong enclosed himself in a room, confined himself within four walls with four cameras to release the rage he felt after a friend's suicide.

However, attempting to make sense of his experiences in China in '82 proved to be a much larger challenge than he had anticipated.

'I can remember in Hong Kong saying, "Fuck. I can't just walk out of Chinatown, this just goes on forever." This is it. I was not in Chinatown. This is China. And because I was with family and people and not what the party-line Chinese government espouses and not what the mainstream filters . . . I was there amongst real people and I couldn't quite deal with it.

'It wasn't the sexy shots I wanted. It was so engrained, like a microcosm. It was like I couldn't look out and yet I couldn't see you either. So I came back and boxed up the Polaroids, super 8 films and photographs, which I've never shown or used. It was so fragmented, as far as I was concerned.'

On the same afternoon we met, as part of the extensive personal tour of Vancouver that Wong was to offer me, I would find myself visiting with his eighty-three-year-old mother. In the very house where he grew up, just off Main Street, I would thumb through a small stack of Polaroids: Wong's fragmented memories from said trip.

In '86 he went back to China—with a different plan. 'I stayed for a number of months and, instead of trying to run around, I just sat still. I went from a village to a small town to a city, and took it a bit slowly and just recorded what was around me.'

The resulting footage became *Ordinary Shadows, Chinese Shade,* released in 1988. It was the first feature documentary made using super 8 video, low-grade video technology.

It was his trips to China that fuelled him to curate *Yellow Peril: Reconsidered*[1] in 1990, a touring art exhibition of twenty-five Asian Canadian artists working in film, video and photography.

'I couldn't find a lot of references, I couldn't find a similar experience of working or writing or people from my own point of view—there was stuff, but it wasn't coming from what I was trying to figure out. There wasn't a lot of it, so it started off with putting together a few screenings of other people's work, linking up with the Asian American community, linking up with a few more people in Chinatown here and Canada. Just softly locating stuff, all toward releasing my own work.'

Yellow Peril: Reconsidered was the first exhibition in the country to feature Asian Canadian work so visibly and prominently, and it led to the development of community identity. The project, which toured from coast to coast, was intended to contribute in a concrete way to the ongoing discussion of race and representation.

In 2007, community identity and discussions of race and representation amongst Asian North Americans can arguably be found or created on the internet. This is the space where my work as a podcaster, writer and promoter of Asian pop culture lives and gets distributed. Thanks to the digital revolution and gadget-savvy Asian youth, access to community is just a few keystrokes away.

'When I go to all these new media conferences with all these new media types, they're talking about the technology,' Wong observes. 'And it's great that one can webcam the world, but there has been a precedent set... it's not anything new, it's just more. But is it changing the world socially or politically?'

I think the question is rhetorical. But he looks at me for an answer.

I recall an incident, during the Virginia Tech massacre, at 8Asians.com, the collective brother blog of my podcast site (Popcast88.com). A contributor, known as Jozjozjoz, had direct access to a student inside one of the locked-down dorms at Virginia Tech, who was feeding out information as it was unfolding.

'We got a comment from a producer at ABC News asking us to contact them for information,' I tell him. 'We found it funny that a major media source—the American Broadcasting Corporation—would come to us, a small independent collective blog that had only been around for a couple of months, asking for information about a major news event that was happening on the other coast.' (Jozjozjoz covered the massacre in Virginia from Los Angeles.)

I continue, 'Has the age of instant digital technology changed the world? Is it changing the world? Now I'm thinking it sort of has because all the major networks are run by five people... People are not going to these media sources anymore. They're going to the web because they get still biased opinions, but not the opinions that the same five people are jamming down their throats.

'An article[2] came out, suggesting that the usage of the internet by Asians in general is higher than any other demographic group simply because (A) we don't see ourselves on broadcast television in North America, and (B) all the Asian stuff—the stuff we want to see—is online. We're so much more connected to one another than we are via broadcast networks because the broadcasters are still way behind what's going on on the Internet. The trend has developed so quickly in the last couple of years that there is much more activism online than the networks care to realize. So perhaps it's changed for the good.'

'A pivotal moment was Tiananmen Square,' Wong says. 'That was the first time the facts and low-digital technology or high-end analog 1988... the stuff that was coming out of Tiananmen Square was stuff that the networks were feeding off. It was still analog, tactile and written for the camera, but it was those who could get access to it and the language thing as it was unfolding.[3]

'Why I did video to start with was because of its instantaneous qualities. Everyone can see it as you're building it: we can see that it's not well-lit, we can see that the sound is poor. I then did a lot of interactive things with video installations and performance stuff because I loved the fresh, instant-access quality that I had with the technology, but also with the viewer and audience because it was kind of involved. And the web completely amplifies a million channels later, but I suppose it's now how to live with, control, limit or manage all of that without going crazy with it all.'

I'm curious. 'A lot of people, especially when they put their lives on the net, whether it be through blogging or video blogging or whatever... a lot of people don't know how to separate the personal from the image that they portray on the web. A lot of people have trouble separating their personal from their public. Do you have such a "personal"—or is everything just out there?' I ask.

'That's an interesting way of looking at it,' he ponders. 'Because my early work, a lot of which I've taken out of circulation and a lot of which never made it into circulation... but there are a lot of pieces that were like that—that caught on—because it was just me and my friends who did the work from the mid-'70s to the '80s. There is a lot of work there that was extremely personal and very revealing because it was so rebel to do that. It was claiming technology and video and image-making. Taking it from the mass media which was only owned by corporations before—there were only several channels, which were owned by corporations, or by government and cable companies—and for the first time since video came out, it was possible to do personal stories that didn't necessarily have to impact the masses, the lowest common denominator, and be sexy to advertisers... I've had a mixed career.

'I come from a place where we purposely made "anti-art" and said it's also art. This is time-based stuff—it's art—its references just happen to be much broader. It's not just based strictly on visual art history and history of painting and Eurocentricity. It's not just about commercial culture and television. It's not just about pop... I actually stopped reading all that kind of stuff that people quote... Why is everyone quoting the same fucking books? Come on, people! I don't have to read the same 150 books; there are hundreds of thousands of other books.

'I'm glad there is another generation of people like you who are continuing on because it's hard being in the front line of fire all the time.

Christine Miguel, sel-ca-ed photograph with Paul Wong (2007).[5]

Always having to argue, strategize, negotiate, compromise and do battle to get a piece of the pie—when in fact I want the whole fucking pie or a different pie altogether, or I don't want the pie at all.

'I always want to make work that is accessible to anybody and everybody—it doesn't matter if someone doesn't understand all of it, so long as they get the emotional and visceral or the visual. That is what I like about the work that I like to do and the work that I enjoy.'

I found it amusing that the rebel artist who made 'anti-art' would call himself the 'King of Main.'[4] Even though the name draws on the Vancouver neighbourhood where he grew up, in the context of our discussions, the play on words gives his self-appointed title a sense of irony. The video artist who at one time 'reclaimed technology' has since become so overloaded with it that he opted to unplug himself. Yet in talking with him face to face, I could see that he hasn't missed a thing.

1. For accompanying text, see Paul Wong, 'Yellow Peril: Reconsidered,' *Video Guide* 11.50 (1991).
2. Jennifer Kim, 'Asian Americans on the Internet,' *East West* (April 2006).
3. Shu Lea Cheang, 'Live from Tiananmen Square' (1989) (P.W.).
4. 'Wong' as in the colour, yellow; or 'Wong' as in emperor or king (P.W.).
5. 'Sel-Ca-ing' (verb): short for Self Camera, a term used by Korean netizens to describe the action of taking photos of yourself via digital camera or camera phone (see Popseoul.com).

'LET YOUR FINGERS DO THE WALKING'

REREADING HO TAM'S *THE YELLOW PAGES*

HO TAM & ALICE MING WAI JIM

Artist and educator Ho Tam, currently based in Victoria, BC, and his influential first video, The Yellow Pages *(1994), were part of the Redress Express exhibition and symposium held in Vancouver, August 2007, organized by Alice Ming Wai Jim, an art historian and independent curator based in Montreal. This conversation between artist and curator took place several months before, in May 2007.*

ALICE JIM: Let's begin by asking you how you started your career as an artist.

HO TAM: My undergraduate studies were in Economics and Social Work. I didn't enter university thinking I wanted to be an artist. Chinese parents never really encourage kids to get into 'art professions,' so I am surprised how many of us end up working in the arts. But compared to the population, I guess it's not a large percentage. I first realized I was really interested in making art was when I was doing a field placement at a psychiatric rehab facility where there was an artist who came in to do art therapy. I remember looking over the client's shoulders and wishing that I was making art myself. And then it was a long road to learn, to experiment, etc. I did community work and office jobs, as well as working in commercial art and advertising. Fine arts then seemed to be an afterthought, but it's something that I'm sticking to now. How did you get started?

AJ: Similar situation, I think. I yielded to economic and parental pressures and got a science pre-university degree in CEGEP (the college system in Quebec), taking studio and art history courses as electives. But by the time it came to applying to university, I had made the decision to study art history. When I started graduate studies in the early '90s in Montreal, one of my biggest challenges was in terms of existing scholarship and support, or lack thereof, in my area of interest; I initially wanted to work on racism in Canadian art (my MA thesis focused on black women artists in Canada). For instance, scholarly writing and curriculum on visual artists of colour in Canada were practically non-existent in academia and to a large extent still are. Work at the university and college levels seemed to lag way behind the flurry of activity happening in the arts and cultural sectors in the late '80s and into the '90s that Monika Kin Gagnon's *Other Conundrums: Race, Culture and Canadian Art* (2000)[1] examines, and in even earlier decades as expanded on in Xiaoping Li's more recent *Voices Rising: Asian Canadian Cultural Activism* (2007).[2] This kind of 'time lag' often takes place in any field or period of study, but here, in its acute lateness, it is very telling of not only the Eurocentric biases in the discipline of art history, but also the problematic orientation of ethnic studies in Canada in general, steered by official discourses of multiculturalism. Even now, Gagnon's text is one of the very few book-length studies critiquing cultural race politics and visual arts by First Nations peoples and people of colour in Canada; Xiaoping Li's may soon be a seminal text on Asian Canadian activism and cultural production. For me, this cultural activism and arts-related activity in the 1990s, though concentrated in Vancouver and Toronto, and building on efforts in previous decades, were hugely influential and motivating for my own personal and academic development based in Montreal at the time, even up until today. Who were some of the people who influenced your artistic formation?

HT: When I think of the contribution and influence of Richard Fung, Trinh T. Minh-ha and many others, as well as artists going back to the civil rights, feminist, and gay and lesbian liberation movements, I mostly want to acknowledge the road that these artists of colour have paved for younger generations like my own. Without them, where would we begin? These artists have created a space where we could enter into the discourse and work from. As an artist, I try consciously to make a difference, to create a new voice and to offer a different perspective that hopefully will contribute to the existing discourse. The work of my predecessors informs and inspires me, but I would like to carve out my own set of tools and focus on my particular interest and research. I'm not interested in making what is already out there. Now that I'm teaching, I realize that my students are doing the same. They want to look at my work, but not necessarily wanting to make the same thing. They want to be 'better,' and I think that's good. The students should surpass the teacher.

AJ: You also studied and had a number of artist residencies in the US. Do you feel that this experience affected your outlook or influenced your work in any way?

HT: My perspective on this comes mostly from my experience in the Whitney Museum Independent Study Program and completing my MFA at Bard College, as well as discourses coming out of critical and cultural studies in Eastern Canada. For me, there is a much greater awareness of the politics of representation at stake in the US, especially given the history of the African American diaspora, along with the complex makeup of the racial groupings there. In a way, I would like to go beyond working with any one particular grouping. I like to see that one is capable of moving beyond one's own ethnic and cultural background. But this move is also based upon a commitment to acknowledging one's own experience.

I moved to Canada from Hong Kong with my family when I was young, and I grew up mostly in Toronto. Currently I am teaching at the University of Victoria, where I've been for three years now. BC is a totally new place for me. I lived most of my life since being in North America in the East Coast–Great Lake area. The areas that I teach in are Video and Drawing; this is a good combination for me because they balance out my own practice. I was a 'painter' for a long time and now I'm considered a 'video artist,' although I don't categorize myself really, and I never think of myself as either. I made my first videos not so much by choice, but because resources became available to me. Once I started I couldn't stop, although I continue to make paintings and photo-based work.

AJ: Do you consider your art practice as cultural activism? Is your perspective different from a decade ago?

HT: I started making art in the late '80s, but it wasn't until the early '90s that I became more aware of cultural race politics in the arts. So far, I've made about twenty videos. Only one is a feature-length work, *Book of James* (2006), which is also my most recent work. I don't make political work on purpose, but my background in community work has a big influence in my perception of social justice. Consequently, a lot of my work seems to be some sort of manifestation of this tendency. I don't set out to be didactic or moralizing, though; that would be very uninteresting. I'm just using what I know, to express how I feel. For example, *Book of James* is about James Wentzy, an artist and AIDS activist; I find there are a lot of parallels between him and me, even though we have very different lives and stories to tell.

Last year, I was part of this exhibition, The End of I.D., at the McMaster Museum of Art in Hamilton,[3] which was about the current state, or the resurgence of identity politics. It was very interesting to revisit the recurring issues; indeed, has anything actually changed over the last ten to fifteen years? There are artists making work that speaks in these terms, but somehow it is seen as unfashionable to be personal or political. The visual arts are quite different from the literary or theatre/dance traditions because, among other things, the audience base is much broader. Perhaps this is why my interest shifted to video and filmmaking, though I think one day I'll actually turn to writing. There are trends and there are undercurrents, but just like everything else in the globalized economy, the art market can sustain only so many artists. Contemporary art is definitely not big enough for all the ideas, especially when most audiences only want to see a Van Gogh or the Mona Lisa. I think, however, that identity politics and the politics of representation have been the driving forces in redirecting the focus.

How has your past experience at Centre A (The Vancouver International Centre for Contemporary Asian Art) influenced and changed your perspective on contemporary Asian Art?

AJ: I've been back and forth between Montreal and Vancouver quite a bit these past four years. My move to Vancouver to work at Centre A was an important one for me, both vocationally and for my own personal goals. I worked there as the gallery's first full-time staff curator for three years after I finished my Ph.D. (on Hong Kong art). Centre A is still the only gallery in Canada that has as its mandate to present work that sustains an open yet critical approach to what the term 'Asia' means, showcasing, though not exclusively, local, national and international artists of Asian descent. As an art historian, it allowed me to gain experience working in the field as an arts practitioner and administrator alongside incredibly creative and dedicated people. But perhaps most importantly, it was a way for me to be a part of, and to contribute to, the shaping of a history that I continue to research and write about. In a sense, you could say that I was keenly aware of taking on the role of being a participant-observer and creating a kind of 'situated critique,'[4] as Himani Bannerji once called it, balancing the writing of an Asian Canadian art history and contributing directly, and as responsibly as possible, to the making of that history.

HT: What are the projects that you working on right now? Could you talk about the Redress Express exhibition and symposium you are curating?

AJ: One of the aspects of Asian Canadian art history that I'm currently researching is its convergence with redress politics. The Redress Express project is a large component of this research. The main objective of the Redress Express symposium is to look back at how far Asian Canadian art and culture have come by critically asking what their current state is and what future directions the field needs to seriously consider in order to ensure its viability as a movement (if it can be even called that), given the outcome of recent political redress campaigns and the backlash against identity politics in recent years. The title for the project is in fact taken from a headline in the *Globe and Mail* last year reporting on the cross-country train ride to Ottawa by Chinese head-tax payers and their families to hear the Prime Minister deliver the Canadian Government's apology to Chinese Canadians for the racist head tax federally imposed at the beginning of the twentieth century and the subsequent exclusion of Chinese immigrants: 'All aboard the Redress Express,' it read.[5] The train metaphor is also extended by the fact that the exhibition venue, Centre A, is located in the historic BC Electric building, which used to be the streetcar terminus for the city of Vancouver before the shift from 'rails to rubber' in the mid-1950s.

Included in the Redress Express exhibition, which explores specifically the Chinese restaurant and the head-tax issue in Canadian art, is your first video work, *The Yellow Pages* (1994). This is a work that particularly resonates for me: not only was it one of the first works by artists of Asian descent that I experienced at the beginning of my grad studies, but it also, precisely because it is an earlier work, provides a historical and cultural primer for the development of Asian Canadian identity politics. Projecting it as part of Redress Express is to critically re-examine the cultural lexicon revealed in the video's 'pages' and how it connects with the current discussions of redress politics that are at a crossroads more than ten years after you made this piece. It makes me think of what it is to turn the pages of history; do you think that we are onto a new chapter in Asian Canadian discourse? Could you elaborate on how you came to create *The Yellow Pages*?

HT: In this post-postcolonial time, I think there is more than one stream of discourse going on. People are all working from different perspectives and coming and going from different directions. This is beautiful but also confusing. *The Yellow Pages* began as an artist's book and was subsequently commissioned as a video work by the arts group Public Access (they also publish the journal *Public*), who were organizing a presentation of video art in Toronto's Union Station. They had invited artists to submit proposals that took the site into consideration. I had just made a self-published artist's book called *The Yellow Pages* and thought that it would translate well into video, and therefore I submitted it. At the time, I'd never done a video before and I wouldn't have had the means; back then, video-making was still quite expensive. My proposal was accepted and I received a lot of support to make my first video, which was projected above the ticket booths of Union Station. *The Yellow Pages* was very much a response to the political climate in the art world at the time, 1993–1994, when it seemed that identity politics was finally gaining recognition and access into the art scene in full force. The video was very much about the chaotic situation where there is no one safe place for anyone to exist. I think I was very fortunate to be in the right place at the right time. Making the kind of work that I was making, I was readily accepted into the arts community. I even found myself a job at ANNPAC (Association of National Non-Profit Artist Centres) as an interim director. With the great effort of dedicated artists and community activists, there seemed to be a lot of opportunities, but also much dialogue and dissonance—for example, the series of groundbreaking conferences and exhibitions on race, Minquon Panchayat and ANNPAC in 1993; the list goes on...

My proposed idea for *The Yellow Pages* was to put the Chinese back into the railway station, since the railroad is so linked to the first Chinese labour importation into Canada and the US. My great-grandfather was one of those labourers, but the family didn't know in what job he worked since the labourers seldom spoke about it. They were just bringing home the money. And then I also considered present-day immigrants from China who drive luxury cars, a scenario that contrasts so sharply with the early class history of Asians in North America. I'm excited that for the Centre A exhibition, this video will return to the site of a train station again, Centre A being a historic rail terminus building. The video is structured like a silent film with a word or text preceding and juxtaposing each sequence. In doing so, some kind of meaning is formed and the viewers are to make sense out of it. The associations are sometimes loaded, sometimes nonsense, and sometimes hilarious and sarcastic, balancing humour and concept. I find the balance helpful because speaking about race and ethnicity is sometimes very heavy and dry.

Years later, I made *Fine China* (2000), which is a little similar, also playing with the stereotypes and conceptions of culture, history and politics. This piece has no text, just imagery. Playing with the idea of the blue-and-white porcelain ware, I was thinking of cultural exchange, diaspora, and imagining a new Chinese identity based on historical and cultural influences.

AJ: For some reason, I think your video works seem to be obsessed with trains and chinoiseries (in all shapes and sizes). Why do I think this? Can we relate this to the idea of 'self-orientalization'? Can these works be read as counter-texts?

HT: Yes, I think you are correct about the use of 'chinoiserie.' Both *The Yellow Pages* and *Fine China* are very much like that: using 'Orientalist' aesthetics and curiosity, and turning them back on themselves. In a way, it sometimes feels like I'm making fun of myself. It's a strategy that I've returned to from time to time. It is part of the critique and is a conscious choice. The train motif is unconscious. Although, now that I think about it, it seems so obvious! *The Yellow Pages, Dear Sis:* (1998), *Dos Cartas/ Two Letters* (1999), *Ave Maria* (2000), *Book of James*: all these videos have trains or some reference to trains in them. And then there are other ones that have buses and cars and passengers and travellers. I think a lot about the transitory space that I exist in, the journeyman in me—here, but not here. Even now I'm working on a travelogue.

AJ: Do you make a distinction between Asianness and Chineseness in theory and in your practice?

HT: I took a more general approach when I was working on *The Yellow Pages* and then got more specific or refined in *Fine China*. It's a fine line when we are doing work in this part of the world. Sometimes it is fluid and other times it is more sensitive and subtle. But then when you get specific, how far will you go? There are territories, regions, and all kinds of differentiations. Even within a city or a town there are differences and borderlines drawn. Class, gender and many other constructed categories separate one person from another. Some of my works explore different kinds of 'otherness.' For example, *Ave Maria* was shot in the New York subway and focused on mothers and children, mostly of colour, to explore motherhood, female subjectivity and race. *She Was Cuba* (2003) speaks about alienation and the immigrant experience through the story of a Cuban woman. *Dos Cartas/Two Letters* is about a mixed-raced relationship in Peru. *Miracles on 163rd Street* (2003) takes the viewer into the domestic world of gay Puerto Rican men.

AJ: How do you feel about participating in queer or Asian film festivals?

HT: I have had mixed feelings about showing work in Asian film festivals or queer festivals. But the more I think about them, the more I feel and appreciate their importance. Festivals like Reel Asian play a much-needed role, perhaps more so these days than ever. I think for a while we had been fooling ourselves that the system would change and perhaps someday these types of events would be obsolete. At one point, queer video- and filmmakers, myself included, thought that we had conquered the mainstream, only to find out later that we had been bought and co-opted. The mainstream takes just what is profitable and usable and gets rid of the rest; what we're left with are *Will and Grace* and some lousy home-design and makeover shows. A similar situation goes on for the Asian characters in mainstream media culture. But today, perhaps there is a return to the experimental—a move beyond the conventional 'screen' into newer territories such as YouTube and Facebook in cyberspace. I remember seeing a highly rated clip on YouTube of a young Asian guy going by the name of Kevin or Kevjumba and speaking about his take on ethnicity and gender issues and sharing his everyday experiences as a young Asian person.[6] It's basically the same thing that some of us have been doing in our work for a long time, but at the same time, it was very refreshing and immediate. 'Kevin' is obviously getting out there and reaching a totally different audience, and I think that's great.

AJ: Can you talk about your creative process in making your videos?

HT: Most of the time, my videos come from my own everyday observations. I could be sitting on the train and an idea would come to me, or walking down the street and noticing something is going on. A lot of the times they are not really anything big or significant. They're just moments distilled. And the people portrayed are not heroes; rather, they're more like you and me, everyday people. By isolating them and re-presenting them, I try to give these stories, moments and people the attention they deserve and perhaps open up new possibilities and readings. Having said that, the videos are never mindlessly produced; often it takes a long time for footage that I've shot to become a video piece. I think through and review the materials over and over before they make sense to me. It's a process of adding and subtracting with contemplation and inspiration. But sometimes the process is only an afterthought and I'm not certain if it's important for viewers to know about it. For example, *Ave Maria* is about mothers and their children, but I'm also making connections between the imagery and an audio recording I taped in Montserrat, Spain, a sacred mountain famous for its Black Madonna statue, which created another layer of meaning. The subway train and the tunnel can also symbolize the journey of life, etc. A long time ago, I had this job in Ossining, NY, which is known for the Sing Sing state prison. To get up there, I had to take the Metro North train, often travelling alongside mothers, girlfriends and children who were making visits to their loved ones. This experience has touched me deeply.

AJ: What are you working on now?

HT: One of the three videos that I'm currently working on is about the 1937 Nanjing Massacre, imagining war and peace and its aftermath and history and how we reconcile with what remains. It's a topic that makes me very depressed and confused, and I'm not sure if another video is what is needed. I am also attempting to work from a female subjective viewpoint, which could be problematic. Why? Perhaps because I do not see a place for men in discussions of war because of the prevalent stereotype of the male aggressor. In this context, how am I, as a male, to even come close to addressing the aftermath of war? But I also believe someone has to take

Ho Tam, still from *Ave Maria* (2000).

this issue on. This video project is an experiment and perhaps the first of its kind; I try to explain that I am a pro-feminist male artist, but most of the time I see only flaws in myself. The other two projects are a little more conventional. One is a personal travelogue-type work and the other is a study on the idea of 'colour.' Well, the one on 'colour' is about more than just aesthetics and the visual; perhaps it will be like *The Yellow Pages.*

1. Monika Kin Gagnon, *Other Conundrums: Race, Culture, and Canadian Art* (Vancouver: Arsenal Press, 2000).

2. Xiaoping Li, *Voices Rising: Asian Canadian Cultural Activism* (Vancouver: University of British Columbia Press, 2007).

3. The Life and Death of I.D., The McMaster Museum of Art, curated by Sally Frater (September 2–November 2, 2006).

4. Himani Bannerji, *Thinking through Essays on Feminism, Marxism, and Anti-Racism* (Toronto: Women's Press, 1995), 13.

5. Tenille Bonoguore, 'All aboard the Redress Express: Next stop, an apology in Ottawa,' *The Globe and Mail* (21 June, 2006): A7.

6. Kevjumba, *I Have to Deal with Stereotypes,* YouTube (March 2007). http://www.youtube.com/watch?v=nbZ9zJ22WfQ (accessed 4 July, 2007).

STILLS

PART II

Ann Marie Fleming, still from *You Take Care Now* (1989).

Ann Marie Fleming, still from *The Magical Life of Long Tack Sam* (2003).

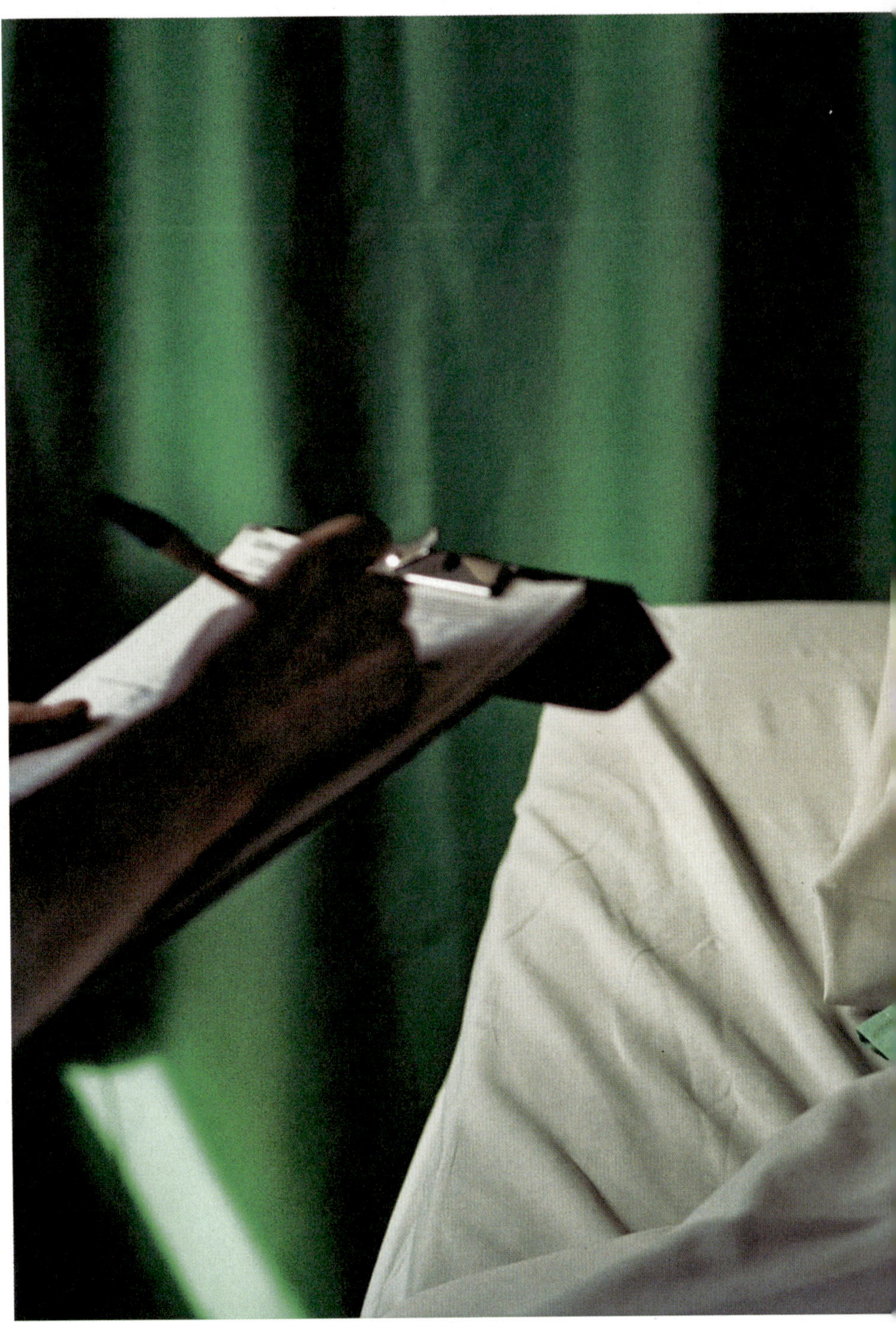

Jeff Petry, production still from *The French Guy,* dir. Ann Marie Fleming (2005).

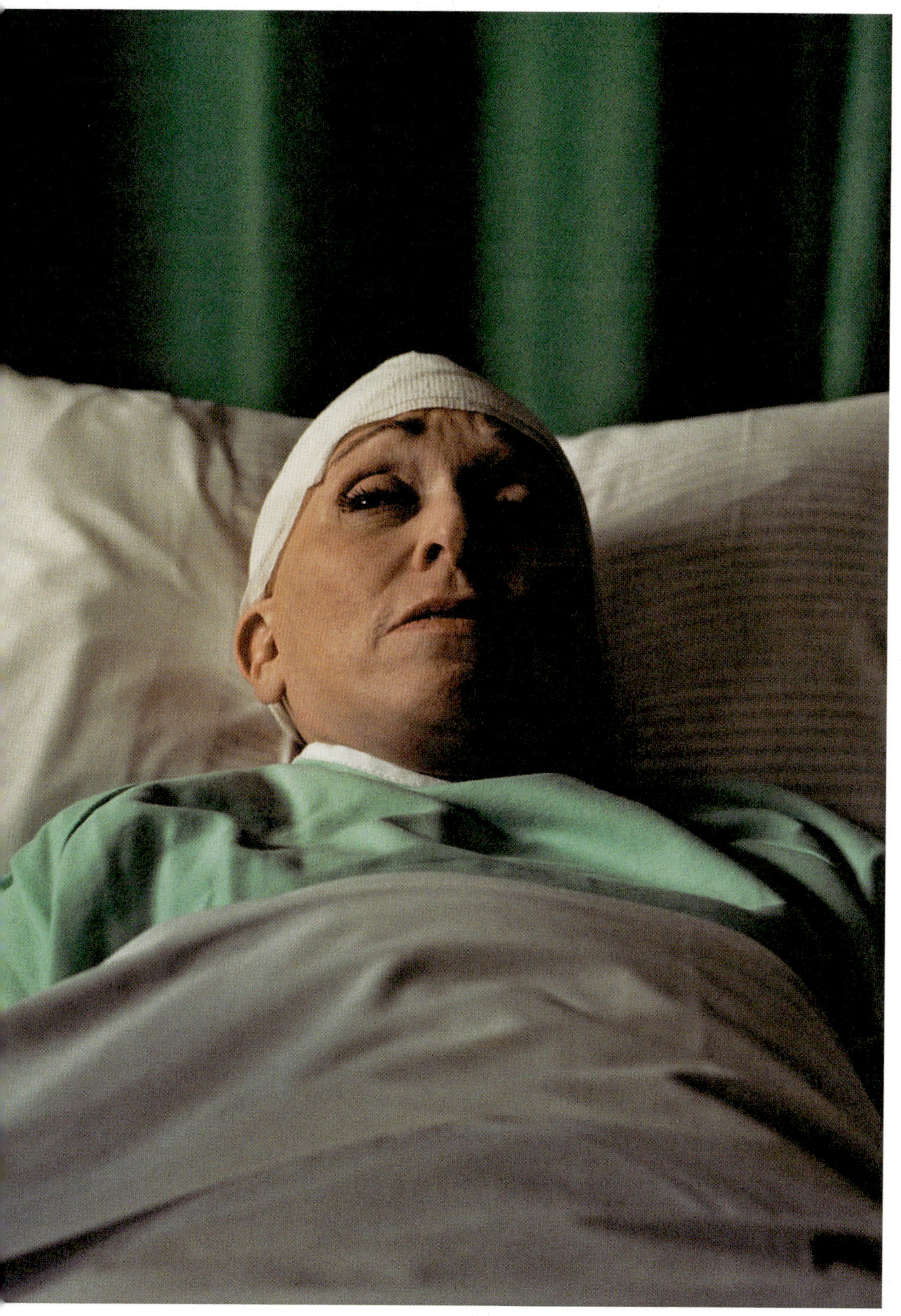

Paul Wong, stills from *Hungry Ghosts* (2003).

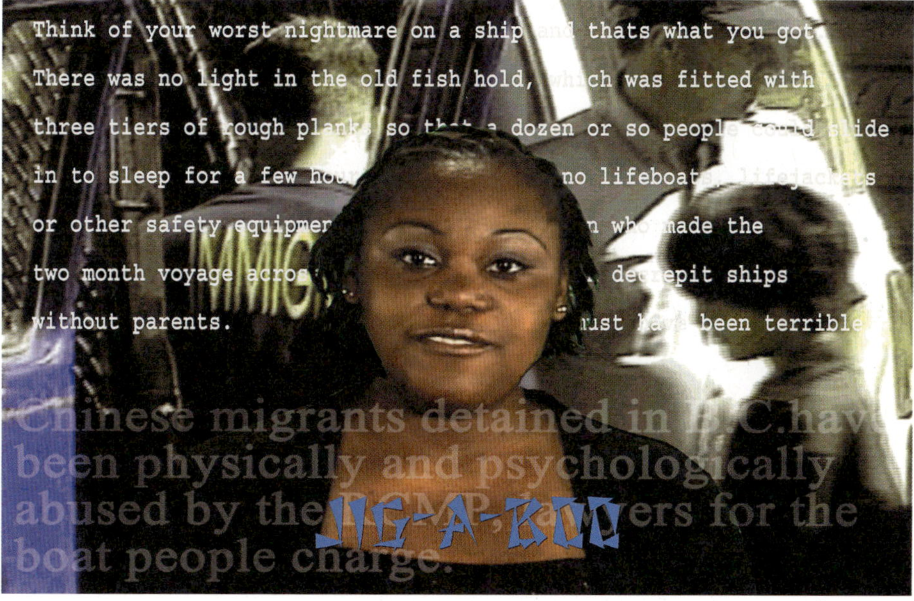

Paul Wong, stills from *Facing History* (2000–2002).

Paul Wong, still from *Chinaman's Peak: Walking the Mountain* (1992).

永垂不朽

Ho Tam, still from *My Memories of Me* (2001).

Ho Tam, still from *The Book of James* (2006).

MEN AND MONSTERS

RECORDED, EXCERPTED

DAVID ENG & LEON AUREUS

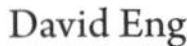

David Eng

Leon Aureus

DAVID ENG: I think we can take it as a given that Asians are seriously under-represented on screen, in film and television, and when they are represented, they're very badly represented: they're the most minor characters, with little or no dialogue, or they're stereotypes. You rarely see an Asian guy onscreen who's anything remotely like either of us. We're Asian, but we're regular guys, and if we spoke to somebody on the phone, they wouldn't necessarily know we were Asian unless we told them that we were.

LEON AUREUS: Yeah.

DE: And that is a problem. But I think we could also try to address why it seems that the Asian community isn't more . . .

LA: Active.

DE: More active, exactly, say the way the black and Hispanic communities in the US have fought for better representation. And they've had some success. I think the Asian community could use a little bit of that fire in the belly. But so far, it seems like sometimes when we raise our voices about it, there's almost a little embarrassment.

LA: A bit of embarrassment, yeah. Many times I feel like I'm fighting against the people that I'm doing this for. I've been at this now for almost ten years, and when I started, a big reason why I wanted to do this was I wanted to help change this poor representation, and it was something that I was very passionate about. And at a certain point in the late '90s, early 2000s, you really thought there was movement with films like *Better Luck Tomorrow.* You saw a lot of growth with a lot of different Asian artists going out there. Then recently, it seems to have sort of plateaued, and the issue has stopped being discussed. The Justin Lins, and in the Filipino Canadian/Filipino North American community, the guys who did *The Debut*: you don't really hear so much from them anymore. I think they really pushed hard, but ultimately they still couldn't break through. And I'm afraid to ask: does the community not really care, or not really need it? Does it not matter whether Asian men onscreen are being properly represented?

When producers do research, they're, like, 'You know what? The Asian community doesn't really care if there's an Asian man portrayed in that role. They're just as happy to see a black man or a white or Latino man.' In the black or Latino communities, they're always going, 'We want to see these faces.' But if you go to any regular Asian guy on the street, for the most part, any Asian Canadian woman or man, they're, like, 'It really is not a big thing for me. It would be nice, but it's not going to really influence how I spend my dollar.' But on the other side of the coin, the white audiences and black audiences don't feel the need. The producers are almost afraid to take a risk by putting an Asian face out there because it's jarring to those other communities as well. They're, like, 'Whoa, what the hell? This is an Asian lead.' For the ending of *Romeo Must Die,* initially it was Jet Li kissing Aaliyah. But when they showed that to the test audiences, they were, like, 'Oh my God! I can't believe it. An Asian guy kissing a black woman? A beautiful black woman? It's like, crazy.' And there was laughter and everything. It's so ingrained in the way Asian men have been and are still being portrayed.

DE: I guess in our supposedly more enlightened multicultural times, there's still, unfortunately, a lot of racism or territorial sensibilities within our ethnic communities. This is something that is not really addressed so much, but I know that a lot of Asians, especially in the old countries—China and Japan and wherever else—have a reputation for being really racist. I don't think that these Asians would necessarily respond well to seeing an Asian man kissing a black woman.

LA: How about if it was a white woman? In *The Replacement Killers,* with Chow Yun Fat and Mira Sorvino, there were glimmers of a romantic interest there, but ultimately nothing panned out, right? So why is that?

DE: Well, this is often the thing with Hollywood movies: Asian women are hyper-sexualized and often treated as sexual playthings for westerners. Of course, not just with *Memoirs of a Geisha, Come See the Paradise,* the famous scene from *Full Metal Jacket*: 'Me so horny. Me love you long time.' Everybody remembers those bits of dialogue. Men, on the other hand, are totally desexualized and demasculinized.

But going back to Chow Yun Fat with Mira Sorvino, I think, strangely enough, one of the aspects of our Asian racism is that we idolize white culture. I don't know that a lot of Asians would have a problem seeing Chow Yun Fat kiss a white woman as much as they would seeing Jet Li kiss a black woman. And this is really sad to say, but I think blacks are sometimes, unfortunately, still held in really low regard, and whites in disproportionately high regard. I think that's why maybe even now a lot of Asians don't get up in arms about our poor representation onscreen: a lot of Asians will identify with the white lead.

LA: Oh dude, yeah, definitely. Speaking from a Filipino Canadian point of view, it's very much that colonial mentality where white is right, or white is much more preferred. Where does the self-hate come from?

Asian culture has its place now, or it's really become quite mainstream in terms of anime and the different art forms being brought into North American culture. They're intermixing, and now there are more Asian Canadians in our society. The younger generation is not seeing so much of the blatant racism. 'Hey, Chink!': you don't hear that as much. They're slow shifts. You're not seeing the Mickey Rooney–type characters from *Breakfast at Tiffany's* on screen so much, though there are still elements of it. But with that slow change there's a greater sense of complacency. 'Things are good. Everything's okay. Why are you complaining?' Yet again, there are no changes on the screen. It feels like there's always a quota. 'Okay, if we want to make it coloured, we'll put in an Asian girl, a cute Asian girl, and either a black guy or a Latino guy. That fits and we don't need anything else. That shows that we're multicultural.' But why is it always that mix? Why? Is it because Asian men are bad actors? It's beyond me.

DE: I think the perception in the film and TV community is that Asians are bad actors and, although I will concede that Asian actors occasionally don't measure up, I think it's thoroughly outrageous and quite unfair. If there was a super-talented actor who just came out of film school but was just given all these bit parts to play, stereotypical bit parts where he only had one line, the equivalent of 'Do you want fries with that?' in every movie, there's no way that he could ever become a solid actor. If Robert De Niro had come out of film school and was restricted to playing bit parts with no lines, or just one line, how good an actor would he have ever become? I think that's the case with a lot of Asian actors. Even if they have a lot of talent, they're not given the opportunity or the experience to develop that talent.

LA: Well, one thing that has to be done is to develop the support of the community. It's our continuing responsibility, as tired as it can get sometimes, to try to nurture each other, try to help build each other in regards to these aspects. You speak of De Niro and those artists, but there was a strong renaissance for Italian filmmakers and writers. And they really worked hard together to push each other in terms of their skills and their talent and their work. For a split second there, you felt that in the Asian community a little bit. That might have been happening a few years back with *Better Luck Tomorrow* and a lot of those other films that were starting to come out. But what happened? Was it because they didn't do well at the box office?

And to address the whole acting aspect of it, that's why we started the fu-GEN Asian Canadian Theatre Company, to really help build the skills of the actors, to give them meatier parts so they could really train and hone their skills as actors. But still so much more has to be done. It's a continuing process.

DE: Well, it's a difficult thing for actors because actors—unless they also become writers or directors or producers—are at the mercy of other people's good will. And yes, unfortunately, there still are just not that many opportunities for Asians. Asians will still tend to be only cast for parts that specifically require some guy's perception of what an Asian is. But there are, at least on TV right now, some prominent Asians on hit shows like *Lost, Heroes* and shows of that nature, but even then, those are stereotypical roles. Masi Oka on *Heroes* speaks mostly Japanese in his role, so he's still an outsider, he's a foreigner.

LA: As is Daniel Dae Kim.

DE: Exactly. Again, they're still not regular guys like us. It would just be a nice change if we got to see ourselves as regular people, as real people, and not some sort of strange, bizarre, exotic, mysterious outsider that's thrown in.

LA: You hear this when you go to panels, you discuss this time and time again, and you go through all the different historical aspects and the political and the social aspects—but really, it boils down to this: we need the producers, we need the writers, we need the directors, everyone continuing to work in that direction.

DE: You're right; it's not going to change until everybody gets on board. Sometimes the actors will blame the casting directors, the casting directors will blame the directors, the directors will blame producers, the producers will blame the studios, studios will blame the advertisers. It becomes one long endless chain of passing the buck. The Asian community has to step up to the plate and say, 'Okay, we do want to see people like us on screen. We're tired of seeing ourselves portrayed as outsiders, or as caricatures or stereotypes.'

LA: A tough part about that solidarity and trying to get that strength of numbers and clout is—and you've touched on it as well—the different sub-sectors, the different types of Asians out there. You're trying to create an umbrella where there are the Japanese Canadians, the Chinese Canadians, the Korean Canadians, the Filipino Canadians, the Vietnamese Canadians . . . They all, for the most part, perceive themselves just as that sub-section. There isn't a great perception of a larger umbrella that really exists. There are efforts, but I don't think they're strong enough.

DE: Well, I think you've done a great thing with fu-GEN. I think with a community like that, there are not separate cliques according to what type of Asian you are. I guess you're right, I have seen it a little bit myself in the general population, in general life. Yeah, Chinese people do stick with Chinese, Filipinos with Filipinos . . .

I just saw *Spiderman 3*, and I really regretted that, trust me. But I was aware, after the fact, that there was one Asian in the entire movie that I remember, and it was such a brief part. It was when Peter Parker was being hassled by his classmates. He has some white guys throwing papers at him from behind and then there's one Asian guy at the front of the class reflecting the sunlight into his eyes, and that was it. That was it for Asians in that movie. But you know, watching that, I actually felt some degree of relief, because in *Spiderman 2* there were more Asians, but they were all horrible parts. Well, there was one scientist, the 'Asian scientist' who was Doctor Octopus's assistant.

LA: That was Daniel Dae Kim.

DE: There was this immigrant family whose house is on fire, and Spiderman rescues the kid. And of course they didn't speak a word of English. And then there was this Asian woman singing the Spiderman theme badly while plucking a single note on the violin. And that got a huge laugh from the audience, but I cringed. I was offended, because I know for a fact that most of the best musicians coming out of the schools right now—like Juilliard, or the Glenn Gould School here—are Asian, more than fifty per cent of them. So yeah, to see that—that's based on some sort of William Hung kind of stereotype; it doesn't reflect any reality about the degree of talent, musical talent, that Asians have.

So that's kind of a dilemma right now: for an Asian actor, you're stuck with no work or embarrassing work. What would you do if you were confronted with that choice? Okay, here's your first role in ages, finally, and it's a substantial role, but it's kind of an embarrassing and stereotypical role that sets back people's perceptions of Asians in general. What would you do?

LA: It's a fine line. It's hard. It's a hard question to answer sometimes.

DE: And that raises another interesting point. If you look at a movie like *Brokeback Mountain,* none of the people involved in that were gay. But it was done so respectfully that the gay community embraced it. And it would be a wonderful thing if non-Asian people were able to do that. It would have been a fantastic thing if that had happened with *Memoirs of a Geisha.* Unfortunately, they didn't really do a respectful job, and the movie ended up being a failure with the Chinese audience, with the Japanese audience and with the North American Asian audience. With the white audience, it did okay, but the movie overall didn't do as well as people had hoped.

And in a way that's kind of a bad thing for us too, because you can be sure that the studios are saying to themselves, 'Okay, well jeez, here we did make a movie with Asians in it, and nobody went to see it. So why should we put Asians in movies?' It is kind of a sad thing to see: the few times they do give us something, they mishandle it so that it screws us.

LA: Your choice of words there is interesting: 'giving us something.' Doesn't that reinforce the idea that it's up to us to do it for ourselves? This is all hypothetical, but can you see the Asian North American community pooling their resources or backing a filmmaker or a project that would be truly worthy of a feature film?

DE: Well, this is a tough thing. Even when an Asian actor or filmmaker wants to do an Asian story, it will be very hard for them to get financial support for that. I remember when Eric Byler, who's a half-Asian-American filmmaker, talked about trying to pitch his idea for *Charlotte Sometimes* to all these different studios. And he was telling everybody, 'I've got this story. It's a relationship drama with four Asian characters and there are no prostitutes or martial arts or anything like that in it.' And almost uniformly, all the studios would ask him, 'Well then, why do they have to be Asians?'

LA: Yeah, exactly.

DE: As if regular Asians don't have relationships. So if an Asian wants to do an Asian story, it will be very hard sometimes to get the backing for that. And when it comes to bigger budget stories, a lot of Asian directors who do succeed—whether they're Asian American like Justin Lin, or from Asia proper like John Woo or Ang Lee—they usually opt not to have many, if any, Asians in their stories. I don't know, maybe what they're trying to do is prove their credibility on somebody else's terms. Maybe they're trying to show that, 'Oh yeah, I'm not an Asian filmmaker, see? You can let me do these films and I won't be adding any Asian content.'

LA: Do you think that's a conscious thing? Or do you think it's the producer's pressure going, 'You know what? If you put Asian leads in this, it's not going to make us any money. So can you switch it?' I'm sure some of these filmmakers . . . Maybe some don't, but don't they also feel that responsibility? Well, maybe not. Whose responsibility is it?

DE: I think there is some reluctance to cast Asian actors, and in a way I understand it. But I think you're right; it would be nice if the filmmakers did take a stand. Black filmmakers aren't judged harshly if they include black characters in their movies. Latino filmmakers include Latino characters, Jewish filmmakers and writers include Jewish characters, Italians include Italians, and so on. Asians should feel no compunction whatsoever about doing the same thing.

LA: That's why I keep thinking there has to be some form of cottage industry, so to speak, to really try to create or greenlight these projects. And start off small maybe and prove yourself. Like Spike Lee started off with *School Daze* and *She's Gotta Have It,* these smaller films, and he slowly built the audience. And a lot of these actors really learned their chops on these projects. So that's the only way I can almost see this ever really happening: if you can pool the resources. And to a certain degree, it's happening. We were doing that with fu-GEN, but theatre and film are . . . They're not completely different beasts, but at the same time the budgets for film are far larger. And it's so much harder to pool those types of resources, those technical resources. But—and I'm throwing this out there—can it be done? I think it's the only way that we can really . . . They've been trying it. They're trying to create Asian television channels in New York and LA where there is a market, but they've been struggling. I've heard a couple have tanked.

DE: That's a hard thing, though. Some of those stations are really geared at the immigrant market. So yeah, that's a tricky thing, because that market is very splintered. There is not one Asian language, of course. But I think there is no equivalent to BET—Black Entertainment Television—for Asians, where it's English-language stuff, with English-language actors, doing everything in English.

LA: But do you feel that there's a market for that? Because again, going back to those studies where it said Asian North Americans are perfectly happy seeing blacks and whites playing these roles. They don't need to see their own faces. It's almost jarring for some of them. It's almost sad. Is it the sad truth? Is it part of our socialization that you can't . . .

DE: Well, yes, I think there is a market for it, of course—just like there's a market for black programming and Latino programming, there's a market for everything, and unfortunately the Asian North American market hasn't been tapped and no one has taken a chance on it. And like a lot of things, it might get off to a rough start—people are going to say, 'See? Asians don't have any talent. Asian actors suck and Asian programming sucks.' But of course that's not the case. Talent is not the sole domain of white people, obviously. And once a television station entered the people's consciousness, it would be successful, and I think there is a market for it.

LA: Maybe in just building an awareness of certain artists already out there in the community—continuing to nurture or create that system where people are aware of their work—you start building a support and fan base around these different artists. So you're creating, you're building that community, you're building the community of artists, and that helps. It really does help. It's just another part of the possible solution, I guess. And it's happening, right?

DE: When you are talking about this pan-Asian thing, it does occur to me that sometimes when we as Asian artists do our stories, sometimes we stick within our own ethnicities as well. And one of the ideas that I'm working on right now is actually something that involves all the various ethnic groups within the broader Asian community. Something like that, if there were more projects like that, it would be a way to bring the different communities together.

But ultimately, as we were saying earlier on, it would be really good to see Asians onscreen in roles where they didn't have to be anyone else's idea of what an Asian was. I was never so aware of my Asian-ness as I was when I decided to enter the film and TV world. Outside, people are people and inevitably you'll run into people of all sorts. But when you enter the film and TV world, people are compartmentalized, and you suddenly realize that Asians are just a tiny, tiny fraction of that world, and usually an insubstantial one. That was quite a shock.

LA: I know it. Some of the time I'm still shocked at how blatant or how stupid casting is, and how Asian males in particular are perceived. A few weeks ago, there was an audition that I luckily wasn't called in for. I heard about it, but I was too tall for what the casting call was. It was for a convenience store chain that was going to be selling one of those iced coffee-type drinks. The story for the commercial was: a guy comes in to the store and he's like, 'Ooh, how do you guys make this?' And so they take the guy into this cavernous lair that's underneath the convenience store where there's a monster—a very Smeagol–Gollum-type monster with a tail. And when you pull the monster's tail, that iced coffee drink comes out of the monster's mouth or something. The casting director or the casting agent is going, 'This is great, guys. You get to wear this really cool costume and just your face is showing.' And my friends are looking around the room and they're like, 'Why is it all Asian guys? Why?' And the casting agent is like, 'But you're wearing a costume.' But their faces are showing—so what does that say? That they're all monsters? The Asian male's face is still visible, and that's the monster. It's disgusting, it's gross. And what pissed me off too was when I brought this up to some Asian friends of mine, they were like, 'Oh, now you're mad that you're getting parts? How about if they cast all white men for that role? Would you be mad that there's no Asian representation then?' I'm like, 'No! But look what they're being cast for.'

DE: When we get so little as it is, when we do get something, a bone thrown our way, and it's something really offensive and unflattering like that, then yeah, that hurts.

LA: Some people walked out of the audition, to their credit. But a lot of people said, 'You know what? Let me just take it. I'm getting paid well for this. It's cool; I get to wear a monster costume.' But aaagh! And I'm not trying to say that there was any sort of malice from the casting agent or the writers who did this. But what does that say about how, subconsciously, we're being perceived or portrayed? It's a distinct aspect of, again, the geeks, the computer nerds, the Asian gangsters, and now the little creatures. It's really strange and disappointing. But then, it's there and you've got to keep working against it, and try and do something about it.

Ultimately, for me now, it's about continuing to do my work and really shining in it so that it can't be denied, so to speak. You just have to really show that your work is amazing—and hopefully I do create something that is amazing—so that it doesn't matter if it's an Asian Canadian thing. What matters is that the story's very strong and compelling and the acting is compelling. You just can't be bogged down. It's there, and you have to live, to work with this knowledge. I don't believe in pretending that it doesn't exist. But at the same time you have to realize that it's there, but find it in your heart to just keep going despite all the challenges.

DE: So, we'll keep doing our work and we'll come back to this in a few years and see how things have changed in the world at large and for us here in Toronto. And fingers crossed, we'll have made some progress.

LA: Sometimes it's so tiring and you're faced with it on so many different levels—in relationships and all these different things. But ultimately, it's just something that you have to feel: this is what I want to do. You've got to do it, and for all the different reasons. But yeah, it'll be interesting to see.

ALBERTASIA: ASIAN CANADIAN FILMS ON THE PRAIRIES

MIEKO OUCHI

While Alberta is not known as a hotbed of dramatic filmmaking in Canada, the province has something that many people may not know about: a long and distinguished history of issue-oriented documentary films. Since the early nineties, a growing number of Asian Canadian filmmakers have come to be part of this development. Linda Ohama, Anne Marie Nakagawa, Michelle Wong and I, Mieko Ouchi, are four examples of Asian Canadian filmmakers who have made documentary films that originate from the Asian Canadian experience in Alberta.

Some of the films explore stories based firmly in the province and its rural roots, like Wong's *Return Home,* which chronicles her journey home to St. Paul, a north-central community of 6,000 people, to reconnect with her Chinese Canadian grandparents; and Ohama's *The Last Harvest,* set during her family's emotional final days on a southern Alberta potato farm. Other films, like Nakagawa's *Between: Living in the Hyphen* and my own film, *Shepherd's Pie and Sushi,* use the experiences of urban mixed-race Albertans to investigate the pros and cons of hyphenated culture and hybrid identity. Stylistically, the films could not be more different. My own work has been strongly influenced by theatre and dramatic storytelling, while Wong's directing style draws on investigative-journalism techniques. Ohama's and Nakagawa's films, on the other hand, clearly show their background and training in the visual arts and contemporary art practice. As stylistically different as each of these films is, however, they do have something in common: they all received support and funding from North West Centre, the regional office of the National Film Board housed in Edmonton.

To fully understand how the North West Centre has become such a hub for Asian Albertan filmmakers, we need to go back to the very roots of filmmaking in Alberta. Filmwest Associates, founded in Edmonton by Anne Wheeler, Tom Radford and P. J. Reese in 1971, seems to have been key in helping to make Edmonton the province's centre for documentary film. In its time, this revolutionary film collective, which at its apex grew to nine members, was at the leading edge of professional film production and distribution in Alberta. Taking rotating roles in different crew positions on each film, members of the collective learned everything from cinematography and sound recording to editing, on top of directing and writing their own films. And they were not out to make Hollywood blockbusters. Emerging from the consciousness-raising movements of the '70s—and parallel movements in other art disciplines, like the Canadian theatre scene, that were actively turning toward Canadian culture and stories—they were, as Anne Wheeler describes it, 'dedicated to making indigenous films that addressed universal issues.'[1] Specializing in issue-oriented social documentaries that emphasized local stories and heroes, their groundbreaking films laid bare the lives of women, local politics and history, Aboriginal reserves and remote and rural communities from all corners of the province. They produced many films, most notably Wheeler's debut feature documentary, *Great Grand Mother* (1975), which drew on personal artifacts like letters and diaries to illuminate the early history and accomplishments of Prairie pioneer women; and Radford's *Death of a Delta* (1972), which followed the battle by the northern Albertan community of Fort Chipewyan as it opposed the construction of the Bennett Dam.

In 1980, Tom Radford opened a Prairie regional office of the National Film Board in Edmonton, and with this new development, emerging Alberta filmmakers began to be brought into the rapidly expanding national fold of the NFB, and to the notice of the rest of Canada. Under Radford's leadership as executive producer, the North West Centre became a hub for personal-POV films, most notably those of Wheeler and emerging filmmaker Gil Cardinal. Highlights of Radford's tenure included Wheeler's multi-award winning 1981 docudrama based on her father's diaries from his time in a Japanese POW camp, *A War Story,* as well as Cardinal's Gemini award–winning 1987 film about his search for his Métis culture and birth family, *Foster Child.*

In 1989 Graydon McCrea came on board as the new executive producer, and under his leadership and with the support of veteran producer Jerry Krepakevich and emerging producer Bonnie Thompson, the array of filmmakers at the North West Centre grew to embrace more culturally diverse filmmakers. This mirrored the outreach that the NFB was doing across the country in the late '80s and early '90s. One filmmaker they collaborated with during this time, Selwyn Jacob (*The Road Taken* [1996]), has gone on to work on many Asian Canadian films through his subsequent and current tenure as a producer at the Vancouver NFB office, Pacific and Yukon Centre, including: Ling Chiu's *From Harling Point* (2003), Colleen Leung's *Letters from Home* (2001), Eunhee Cha's *A Tribe of One* (2003) and Linda Ohama's feature documentary *Obachan's Garden* (2001), co-produced by Jacob and McCrea. It's clear that in the west, the NFB

North West Centre has evolved into an important incubator of Asian Canadian filmmakers.

I'm one of them. In 1992, right after graduation from a professional theatre school in Edmonton, I was approached by a high school friend, Craig Anderl, to see if I wanted to write a film project for him to direct. Although young, we weren't complete newbies to filmmaking. Since we had met and worked together in high school, Craig had completed his diploma in film production at Confederation College in Thunder Bay, made several award-winning student films and was working in Vancouver as an IATSE camera assistant. During that time, I had received training on the other side of the camera. I had completed a BFA in Acting from the University of Alberta through their classical theatre program and had done extensive work as a principal actor in local industrials, and in national educational series and commercials. When approached by Craig for a subject for a new film project, I was surprised. For the first time in my professional career, I was being asked to create instead of to simply interpret. I decided that if this was to work, I would have to start with something I knew intimately: my own family. I resolved to write a script about something that had been on my mind for a long time: my Japanese Canadian grandfather. While I knew enough to know he was somewhat 'famous' in the Japanese Canadian community—I was constantly asked if I was related to Edward Ouchi—I certainly had no idea what for. The objective of this project would be to discover who he was and what he had done to earn such respect from his community.

The result was the forty-five-minute CBC broadcast TV documentary *Shepherd's Pie and Sushi,* a co-production between the NFB and Craig's and my own company, The 100 Miles Film Group. The film developed into a personal examination of my grandfather's life and work—which included a major role in the fight for the franchise, or the right for Asians to vote in Canada, and his work as financial manager of the seminal Japanese Canadian newspaper, *The New Canadian*—and grew to include the rest of my family, including, after much hesitation, myself. The film became structured as two parallel stories: first, the chronicle of my own journey as an actor lucky enough to land a starring role to relive history in, ironically enough, Anne Wheeler's CBC movie of the week about the Japanese Canadian internment, *The War Between Us*; and secondly, the true story of what happened to my own family during and after the Second World

War. More importantly, the film evolved into a discussion of my mixed-race heritage, investigating the widespread sociological phenomenon of interracial marriages that grew out of the war experience in the Japanese Canadian community.

One of the most interesting things about making my first film was the research I conducted at the beginning of the process, to find out what films might constitute a pre-existing Asian Albertan canon. At the time I began making *Shepherd's Pie and Sushi,* I was able to find only two films made in Alberta by Asian Canadian filmmakers, and one of them was still in progress at the time: Linda Ohama's 1993 CTV documentary film, *The Last Harvest.* Surprisingly enough, the other film, the 1992 NFB production, *Return Home,* by Calgary filmmaker Michelle Wong, had just been completed a few months before we started work. The canon was one year old.

The Last Harvest beautifully and heartbreakingly documented the Ohama family's last harvest on their potato farm in Southern Alberta. In this, her first film, Ohama, who began as a visual artist, elicited the long-hidden history of the internment of Japanese Canadians in Southern Alberta and examined the ramifications of this forced relocation on the psyche of the next generations, using a visual style that drew on the dramatic rural landscape of her family's farm. In her film, Ohama revealed details of the internment that had been hidden even from her by her own family, and interwove her family's poignant past history with a present in which they were being forced to leave their land once again.

I related strongly to Ohama's story of Japanese Canadian experience in rural southern Alberta, but even more with Michelle Wong's *Return Home.* The parallels between the premises of our first films were stunning and unmistakable. Both *Return Home* and what I was beginning to write for *Shepherd's Pie and Sushi* began with the simple desire for reconnection with our grandparents. In Wong's case, it was a wish to build a deeper connection with her emotionally distant Chinese grandparents in St. Paul, Alberta; in my case, it was a need to rediscover my family history through a renewed relationship with, and through the story of, my Japanese Canadian grandfather, who was living in Vernon, BC. At the time, I remember thinking, 'What is in the water?' When I conceived of my story, I had never heard of Michelle or her film and was stunned that someone else was embarking on a similar journey.

What was driving us to make these kinds of films, to tell these kinds of stories? Would I be able to make mine when a similar film had just been completed? What would make them different from each other? What was I saying, if anything, that was fresh and new?

Through Bonnie Thompson, who at that time was the head of marketing and running the Studio D women's program at the North West Centre, I was able to talk to Michelle and eventually meet with her in person. Together, we talked about what she had gone through making her film, and what I wanted to do with mine. This conversation was a powerful moment of recognition and revelation: many of the things that I felt as an Asian Albertan were echoed by Michelle. However, I was also struck by the differences between our stories and our experiences. For one, Michelle was the child of first-generation Chinese immigrants and was raised in a small town, while I was the mixed-race child of third-generation parents: one Japanese Canadian, and one of European descent who had grown up in oil-slick Calgary. We experienced life as very different kinds of Asian Albertans. And our socio-cultural backgrounds weren't the only point of divergence. My chosen career of acting had made race an urgent and pressing issue for me whether I wanted it to be or not. It came up every time I auditioned for a part and every time I was offered one and was asked to play Japanese, Chinese, Korean and even Inuit characters. Wong grew up as one of two Asian families in a close-knit town community, and had extensive friendships with her family's café customers. These friendships, she admits in her film, shielded her from a lot of racism and allowed her to disregard and even put aside her ethnicity. My early discussion with Michelle convinced me that rather than give up and find another story, I should persevere and continue to develop my own story. I felt the community needed more stories about the experiences of Asian Canadians and their struggles to come to terms with their hyphenated culture and identity. Let others argue that these films were similar; I knew that our experiences and our films were not. I have discovered since then that these early 'identity' films were not just an Albertan phenomenon amongst a few filmmakers; Wong and I were actually part of a wave across North America of second- and third-generation Asian Canadian and American filmmakers digging into their family roots, and, in ways as distinctive as each of us are, exploring the road home.

For Wong, the road home had a few detours early on. After studying Education at the University of Alberta with a major in Drama, and working successfully in theatre for a while, Wong taught junior high in the small community of Beaumont, Alberta, for several years before the film bug bit. She almost returned to school, applying to the Southern Alberta Institute of Technology, where she was accepted into the film production program. At the last moment, she decided not to attend, opting to take a more practical approach instead. After several years of working as a crew member in many different capacities, Wong made the 29-minute film *Return Home.* Completed in 1992 with the NFB North West Centre in co-production with her own company, Fortune Films, and Studio D, the Women's Initiative Program, the film ultimately went beyond Wong's desire to renew a relationship with her grandparents. Through her interviews and time spent with them in the family-run Boston Café, the film revealed the reasons behind the seemingly distant relationship: Michelle's long-held interpretation of their silence as a lack of feeling, and her deep disconnection from her family history and ethnicity. The film was poignant for Michelle's self-confessed naive understanding of her grandparents' lives, as well as for her bold interview questions, which transgressed traditional taboos. Because she was a beloved grandchild, and was so interested, her grandparents surprisingly didn't clam up as she imagined they would. Instead, they opened up about many things, including stories they were clearly uncomfortable talking about, like the difficult early years the family spent in Canada dealing with the crippling head tax, and her grandmother's revelation that her brother was 'bought.' The film also marked the first time that the NFB made a Chinese-subtitled version of a film. This version has screened very successfully and is still available on video through the NFB.

Much of the film addresses Wong's discomfort with being 'Chinese' and her early desire not to be associated with her first-generation parents and grandparents. As a second-generation Canadian she felt distant from their immigrant concerns. And yet life in the mainstream, especially in a mostly white rural community, was fraught with issues as well. In an interview with Chinacity Entertainment in 1992, she talks about the fact that she 'grew up uncomfortable with being Chinese. I had internalized a lot of Western stereotypes and negative images of what a Chinese person was. In the Chinese community, I was not Chinese enough.'[2] Later in the

Mieko Ouchi, still from *Shepherd's Pie and Sushi* (1997).

same interview, Wong remarks that 'during the making of the film, I was able to unravel the negative images and stereotypes I had about being Chinese. I finally understood what it means to be Chinese myself. Now, I can appreciate and not be afraid to accept my Chinese heritage.'[3]

Working on my own film, *Shepherd's Pie and Sushi,* I was coming to some very similar conclusions. As an actor trying to make a career in the mainstream media, I struggled against cultural and racial stereotyping, and had attempted for several years to move past seeing my ethnicity as a liability. Being cast as the lead in Anne Wheeler's *The War Between Us* was a watershed moment for me. As I say in *Shepherd's Pie and Sushi,* 'It was the first time that I was cast *because* of how I looked, instead of in spite of how I looked.' In *Shepherd's Pie and Sushi,* I was able to share the unique experience of reliving the tragic history of the Japanese Canadians during the Second World War that *The War Between Us* afforded me, while simultaneously delving into my own family's painful experiences during the war and their relocation to Vernon, BC. Through these two parallel stories, I was able to explore, from the inside, the lasting effects of internment on the cultural identities and lives of subsequent generations of Japanese Canadians in my family.

Mieko Ouchi, still from *Shepherd's Pie and Sushi* (1997): Edward Ouchi.

I found myself struggling with many of the same issues that Wong had articulated in her film, but in my case, through the lens of my mixed-race identity: the sense of feeling like a fraud, of being a 'fake' Japanese Canadian. For me, the cast of the film represented the largest group of Japanese Canadians I had ever seen assembled in one place. The pressure I felt to accurately and authentically represent their stories and history, and the fear of being rejected as a mixed-race person, of not 'passing,' weighed heavily on me. Ironically, I quickly discovered that I was not the outsider I feared. Their knowledge of my grandfather, Edward, and the rest of my large extended family, meant that I was far from an outsider. In fact, my mixed race mirrored that of the community elders' children and grandchildren. I was 'family.' Unbeknownst to me, I had had a community all along. They were just waiting for me to realize it. What I discovered while looking at the canon of Asian Albertan films and making my own film is that these powerful feelings of not fitting in are not something that only actors think about—and, indeed, are not the sole domain of first-generation immigrants and their children. These are things that many third- and fourth-generation (and beyond), and mixed-race Albertans, and indeed Canadians, continue to relate to and feel. Moving past these initial feelings to deeper understandings of our history and our future place in this country, however, is the next step.

On that note, the most recent Asian Canadian filmmaker to make a documentary at the North West Centre has been Calgary filmmaker Anne Marie Nakagawa. She came to work with the NFB via a much different route than the one that Wong and I took. Before bringing her project to the NFB, Nakagawa studied at the Parsons School of Design in New York and received her MFA from the University of Calgary in 1999. Over the last ten years, Nakagawa has completed six short experimental films, including *Transit* (2003), *G-8 Gazing* (2003), *Omukai: Facing the Window Seat* (2002), *Strip Mall Tease* (2001), *Peoplescape* (1997), a short documentary called *Reading Faulkner* (2002) and a short mockumentary entitled *Encounters: Kurt Weinar Speaks* (2004). Completed with the NFB in 2006, *Between: Living in the Hyphen,* Nakagawa's first hour-long TV documentary and eighth film, dives directly into the complex issues of mixed-race culture. The film examines how people of bi-cultural and biracial origin construct their identity. Using standard interviews, but also embracing the enigmatic language and spoken-word poetry of mixed-race subjects like writer Fred Wah, and expressionistic images and posed photography, Nakagawa layers meaning and questions with the deft hand of a painter. The film uses seven 'hyphenated' Albertans (and, one could argue, herself as the eighth) as examples of different perspectives on culture and race, focusing particularly on the darker challenges of living with and between multiple cultures within a larger mainstream culture. Nakagawa's film moves past the Asian Canadian 'identity' films of the '90s to work on a larger canvas. The film pushes past the current nationally encouraged policy of celebrating diversity to expose harder and more complex questions around issues of racism, labelling, stereotyping and people's continuing need to sort each other by race, colour and ethnicity.

Since completing our first films with the NFB, both Michelle Wong and I have made numerous other projects. In kind of a reversal of Nakagawa's filmography, I made several dramatic, experimental and documentary shorts *after* completing my initial film, *Shepherd's Pie and Sushi,* with the Film Board, including the 13-minute experimental short *By This Parting* (1999); the NSI Drama Prize film *Samurai Swing* (2000) and the accompanying music video, *Call Me Irresponsible, Saiki: Regeneration* (2002); a short documentary project for the Japanese Canadian Redress

Association; a short mobile film, *Papercut* (2005); and a dramatic short, *Assembly* (2002 and 2007). *Minor Keys,* my second TV documentary with the NFB was completed in 2005.

Wong has also continued to work as a filmmaker and producer in Alberta and across the country, including work as a segment director on W Network's *Beyond Medicine* and as segment producer on Vision's human-affairs program, *Skylight.* While working at Voice Pictures from 1996 to 2004, Wong co-produced several mainstream MOWs and two series, including *Surviving, Word of Honor, Undercover Christmas, Twelve Mile Road, Picking up and Dropping Off* and *Karroll's Christmas,* and two series, *Into the West* and a new version of *Little House on the Prairie.* Her most recent film is called *One Dyke Wore White,* a documentary on gay marriage. She has also completed a second personal-POV documentary with the NFB in 2004, called *Pieces of a Dream: A Story of Gambling.*

Interestingly enough, both Wong's and my second TV documentaries with the NFB do not directly address Asian Canadian issues, although our cultural backgrounds and personal perspectives on ethnicity come strongly into play in both films. *Minor Keys* takes viewers on an eighteen-month journey through the lives of two child violin prodigies, Ewald Cheung and Jessica Linnebach, and their master teacher, former child musical prodigy and Edmonton Symphony Orchestra concertmaster, James Keene. The film, a full production of the NFB, was commissioned by CBC's flagship documentary science program, David Suzuki's *The Nature of Things,* and aired in 2005. While the film did not set out to be about Asian culture, it examined several issues in the Chinese Canadian community in indirect ways. One of the young prodigies, Ewald Cheung, and his parents, who are first-generation immigrants from Hong Kong, demonstrate a culturally supported respect and appreciation for classical music and formalized music training. The support of his large extended family, as they work communally to support Ewald's career, is a strong reflection of their cultural values. His successes are clearly seen as the family's successes. While I was not aware of this when I began the film, upon reflection I feel that my ethnic background and my sensitivity to cultural specificity and difference offered me a powerful insight into the Cheung family. I believe it allowed me to draw the viewer's eye to the unspoken and delicate dynamics of their family unit and helped me find the ways to ask difficult questions around issues of money, community, respect and honour.

Wong's second film for the NFB was 2003's *Pieces of a Dream: A Story of Gambling,* which also aired on CBC. The film documented Wong's forensic search to understand the gambling addiction that had devastated her brother, Phillip, and led to his tragic suicide at age thirty-six. While the film is obviously a deeply personal inquiry into her brother's sudden and surprising death at his own hands, her keen and evolving understanding of the place that gambling holds in the Chinese community and in her family turns out to be an important piece of the puzzle. As well, the deep reticence her family has about talking about personal things, which in her mind may be culturally determined, also seems key to understanding why her brother's addiction escaped her family's detection for so long. Wong also asks hard questions about the Chinese concepts of honour and 'losing face,' in relation to her brother's fall from grace and his desperate attempts to win back his family's respect—issues that have haunted Asian Canadian families for generations. Finally, Wong also considers the family's place in the St. Paul community, where as a member of one of only two Asian families, and as one of only two Asian students in the local schools, Phillip was forced into a leadership role. His fear of having to take over the family Chinese restaurant business is part of what Wong believes drove him to Las Vegas to live with their mother after their parents divorced. Rejection of a culture and the stereotypes associated with that culture may have contributed to other life choices. None of this is easy to talk about, but Wong never shies away from these kinds of hard questions about her family and her culture in the film.

Both Wong's and my sophomore films have moved past the initial personal coming-of-age stories presented in our first works. As filmmakers, we are beginning to bring our perspective to other stories, to other issues. It may not be directly obvious to the average viewer, but for me, that perspective is clearly present in both works if one looks for it.

So where does Alberta Asian filmmaking go from here? Ohama now lives in Vancouver and has made many more films between *The Last Harvest* and *Obachan's Garden,* including *Neighbours: Wild Horses and Cowboys* (1997), *Watari Dori: A Bird of Passage* (1998) and *The Travelling Reverend.* She also continues to make films and to exhibit as a visual artist. Nakagawa has only just completed *Between: Living in the Hyphen,* so it will be interesting to see what direction her future work will take. With her strong background in visual art, like Ohama, she continues to exhibit and curate projects that explore hyphenated culture and identity. Wong now works full time as a producer with NUTV, the community television station at the University of Calgary, and I continue to straddle the worlds of theatre and film and TV.

In a province that is only now beginning to open its eyes to issues of diversity and culture, I hope that both senior artists and emerging Asian Albertan filmmakers will keep making films that reflect the complexity of the differences in our society. Films that examine our concerns from the inside, and continue the important job of telling and documenting the histories and stories from our communities. Films that touch on the rural roots of the province, but that are also unafraid to tell urban stories and to look at the larger world around us through our own eyes. Hopefully, under the recently announced temporary leadership of executive producer Derek Mazur, the North West Centre will also continue to be a jumping-off point for Asian Albertan filmmakers, who will find there, as I have, a soft place to fall and an organization eager to support new work from an increasingly diverse population.

1. Anne Wheeler, 'Anne Wheeler: Biography' (Anne Wheeler 2001). http://www.annewheeler.com (accessed 15 May, 2007).

2. Chinacity Entertainment, 'Alberta Filmmaker Michelle Wong Returns Home' (Chinacity Entertainment, 1992). http://www.asian.ca/media/chinacity/return.htm (accessed 10 May, 2007).

3. 'Alberta Filmmaker Michelle Wong Returns Home.'

FOR SALE

home misses you

EXCERPTED

NOBU ADILMAN & ROMEO CANDIDO

Tastyyes

romeo candido

This is a transcription of an IM conversation between Nobu Adilman, who is in New York City, on Wednesday morning, May 23, 2007, and Romeo Candido, who is in Manila, Philippines, on Wednesday evening twelve hours later. 'Tastyyes' is Nobu, and 'romeo candido' is . . .

AIM IM with Tastyyes

[9:36 PM]

Tastyyes: yo
Tastyyes: i've got an hour on this card. do you know how to save the chat?
Tastyyes: check to make sure first

romeo candido: let's go

Tastyyes: oKAY this is it:
Tastyyes: How's it going over there?

romeo candido: ok.

Tastyyes: What are you working on these days?

romeo candido: right now i'm starting to pitch and sell myself. i just pitched to the big studio a romantic comedy that they really liked. i'm pitching a martial arts film to another company. and a series to MTV Philippines
romeo candido: but for the immediate, i am hustling for commercial gigs to pay the bills

romeo candido: and to get on set again
romeo candido: how about you?

Tastyyes: I love hearing about all the projects you've got on the go. Before you went to the Philippines you always had a million things going on in Toronto but somehow in Manila there's even more and it's all really big.

romeo candido: it's as intangible as it was in canada. i just have more access to people.
romeo candido: it's like dating...
romeo candido: you gotta put it out there
romeo candido: risk the rejection
romeo candido: the heartbreak

Tastyyes: In Canada there was a focus of work that you would pitch. In the P'pines, it's really all out there.

romeo candido: or you're just at home masturbating
romeo candido: well, it's all the same. It's about Filipino identity, whether it's a musical, a comedy, a horror

Tastyyes: Or a masturbation musical

romeo candido: haha
romeo candido: listen. i've done that

Tastyyes: I've heard the mermaids singing

romeo candido: is that what you hear when you're jacking off...
romeo candido: ok

Tastyyes: I just wrapped second season of *Food Jammers*

romeo candido: food jammers. i am a fan and totally part of the target demographic

Tastyyes: Thanks man. We're waiting to hear about a third season
Tastyyes: Now, we're pitching new show ideas to networks in the States

romeo candido: god. that's so great.
romeo candido: i totally think that's where it's at.

Tastyyes: I like working in television partly because so many people get to see my work

romeo candido: i'm certain i will see you on syndicated television some day
romeo candido: in manila
romeo candido: or bangkok

Tastyyes: I cringe when I see so much hard work that has gone into a film and see it disappear at the theatre in a few days

romeo candido: dude

Tastyyes: I would love to be in a Thai TV series—hook me up!

romeo candido: yeah, you'll make a hot girlie boy
romeo candido: we can make it a musical. it'll be huge
romeo candido: anyways. did you ever want to do something longer format. like *I Pie*...the feature length?
romeo candido: or apply your style to something longer narrative?
romeo candido: i'm watching on the lot. i would eat these white kids up.

Tastyyes: I really want to get back to making films, longer ones. I feel like I was on that track then got ensconced in the world of television

romeo candido: i just like the fact that you know how to say a word like ensconced

Tastyyes: But my bro, Mio, and I did make a one hour dramatic comedy for the CBC titled *Shooting Stars* last year. It has a cameo from David Suzuki in his first ever dramatic role. He was great. It was the first time Mio and I really tackled something longer, more nuanced and way more complicated from a production perspective. It was a great experience and if the CBC ever airs it, you'll get a chance to see it!

romeo candido: i've made a pilot too. there's such a crazy let down if it's not picked up.
romeo candido: *St. Jamestown* was the one we did for Vision
romeo candido: earnest 'media club' in the 'hood' of st jamestown degrassi type thing
romeo candido: that was the first time i worked with network
romeo candido: and that's a whole other dynamic
romeo candido: now that i do commercials
romeo candido: i totally get the 'director' not as auteur thing. it's an art in itself to collaborate.
romeo candido: what are we supposed to be talking about?
romeo candido: filmmaking in canada?
romeo candido: are you still typing? you're slow.
romeo candido: ensconced

Tastyyes: I remember being really psyched for you when that was being made but when I saw it and heard about the constraints placed on you, I felt that you could have been far better off if everyone had supported you more in terms of dollars and stayed a bit out of your hair in terms of story. I was glad you had the experience but wondered what they were thinking in terms of getting something big started.

romeo candido: i think they had to spend the money...i think they got funding based on doing some 'diversity' stuff. none of us knew what we were doing.

Tastyyes: we're supposed to be talking about our experiences in the world of making film/video/tv etc. it's better if one person says something, then waits for the other to respond, then ask another question for the other once the thought is finished
Tastyyes: don't be an ichat hog bitch

romeo candido: working with you and mio on *Brotherhood* was my big script writing school
romeo candido: i learned the 'beats,' the 'weave' and all 'writing room' dynamics. i still use that...here in the philippines.

Tastyyes: That was another development story that kind of went nowhere but a lot happened along the way. A lot of learning. The CBC has been really good to me.

romeo candido: i read somewhere in a blog that you are the next David Suzuki.
romeo candido: maybe i wrote it. . .

Tastyyes: I know that I learned the most in my time working in the story department of *Emily of New Moon,* the tv series I worked on in PEI for years in the mid-late '90s. Every week we built up a script, tore another down, re-wrote, figured stuff out and had it filmed the next day. I think the more time spent on a script or a number of scripts will make the film/tv show/whatever you're making, so much the better
Tastyyes: I have been approached by many people, both drunk and sober, both Anglo and Franco, who thought I was David Suzuki. I told him that when we met and he, for real, said that based on our looks we could be related. Maybe we are related. That's why you've got to write a letter to CBC and ask them to air *Shooting Stars.* It's all in there.

romeo candido: yeah, and in your letters, tell them you want me to direct a couple episodes.
romeo candido: i can't believe i haven't done anything with the CBC yet... other than a cool radio drama... again, a 'diversity' initiative thing

Tastyyes: Why is that? Why is it that you're working like a dog in Manila but have such a hard time making ends meet as a filmmaker in Canada?
Tastyyes: Seriously...

romeo candido: i dunno. i can't help but think it's a culture thing
romeo candido: all my work has been focused on filipino identity

Tastyyes: Culture thing? Like you've got none?

romeo candido: as my way of expressing 'canadian' identity
romeo candido: and it was my focus on 'filipino' stuff, that helped me get funding, which helped me get on set

Tastyyes: Why do we have to focus on Canadian identity? Why does it matter?

romeo candido: but then
romeo candido: the 'colored people' money isn't such a hot funding initiative any more
romeo candido: so, as a 'filipino' storyteller, i have to go to the motherland.

romeo candido: but with all my 'canadian' training
romeo candido: like writing rooms with jewish guys

Tastyyes: Do you only want to tell 'filipino' stories?

romeo candido: no
romeo candido: oh. I heard a good quote
romeo candido: 'I want my work to be culturally specific but universally affecting.'
romeo candido: i just look at the mexican 'new wave'
romeo candido: and they can do it within their culture
romeo candido: they're crazy good
romeo candido: and south american is hot. spanish language films seem totally marketable.
romeo candido: anyways, they get their own book. more on asian canadians like nobu
romeo candido: so, are you going to ever address your dual identity in your work?
romeo candido: or have you already?

Tastyyes: I agree with that. My very first film, *In Search of the Rising Sun,* was a short about a Japanese Canadian guy who has an audition for a film where the producers want him to be Japanese. He gets really tense in the days approaching because he doesn't feel very Japanese so he bones up on the culture but in the end is too Japanese for the producers. I don't think we can ever get the balance right. The rest of my work has never specifically been about Asian culture. I feel that small actions say a lot about a person. And if you show those actions then you'll get to know and understand where they're at. And in some kind of abstract way, a sense of culture or identity will come through. We don't really need to hit the nail so hard on the head, which is what i feel happens a lot

romeo candido: holy shit. why don't you ever press enter.

Tastyyes: YOU'RE A MONSTER!!!
Tastyyes: AN ANIMALLLLLLLL

romeo candido: ha ha. i'm a fucking cultural sellout
romeo candido: the thing about 'hitting them over the head' is it's part of creating 'representation'
romeo candido: we gotta start somewhere... i think because i had none... because filipinos had no visibility... i just felt i had to make it for filipinos...

Tastyyes: And you have.
Tastyyes: And you will continue to do so, which is great.

romeo candido: but, here in the philippines, it is really brought to my attention that i'm a 'white' guy

Tastyyes: How so?
Tastyyes: Your money? Your status?

romeo candido: because i don't speak Tagalog

Tastyyes: Is that a board game?

romeo candido: haha
romeo candido: Tagalog is the lingua franca of da pilipeenz
romeo candido: anyways. so now what mr nobu.

Tastyyes: sounds french

romeo candido: what do you want to do... in film?
romeo candido: I guess. cuz this is a film book

Tastyyes: I want to work with people, whether it's a music video or a film or a television show or playing music. It's all related and all important in my opinion. I want to make longer films that people will be entertained by. I want to keep it simple because the second I get complicated I get nothing done and no one understands what I'm trying to say
Tastyyes: Including me
Tastyyes: I'll answer your question about my dual identity now.
Tastyyes: since you've been such a good boy

romeo candido: ok. i totally got a bowl of food while waiting for you to type.

Tastyyes: Because I grew up in a really mixed neighbourhood with a Japanese mother and a Jewish Canadian father, I never really felt out of place. Everything was normal. It's when my brother and I got into our teens that we started noticing some differences. You know, no Asians were represented in the media, on the billboards but when I was at school or out and about, I never felt marginalized. Then every once in a while you'd get a whiff of the prejudice. Some guy at the cheese store I worked at made a slur. It confused me. Then I went to PEI where we have a cottage and suddenly there were many comments about our Asian appearance. Overall there was very little tension about identity besides the norm of growing into my own as a human. Everyone was always so so so interested in what it felt like to be a Japanese Jew so it really felt more like a party trick than anything else. Something to entertain others with.

romeo candido: oh my god.

Tastyyes: Not finished

romeo candido: i'm 'oh my god'-ing because he never presses enter... reading on...
romeo candido: was i the first one to say Jew-panese to you...or was that already a cliche when i thought i was being funny...

Tastyyes: But when I started to take a look at it, I also realized how special the relationship was. The relationship between my father and my mother. How they came together. How strange that would have been in the early '60s. How much they overcame to be together, and how much they benefited from the sharing of one another's cultures. After thinking about all that stuff, I think that I would like to address the dual identity but how I would do it is something that will take some time to figure out.
Tastyyes: Jew-panese was new. There's also Japuish and the real JAP.

romeo candido: nah. Jewpanese is the best.

Tastyyes: Ya, I think so
Tastyyes: Now that you've made a large budget crazy feature film in the 'pines, do you feel you've arrived as a filmmaker?
Tastyyes: Or did you feel that before?

romeo candido: well
romeo candido: i feel more in 'ownership' of my 'role' now.
romeo candido: in canada
romeo candido: it feels delusional to say you're a director

Tastyyes: How about a plan to translate that into regular work in North America?

romeo candido: when you're not paying your rent with it
romeo candido: i just need to get work in canada

Tastyyes: but you are paying your rent with director work
Tastyyes: and keeping a maid

romeo candido: i'm hoping to come back to canada and direct episodes of *The L Word* that i think films in vancouver.
romeo candido: i miss home
romeo candido: like crazy

Tastyyes: home misses you
Tastyyes: ok so . . .

romeo candido: i hustled in advertising too.
romeo candido: it's in manila for me

Tastyyes: making crazy commercials
Tastyyes: ok so . . .

romeo candido: ok so

Tastyyes: ok so . . . listen TO ME

romeo candido: haha

Tastyyes: let's leave it at this

romeo candido: enough about fast typing romeo . . .

Tastyyes: you are a gimp-no
Tastyyes: LISTEN TO ME

romeo candido: it's all about deep thinking nobu

Tastyyes: you will continue to focus on making features, with the ambition of moving back home to continue your work. i will continue making tv with the ambition of making a longer film piece. and we'll leave it at that.

[10:25 PM]

romeo candido: ok. so we're done right?
romeo candido: asian film book? god
romeo candido: that can be so boring

Tastyyes: god no

romeo candido: i wouldn't read it
romeo candido: i would not read this book if i wasn't in it and i'm a canadian asian filmmaker

Tastyyes: i wouldn't read anything that started with 'romeo candido says...'

romeo candido: haha

Tastyyes: ha

romeo candido: i say we send it
romeo candido: sending as is. bye. love you bro.

SEARCHING FOR THE WHITE-HAIRED GIRL

RECORDED, EXCERPTED

KARIN LEE & LORETTA TODD

Karin Lee and Loretta Todd

Vancouver-based independent filmmakers Karin Lee and Loretta Todd discuss idealism, community and activism among Chinese and First Nations filmmakers of the West Coast, and issues of access, support and their creative voices.

LORETTA TODD: Maybe it goes back to what we were talking about before, just the numbers of Chinese Canadian filmmakers and videographers: the numbers haven't really changed that much in the last ten years or so. You were talking about the '90s when there seemed to be a kind of flourish in terms of access, but it seems that not much has changed since then. Why is that? Is it possible to think of new modes of production that could potentially change that?

KARIN LEE: The other day, I was chatting with someone and counting on my fingers the numbers of film- and video-makers—independent filmmakers as opposed to visual artists, of which there are many. So few of the many, many film- and video-makers in Vancouver are Japanese and Chinese Canadian. Fewer still are South Asian Canadian, even though the South Asian community here is so strong and large. I wonder if the kind of support here in Vancouver is very different from the kind of support available in Toronto or other centres. I don't know why we don't have stronger support. Maybe during the post–identity politics era, people started thinking that what we needed to articulate was not identity, but something beyond and outside of that. There was kind of a rebellion against being identified: not being identified was better than being identified as something as specific as a Chinese Canadian filmmaker or video artist. I think that we need to rebuild and continue to develop the kinds of workshops or the kinds of networks that I think were stronger within video for many years. There might be a stronger support network in cities like Toronto, although we have a burgeoning film industry here. But again, it doesn't reflect and it doesn't trickle down to the local population of independent filmmakers, whether you're Asian or not, a person of colour or not. The main concern is with developing venues in which the work can be seen; that's still a closed door so far as broadcasters are concerned. We're just very few and far between, and the way the work has to be contextualized for the larger audience is that it can't be community specific. It has to relate to the mainstream. So how do you tell your stories that focus in on certain themes around community to a larger, mainstream audience?

LT: I always thought it was funny when people said 'identity politics' were dead and gone: well, what do you think Hollywood is? It's all white-boy identity politics. I mean, what's up with that? It's interesting because in the native community, it's the same split: there are a lot of visual artists, some who work in media/video, but it seems that the actual independent film community is actually getting smaller. I see a lot of Aboriginal filmmakers coming out of activist movements. So people are caught between art and activism. I mean, obviously there's limited access to few resources, but sometimes there's also that, too—that division or tension where you can't just devote yourself to your art work because there's so much that needs to be done. Caucasian filmmakers, on the other hand, don't often have the burden of having to deal with social activism. Many do, but the majority can deal with their own careers and not be torn to do community work. Would you say that happens in the Chinese community as well?

KL: I would say that definitely happens in the Chinese community to certain kinds of film- and video-makers. And I think that you see less activism from people mired in traditional ideas of film than you do from those who are making documentaries or who are media artists. If you are a media artist you'd probably be more engaged in activism and community issues and contemporary social themes than filmmakers. You say you've got APTN now, so that means that there is a greater chance for your work to be shown and seen. But why isn't there a huge flourish again of film/video-makers in the aboriginal community, then?

LT: I think the film/video-makers in the aboriginal community, particularly those in the independent communities, are now becoming more assertive in saying, 'Well, we can be those major players.' We don't just need to have a non-native group/community do the work. We can be that major company that can generate this work. We can work with non-native people, we can work with Asian people, we can work with whomever we want, but we could be the drivers of this production, whereas before, the industry thought that 'you guys don't really know how to do this, so you have to rely on these experts,' which is kind of this treadmill they've kept us in for so long: basically to have a lot of non-native people getting rich off natives. But one of the things that could change that dynamic is more collaboration between Asian and Native, and South Asian communities, which would help build a larger community, but which to some extent would also reflect a larger community. I think University of British Columbia Professor Linc Kessler said that we really should be talking to the Asian community, especially the new Asian community, so that they know our histories, so we can have that dialogue. So some people have talked about new modes of production. Within our own cultures, we should maybe build our own production models. Any thoughts on that?

KL: Well, I was just thinking, when you mentioned the APTN, about the number of Chinese-language broadcasters that are actually here—Channel M and Fairchild—and I think there is a distinction in the aesthetic between what is produced in Hong Kong and what is produced here by Asian filmmakers or video-makers accessing a different language audience. If you're second or third generation, you're always going to be working in English, although I work in English and Mandarin. But it's difficult to cross over and get on to those stations, because they're more concerned with Chinese-language presentation and that Hong Kong aesthetic because they're Hong Kong broadcasters, although Channel M does have Mandarin news and a news magazine. But again, it's a completely different audience. I went to Beijing to talk about doing a co-production with Chinese television: I was adapting *Diamond Grill,* a book by Fred Wah[1] about three or four generations of a Chinese Canadian family running a café in the interior, in the Kootenays, and they were really interested. There's this thirst for what Chinese North Americans do and how they live. It's almost a fascination with how the other side works many, many miles away. But the head of the broadcasting department said, 'We actually don't know what our audience likes. We just put things on and we can tell that things will work from time to time, but it's a very fickle crowd because television and media have developed in such a different way than they had been over the past fifty years, when the media was mainly used as a propaganda tool.' So now there are all these other shows that are coming in, and when that audience comes here, they're not concerned about local issues. They're concerned about what's happening in their homeland. They're concerned about how their people are adjusting to being immigrants here, and the same is true of Cantonese-language-based broadcasters. They're a bit better in that they cover more local news because the Cantonese-speaking Hong Kong community has been here for three or four decades, so they're more immersed in the local issues. But identity and the work being made by third- or fourth-generation Chinese Canadians or East Asians don't have that same resonance to them because they didn't have to deal with those issues from early on. And I think that many of us who are making work that reflects our reality here don't cross over into that crowd, so you always feel that somehow you're on this island and you know that you're related to the ones across from you, and that it's just a matter of finding the formula for the common place between us all because it is so diverse, and it's distinct by dialect or generation and more specifically culture. The cultures are very different between Asia and here, so I'm fascinated by how we can create those links and whether or not we can cross over in that way. Chinese filmmakers have an incredible sense of confidence in what they reflect because that is their country and they know that their issues are the kind that resonate with everyone. Here it's much more difficult to pin down who your audience is. And then these other networks, YouTube, or podcasting, or all of those other kinds of things; it's true, you're casting a wide net. To whom? You're not really sure. And what do they want? Like the guy at CCTV said, 'We don't really know until we put this stuff on' who's seeing it, what they like, and what they're going to enjoy. Do they like these things from Germany, do they like the Academy Awards from Hollywood? Do they like the films of the '90s filmmakers? Most likely they don't really care about the '90s filmmakers' films because they're concerned with the issues of contemporary Chinese society, which are slightly more conceptual than the mass TV audiences would be interested in.

LT: Well you get APTN, and APTN says that, as a non-profit society, what they've done is looked at the community and the community has these needs. And the needs are: youth, children, language retention, language learning. But then that was the past and now what they're saying is: 'Well, those are still our priorities, but we can do those in different forms.' I guess, in a sense, like you say, there's no unified Chinese community, nor is there a unified native community. It's almost as if there needs to be that kind of activist sort of progressive Chinese or Asian or diverse channel that gives voice to that. Do you think that might be a potential model? That's another thing for you guys to do.

KL: It would be great if we could find someone that would put some money behind that. It would be more likely that the kind of patron that would do something like that would be a kind of a Bing Thom: someone who, as an architect, is also really engaged in social issues. I know he was around when my parents were actively engaged in the community and he also goes back and forth between China and here, and he has that kind of rapport, and those links, and tries to translate that kind of (it's not really even a hybrid) development into something that brings us closer to culture and language. You see the kind of works he's doing and the way he's trying to reflect that. Someone like that would be perfect to back up a new broadcaster of some kind that could draw out a number of different approaches and cultures and the diversity within the Chinese community.

LT: Well, I hear that Paul de Silva did go before the CRTC with a digital channel called Channel One, which was supposed to be a diverse and aboriginal channel focusing on English-language drama. Of course the usual cable companies were interveners against it. But perhaps Channel One will be successful and we'll see some movement there. But at the local level, perhaps patrons or our communities need to invest in a long-term strategy, because there's another thing in this whole mix for us as independent filmmakers. We can't just work within co-ops, we have to work with larger budgets, crews and so on. So that means having to interact with mainstream broadcasters and mainstream financing sources and so on. And yet we're faced with this other weird thing going on in Canada right now, and that is the broadcasters buying each other up ... CHUM selling, CTV buying, CanWest, Rogers, Global and many more companies looking to buy, and you see this whole change in the media landscape in Canada that potentially puts us even more in the margins. Is there a discussion going on in the Asian independent community?

KL: Well, the sad thing is that there really isn't a lot of discussion that takes place in the Asian independent community, maybe at isolated times during film festivals and so on. We don't have a strong film festival here that has a large criticality of work that they exhibit, and I think that's a problem—that we don't have an organization that develops some kind of dialogue with community. Maybe it's a bit stronger in Toronto with Reel Asian. And Montreal, I know that they're struggling as well. They don't have the money to go forward. And even though we have what they call Asian Heritage Month, again, there's no criticality in the programming there, it's really a celebration. And so because arts—there should be support networks—aren't strong in that area, we haven't developed a lot of dialogue around those kinds of issues, which is unfortunate. What usually happens is that those artists who have a sense of critical issues, when they're engaged and active in the community, it takes so much energy and so much time that they haven't enough time for their own art practice, for their own media practices. When there's not enough money to fund these sorts of organizations, institutions, then those kinds of discussions are left at the sidelines. What I'm seeing now is an emergence of scholars who are becoming more numerous in academic institutions. And because that's developing, and they have tenure and this wonderful economic stability, they can bring on these kind of discussions. I think there's a sort of renaissance starting to take place, especially here in Vancouver. A number of key people at Simon Fraser University, Emily Carr College of Art and Design, and the University of British Columbia are starting to create that dialogue. But again, it's stronger in the visual arts and the academic communities than it is in the filmmaking community.

LT: One of the things that I find interesting is that the academics, a lot of them, are telling histories. And what's interesting is that when you talk to the mainstream broadcasters, they'll say, 'Well, we don't want to see any of these native history stories. We just want to do more contemporary things.' And, of course, the native communities are kind of tired of them too, because they were done so badly. It was all about dying Indians, or Manifest Destiny or the Canadian variation of that, so they were never really dynamic or beautiful. But that seems to be one of the biggest things in Canada: Canadians don't know their history. They don't know the histories of Asian Canadians, we all know just the very surface. They don't know aboriginal history and some don't know that we have our aboriginal titles and rights. So what's that all about, do you think? Why do you think there's a resistance to these histories from the broadcasters with their perceptions of the mainstream Canadian audience point of view?

KL: I think because, as you said, there have been certain histories that have been told and told badly, maybe, by the CBC and the NFB, and they're trying to make up for some of the works. But there are certain producers who've said, 'We've heard it once, we don't need to hear it again, and how many variations can you make on that theme?' And I think that's something that has to be developed in the film- and video-makers. I'm working on a piece about my grandmother in Barkerville. It's about history, but the themes around it are about resistance on her part, on female, feminist resistance during that era. So for me, it's easy. I have so much material that I can draw from, so much history that I can draw from, in creating these kinds of works. But I don't want to just be retelling history in a didactic way. I want to deal with a number of themes, but utilize those events in history to illuminate them. *Cold Mountain, Almost Famous*: it doesn't matter in the mainstream what era you're recreating. You're not going to hear somebody saying, 'You know what, the '70s have been done already. We don't want to do the '70s again.' They do the '70s over and over again. They do the First World War over and over again. It's always there, so why does it always come up for people of colour that 'we're tired of hearing your history'? Well, maybe it's because of the form, that we're retelling our history in a particular kind of form. But the fact is that we have an appetite to know about the past. Even my daughter will say, 'Well, in the old days, you told us that you used to jump out of trees and played this and that,' and she's fascinated with what happened in the old days. How do we tell the stories about what happened in the old days? Well, I don't want to be like some veterans—and I totally respect war vets—but it's like hearing the same story about what happened in the war and so on and so forth. If you approach the past in different ways and deal with themes that are related to the human condition, then it becomes more palatable. But if you go straight on and say 'Well, I'm making a story about so-and-so up in Barkerville,' they go, 'Barkerville's been done before.'

LT: Well, I want to see contemporary films, I want to see futuristic films, especially as a sci-fi nerd. It's not that I'm stuck in the past, but keeping the histories unknown is a way of silencing. I mean, Canada wants to see itself as not racist; it sees itself as fair and benevolent, and those histories are in stark contrast to that self-image. But ultimately you're right. It's also about that human condition. It's also about the fact of human beings resisting oppression and finding some way to make sense of their lives despite that, and to draw on the strengths in our own lives. You certainly see that in your works. You talked about that story of *The White-Haired Girl*[2] and there was a kind of sadness to that story even though she was optimistic. How does that relate to your own father's story? Because he was that idealist; he wanted there to be a good world for everyone. Your dad was the White-Haired Girl in the sense that he had this belief that the world could change, and you inherited that. Your father died an idealist, and he also suffered for being an idealist. You see this a lot in Asian Canadian work: on the one hand this idealism, on the other this sadness. It seems that the ideals can't be achieved, which might be in contrast to the American dream. I see you as the White-Haired Girl with all this idealism, and then you make a film about the loss of that idealism: *Comrade Dad* (2005).

KL: My father definitely tried to hold on to that idealism and was grasping at reasons why he should, and was really stubborn until the end—to hold onto those ideals, in a way, to tell us not to lose the hope that is out there. And it's true that kind of idealism got passed on to me. When I went to China and saw these artists developing works and writing poetry, and I was translating a lot of the poetry at that time, I was just so excited, because I realized that what had stopped in my father's life, and what had stopped for those people who were active post-revolution and who became disillusioned and victimized during the Cultural Revolution... that there were still threads continuing in Chinese society, where just the sheer massiveness of the population means that it's going to be rife with difficult problems. I think it was definitely the death of idealism for a lot of people, and that's why I had so many problems getting people to be involved in the film: once stung, twice shy, it's over. I spent a lot of time in Beijing, and then I realized back in Vancouver that I was doing the same thing my parents did: trying to develop community and engage in activism and feel like it was going somewhere. I didn't want to be burdened or saddled with having to be the voice of a community. But it's one of those things that come into your work. I don't think that I can really separate personal identity, cultural identity, history and community from my work. I want a lot of those things to imbue the work. At the same time, I'd like to focus on universal themes.

1. Fred Wah, *Diamond Grill* (Edmonton: NeWest, 1996).

2. *The White-Haired Girl* was a modern revolutionary ballet and Peking opera whose heroine, a young woman, escaped from the landowners' mistreatment and helped the Red Army to rescue fellow villagers. These operas and ballets, propaganda materials for the Cultural Revolution, exalted the proletarian classes and were most popular during the 1970s (K.L.).

LETTERS FROM SEOUL

HELEN LEE & MIKE HOOLBOOM

It seemed that we became friends on the eve of departing, or at least in its shadow. Hello was also goodbye; the front door doubled as an exit route. Because we are adults (at least in age), we are condemned to interact through the medium of language, with the inevitable distances and abstractions that language creates. Whenever we meet we like to eat—in fact, why not say it out loud—we like to overeat. We like to stuff ourselves so we can hardly move. We eat like two jazz musicians working up a slow riff, until we are inert and bursting, and we have looked at photographs and shoes and spoken about difficult matters easily. Why not fry up something savoury while reading the interview? It might put you in the mood.
—M.H.

As improbable as it sounded then, Mike represented some kind of 'establishment' to me back in the late '80s—some kind of Toronto avant-garde with which I felt some kinship cinematically, but came up blank in terms of race or women. So I was surprised to find us becoming friends, this after an immense flowering of Mike's work and my own turn into narrative film. About ten years ago, he invited me to participate in one of his interview books[1] (if you know Mike at all, you know how incredibly prolific he is). Through the tumult of our personal lives and work, we kept talking. How lucky we are to be able to sustain this dialogue and our friendship, despite the distances.
—H.L.

MIKE HOOLBOOM: Helen, I am just back from the Media City Festival in Windsor, a gathering of fringe moviemakers bent under a rigorous light. Landscapes rule, okay? Silent movies are better than sound. It was a stern demonstration of a cinema that remains abstract, first person, sometimes lyric, reflexive to a fault, an examination of the apparatus and of the act of seeing itself, and, of course, it was helmed by white males. Everywhere I looked there were more white males, like me. And I found this distressing, that this genre had been commandeered, once again, without anyone saying a word, by more white males—as if dominance in the dominant genres weren't enough. Of course we were all crouched behind our marginal attitudes, our first-world poverties, and whenever I brought up the fact that this festival was dedicated to staging a white aesthetic, people looked at me as if I'd swallowed all the blue pills and not the red ones like I was supposed to. Have racial politics taken a giant step backwards over the past decade? Has the constant bludgeoning of the neo-con right won out after all, and allowed, even in the grottos of the fringe, a white male supremacy to rule again?

HELEN LEE: To announce that cinema itself, at root and centre, is a white male enclave seems to be stating the obvious, and people don't like to hear it, not then and not now: how boring, oh do we have to bring that up again, get over it already. To have the same sentiments reinscribed in what's assumed to be a more progressive, now-rehabilitated environment of indie experimental makers, well it's a bit galling, isn't it (as if we expected better from our peers than the more commercial arena of feature films)? What being male and white (gay or straight) endows is, of course, not a natural aptitude or in-born talent for cinema, but rather a feeling of enfranchisement, that yes I'm able to go out and make movies as it's my right. Thank God there are some women, and increasingly more and more, who believe they are equally entitled. I don't think anyone was ever happy with the term 'people of colour,' but we created that space for ourselves, pried it open, carved it out, squatted it and made our own uses of it. So, Mike, now you're back in Windsor and it's feeling so old-school again, that's a bit demoralizing. I did love that scrutiny, the precise and passionate attention to cinema itself. The revitalizing gestures of reflexivity were part of a time when I discovered cinema in the mid-'80s, and were part of the sea change that occurred a few years later where social and political matters went hand in hand with aesthetic considerations, making the work all the more strong, pressing and provocative. I'd hate to think of a backwards movement, or even a lateral one—more of a co-existence perhaps, whether one likes to acknowledge others or not.

MH: Could you speak about your relation to the avant-garde? Do you believe this is a historical consideration, something that used to exist, for instance, in Russia during the 1920s, but not any longer? When *Sally's Beauty Spot* came out it really lit up imaginations around the globe, in its own small, avant way of course. It seemed part of a generational agon around issues of racial representation that remains ongoing. But your work represented part of a new frontier of visibility and intelligence, a new way to address racial politics perhaps, a new kind of aspiration and a new sort of pleasure. I don't need you to mull over whether you were more avant

Helen Lee, still from *Sally's Beauty Spot* (1990).

than the next liberation theorist, but I'm hoping you could describe something of this heady time.

HL: There is certainly that avant-garde you speak of, which includes *Battleship Potemkin,* Dziga Vertov, Kuleshov *et al.* that we learned about in our cinema studies classes. Of course it's inspirational, but historically circumscribed and reified—possibly exactly what the avant-garde is exactly not about—it's become a genre in itself. It has an 'experimental look,' a 'music video feel'—you know what I'm talking about. I was exposed to art and art-making early (my parents, particularly my mother, believed in art) and started to view the world aesthetically at the same time as sensing my own foreignness in early '70s immigrant Canadian culture. My grade school coincided with the era of Trudeau's multiculturalism as official government policy, colliding with the changeover to the metric system and visits to Ontario Place. It all seemed extremely modern and shiny! Finding words for a racialized identity and then moving towards cinematic expression was altogether organic with the artistic and intellectual goals of my education, which culminated in that time you speak of. I was studying in New York in 1989 at an astonishingly vibrant time for critical and cultural studies, learning from groundbreaking figures like Homi Bhabha, Mick Taussig and Faye Ginsburg. My illustrious teachers at NYU and the Whitney were wondrous, and we students were tadpoles in a very deep pond. At the same time, nobody was saying anything exactly about my experience in the Asian American world, the way I'd like to see it—which is more sideways and askance—in the critically challenging way that was exciting me at the time. In that sense, criticism and theory (Stuart Hall, ideas of Third Cinema) came slightly before the filmmaking, but very quickly they arrived hand in hand (Trinh T. Minh-ha, Sankofa and Black Audio Film Collective), inseparable and stronger for it. Like the Soviet experiments, the most compelling artwork is almost always socially engaged.

MH: In *Sally's Beauty Spot* (12 minutes, 1990), you make ample use of clips from *The World of Suzie Wong* by Richard Quine (starring Nancy Kwan and William Holden). We see Sally watching this movie; as she takes cues for her own life, she offers us a model of picture reception. She is the first audience, and we watch the movie over her shoulder, or at least part of it. Why was it important to insert the viewer into the frame? How did you come to choose this movie, and how does it function within your film? And how does the complicated exchange of looks 'work' in your movie?

HL: It was important to assert Sally as an active and interested viewer who took pleasure in the images of Suzy, a stereotypical 'dragon lady' and 'hooker with a heart of gold.' Although *The World of Suzie Wong* is addled with clichés, it was one of the few attractive mass-media images, one of the few images whatsoever, for young girls like us growing up in North American suburbs in the '70s, and this old 1960 film seemed to be on TV all the time. She looks smashing in a cheongsam; her sassy attitude and flagrant sexuality was part of the hook (and even more so if she had actually spoken with the British accent that Nancy Kwan must have had since she was raised in England—how interesting would that have been). So Sally's viewing provokes a discussion about how we find pleasure in things that are supposedly 'bad' for us, in reputably racist images such as Suzie Wong. It upends the rather simplistic argument that only 'positive' images are good for us, for the so-called model minority citizens that Asian Americans are purported to be. But then I wondered: isn't it just another kind of simplistic reflex to position Sally as a viewer in front of the film? And then I realized that film is fundamentally full of simple gestures, basic human responses and behaviours. Sally is no longer ignored or invisible, but rather becomes a 'reading against the grain' kind of viewer, to create our own model of spectatorship. Because that's the only way to look at old films or old pop songs—otherwise we revert to nostalgia and sentiment. We have to invent a new historicity to make it relevant to us, how we live now.

MH: One of the voices in the soundtrack says, 'Skin as the key signifier of cultural and racial difference in the stereotype is the most visible of fetishes, recognized as common knowledge in a range of cultural, political, historical discourses, and plays a part in the racial drama that is enacted every day in colonial societies.' Do you still believe this to be true? It is rare to hear statements like this made in movies made today—why do you imagine that is?

HL: Yes, it does sound rather totalizing, doesn't it? Especially for most of us who don't see the world in that way, despite the dialects of North/South, white and black (or brown or yellow), master/slave, because history can't be ignored. But probably class and economics penetrate all this. I mean, practically anyone will work with anyone and put prejudices aside if the money is right. That's probably too crude or, rather, jaded. I think in cities like Toronto or New York you'll find both race-identified clusters and also a cosmopolitanism that tends to elide or mask the conflicts—but they're there, especially in terms of class (as other places such as Los Angeles and Paris suburbs have found), or obviously in terms of religion (London, the Middle East), and the perceived threat of difference. Everyone likes to believe there's progress and tolerance, and that education and assimilation are working, but the issue of race remains. It may be parodied in Hollywood, or commodified and niche-marketed, but it's still an 'issue.' It's not often talked about as 'skin' per se because that would be so wrong and retrograde, wouldn't it? French films that take up race with a heavy skin factor at play, like *La Haine* and some of the earlier films by Claire Denis (whom I immensely admire), seem to be made under the ghost of Frantz Fanon[2] and the spectre of Otherness, like it's an inescapable legacy. No matter how far away from a post-colonial environment we think we may be, we're always confronting the Other, and in turn, ourselves.

MH: In *My Niagara* (40 minutes, 1992), each of the characters lives a double life because of their ethnicity. He's Korean trying to escape the Japan he grew up in, while she longs for the Japan she's never seen (and hopes to find in him). This double vision that troubles the transparency of representation is typical for makers of fringe movies, which include a disproportionate number of first-generation transplants. Their (our) parents grant us an irresistible sense of another world, even as we are busy growing up in this one. Your movie articulates this double vision, both content-wise and in its stylings and vagrant attentions. Can you elaborate on this theme and why it is important for you?

HL: At that time, in the late '80s and early '90s, there was so much critical theorization around otherness and alterity, postcolonialism, Third Cinema, oppositionality, marginality, fringe films—it nearly busted my brain! Here I was in cinema classes studying Wittgenstein, the Frankfurt School and continental philosophy, and I thought I was supposed to be studying film! (At the time, cinema studies was concerned about its position in the humanities and institutionalizing itself in the academy.) It was so much more pleasurable and productive, I thought, to try to apply these interesting ideas to making films. So I was extraordinarily preoccupied by these themes; they were there first for me, preceding the filmmaking apparatus and production skills that I learned in conjunction with the making of these films. These projects were, at first, a critical enquiry or investigation, and then a film proper—as if I was making films instead of writing essays. Making *My Niagara* was so much about the way its characters were seared by marginality, but we didn't want to portray only that. Their ethnicity and backgrounds were a given (race wasn't 'the story,' so to speak), so that we could contemplate something else about them, their particular foibles and self-projections. I was also obsessed with tracing a kind of subjective cinema, and how to shoot a film that let subjects speak from a naturally empowered position, not as objects of sociological or anthropological interest. Which is still why I am asked, when someone finds out that I'm a filmmaker, 'What kind of films do you make, documentaries?' Because if I'm an Asian woman, then it's about sociology first and films second. The challenge is trying to bring a cinematic structure to this 'double vision' as it's so aptly called, wherever that doubling or tripling may take place—on the level of aesthetics (experimental films), gender (feminist films) or race and ethnicity (films by 'people of colour'). Don't you love that line in Miranda July's film, *You and Me and Everyone We Know,* where Tracey Wright's curator asks about an artist, 'Is she . . . of color?' It's such a knowing comment about the contemporary artistic cultural environment, isn't it, along with its jaded, aren't-we-all-past-that posture. Well, no, we aren't.

MH: *Prey* (26 minutes, 1995) is a self-assured drama about Il Bae (or Eileen) who works in the family's convenience store and falls in with a young drifter. Could you elaborate on the title, *Prey*? This is a movie where every character seems both preyer and preyed.

HL: *Prey* sets up a kind of narrative in the title, and it has a metaphoric dimension. But it's not meant to be literally interpreted. Although there is that section in the film where Il Bae sits down with her grandmother, Halmoni, to watch a nature documentary on TV. This is shortly after the surprise encounter with her semi-naked, now banished Native lover in the same room. Avoiding the obvious, Halmoni remarks on a lion devouring its prey, correlating it with Korean survival, not without nationalistic pride. But then she's completely oblivious to calling this Native stranger a 'foreigner.' Who is foreign, Native or other here? The immigrant still trumps the native on Canadian soil, both economically and socially. In terms of enfranchisement, visibility and power, it is still, ironically, immigrant lives that have advantages over Aboriginal people. And it's a sorry state, isn't it, to be comparing and contrasting oppressions, but these differentials in history, educational and social opportunities must be taken into account. Factor in the privileges of whiteness and class, and there's a minefield of difference at play. There are no 'white people' in *Prey* (save the pawn shop owner) who act as a 'base' from which people of colour are positioned as being different. And that's the one thing that's common in all of my films: we are the 'base.'

MH: Amongst other matters, *Prey* relates a story of young lovers (whose desire makes prey of one another). Does love occur only where there is something missing—a deficiency to be mortared over, smoothed through touch and language? Despite their wounds, both Il Bae and Noel appear to be trying on roles, posing with guns and lovers, sometimes shopkeeper or juvenile delinquent or dutiful family member. How do the pictures that surround them, which they are busy occupying, help or hurt them in coming together? Forgive, please, this dangerously naive question, but might your movie also suggest that ethnicity itself can be a pose or position?

HL: There is a certain amount of positioning that occurs as soon as you place a non-white character on screen. You automatically do the mental calculus from your position as a viewer—it depends where you're placed or how you place yourself as a spectator, how you can thus read the character. An insider can have 'special knowledge' or assumptions about the character, and that means less explaining needed, or rather, a different approach. We already know that backstory. Can the same be said of, say, gay characters in a movie? You can only go so far with that logic. Because then we're relying on generic stereotypes, even as we play and manipulate them. Il Bae and Noel were entirely independent creations, but they are constantly flirting with each other on that edge of race, ethnicity and gendered expectations around desire. The challenge was to frame it in a dramatic story that seduced you and shook up your expectations.

MH: Il Bae has lost her mother, Noel his sister, Il Bae's father has lost both his wife and homeland. Is the displaced place of the immigrant always one of loss, is every gain measured by what must be left behind? Is that why you conjure this geometry of loss?

HL: I do think of the immigration story as one suffused by loss, and not only the gain of a new life in a new country. And somehow there's this conflation of mother and culture in my films; this yearning for cultural connection is symbolized by the lost mother. The relationship between Noel's loss of his sister and Il Bae's loss of her mother, tenuously linked in the story, is also a linchpin for their connection—not that they should be defined by negatives, however. They've both known sadness in their lives, that much is shared. And how does one calculate loss, particularly a concrete one such as a family member? I can imagine that one feels that loss in the body, like the perpetual pain of a phantom limb. If you leave your homeland, the loss can be as profound as the gain. I think of my aunt, whom my father sponsored to Canada in the early '80s. I don't think she stayed six months, not even two changes of season (maybe it was winter, that would drive anybody away), before returning to Korea. Of course it was because she was in love with a man from her hometown, whom she eventually married, but the connection to the homeland can remain forever compelling. Look at all of Canada's immigrants who return 'home' on a regular basis, to the point of buying land with the expectation of retiring there. So where is home, really? In the most positive light, it's like having two homes, which isn't a bad deal at all. But of course you need economic flexibility for this. Or, conversely, economic burden—for all the people who make monthly remittances to their parents or relatives—another familiar immigrant duty.

MH: *Subrosa* (22 minutes, 2000) is a pop-coloured monodrama about a twenty-something Asian woman, newly landed in Seoul in order to find her mother. This quest narrative ends with little resolution; the city turns into an increasingly blurred and abstract backdrop as she uncovers few clues. Why this story, which refuses storytelling, these arrested moments shirking any sense of closure?

HL: I never feel like my films are at all autobiographical, but the desperation and futility of the protagonist was something I felt while making *Subrosa*. The film originated as a kind of prequel for the feature film I was developing at the time, called *Priceless* (which was never made), which dealt with the same character five years on, still living in Seoul, still engaged in a fruitless search for her mother, among other trials. I'd been enamoured with Korea for a number of years. It's the place of my birth and, at the time, a country I knew very little about, so of course it had a huge place in my imagination—a sort of inversion of the conventional immigration story. I think for immigrants there are two contradictory impulses about your home country: one is to negate or ignore it, and the other is to romanticize it and puff it up. I did the latter. I had wanted to make a film in Korea for a number of years, but had a hard time finding the right shape for it; it is indeed a kind of inchoate, all-consuming feeling that you're trying to hammer out into script form—a difficult task for me. But because of all the constant rewrites for *Priceless*, the script for *Subrosa* came out in a couple of days. Yes, there was definitely a sense of: the closer she got, the further she was, and that her search was less about finding her mother than about losing herself. I think it's a self-obliteration story.

MH: The lead is often lensed in extreme close-up, whether she's taking in her first impressions of the city, talking on the phone or checking out floral arrangements. The camera proximity centres the action and grants the viewer an anchor. We are always seeing with her, alongside her. But is the closeness also a kind of deception, because we don't find out so much about her? Like her lost mother, she is close and far at the same time. We discover little about her in a strict biographical factoid manner—perhaps there is another level of knowing which arrives before that, and which is finally more powerful, and more cinematic?

HL: Again, I wanted our knowledge of this character to be organic, and not psychological. I think you may be detecting a kind of anti-psychological refusal of character, at least in the Western sense, where one enunciates oneself all the time about who we are, our tastes, our status, our opinions, our sense of ourselves in every way, from what we like to eat, where we went to school, our favourite authors. This is a conception of individualism that is wholly Western. We know very little about this *Subrosa* character. She wears a red coat. She speaks English in an off-accent—although in fact she speaks very little. I think there's a diaristic feeling to the film. The close-ups you mention are part of an exploration of subjectivity that had been obsessing me for some time. But those decisions also came along with tiny, hand-held cameras that allowed us to fit into tight spaces and produce tight frames. There's something about seeing someone so large on screen, getting to know an eyelash or a mole; sometimes that says enough about the character because that's all she's willing to tell you. The danger, especially dangerous for Asian characters, is to end up being called 'inscrutable,' because then you're finished. The viewer doesn't have an entry point and it's game over. There's that fine line between enigmatic and unknowable, a line that many art cinemas graze against, that may be compounded by ethnic or cultural differences that further frustrate or intrigue the viewer, depending on who s/he is. As the main character plunges deeper into an unknown Seoul, she loses herself even more. When she plunges into the river and emerges, she arrives at a zero point. As if she's been born again.

MH: One of my enduring frustrations is the coverage of 'independent' media. Cover after cover, month after month, there are stories that take readers behind the scenes, the making of, this month's big flash. But there is a story much larger than any of this which is seldom told. I've yet to speak with a feature maker who hasn't been cast into the wilderness, wondering if they would ever make another movie, unable to raise interest or money in their new project(s), no matter how successful or heralded their past efforts. You have also gone through this experience, and I can't help but wonder whether questions of ethnicity and gender exacerbate these problems.

HL: Regardless of gender and ethnicity, every filmmaker has had these problems (although I believe that gender and ethnicity are also enablers of my filmmaking—they're fundamental to the work). In any case, perhaps it's best to think about these stop gaps not as 'problems' per se, but just a natural, inevitable part of the process of filmmaking. And the process can be soul-destroying, it's true. Most of my peers from my twenties have fallen away to other professions outside of film, adjacent to filmmaking (such as teaching) or steady paying gigs (jobs in TV) or, like myself of late, to other creative and personal endeavours such as motherhood. The irrefutable, practical aspects of making a living and feeding yourself come to the fore, never mind taking care of a family. It's okay to starve for your art in your youth, but few of us have the means and heart and single-minded devotion that independent cinema demands. You may have garnered some good reviews, sure, and attended some festivals, and make the rounds of university classes or have the occasional speaking or guest teaching gig, but at the end of every project you're left with a blank slate—returned to zero, as you say. Of course my feature, *The Art of Woo,* how it got made, how it played, etc., is a whole other story. But, like *Subrosa*'s heroine and every other filmmaker at the crossroads, I hope to come back from the wilderness some day.

1. The full version of this conversation will appear in Mike Hoolboom's forthcoming book, *Practical Dreamers: Conversations with Movie Artists* (Coach House Books, 2008).

2. Frantz Fanon, *Black Skin, White Masks,* trans. Charles Lam Markmann (New York: Grove Press, 1967).

Helen Lee, still from *The Art of Woo* (2001).

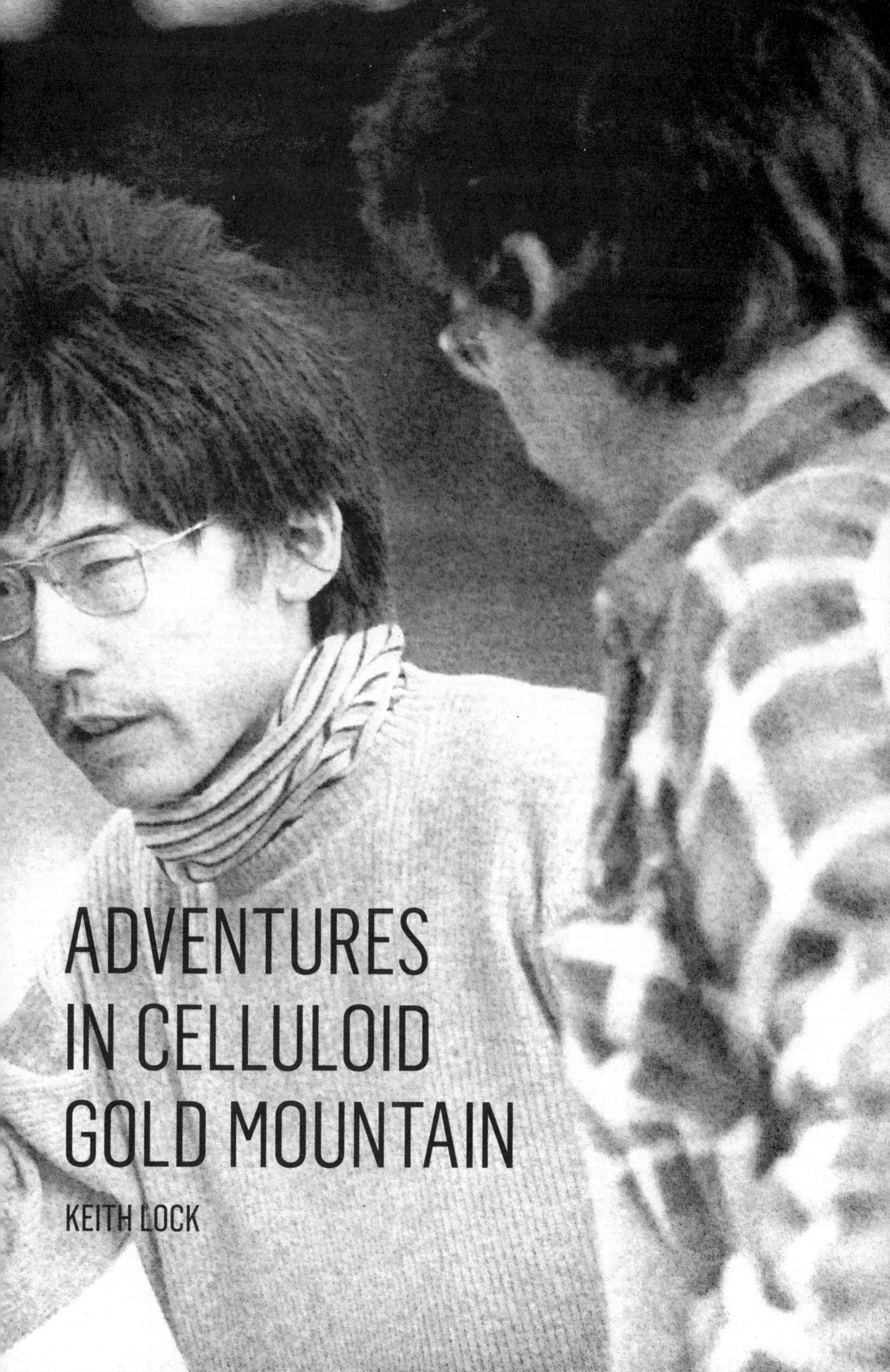
ADVENTURES
IN CELLULOID
GOLD MOUNTAIN
KEITH LOCK

As a returned war veteran, my father could not be denied entrance into University of Toronto. He and his friend, Sam Chin, were the first two Chinese Canadians to graduate from the U of T Pharmacy College. My father's drugstore, Tom Lock Drugs, opened in Chinatown in 1954, the first Chinese-owned pharmacy for western medicine east of the Rockies.

I was born in 1951 and it must have been around this time that my family closed the hand laundry that had been their livelihood. To say my father had a lifestyle that didn't sanction spending money would be a huge understatement. Yet when I was seven years old, he gave me a camera and showed me how to use it. He had wanted to do photography and had even bought some equipment. For this he had been severely scolded by my grandmother. However, he had kept his enlarger and set it up for me in the basement of the drugstore. The drugstore sold film and had a photo finishing service. My father would sometimes give me expired film to use.

In 1967 our high school geography class was assigned an essay. A friend and I thought it would be more interesting if we made a film. At this point my interest switched from still photography to making 8mm films. My father obliged by letting us use his home movie camera and turning over any short-dated film. There was a buzz about Canadian film in those times due to Expo '67. There was even a film shot in Chinatown around this time by David Secter, *The Offering,* which a lot of people, including my father's partner at the drugstore, auditioned for.

My school filmmaking friend, James Anderson, suggested we take a filmmaking course offered at the Three Schools art school on Bloor Street. Using the school's super 8 camera, we made a film with a real soundtrack using my little brother's toy soldiers. By taping a magnifying glass to the front element, I was able to get extreme close-ups with very little depth of field. The resulting film looked great. My friend James was a rather introverted person. One day he showed me a film he was working on using Norman McLaren's technique of hand-painted animation. I was really amazed by it and suggested titling the film *Scream of a Butterfly.*

These two films, the super 8 film that we titled *Flights of Frenzy* and James's animation, were seen by someone and selected for a UNESCO festival in Holland called the 10th Muse International. A little later, we received word that *Scream of a Butterfly* had won the festival Grand Prix and *Flights of Frenzy* had won the best super 8 award. The awards were accepted on our behalf by the Canadian Ambassador to the Hague. The *Toronto Star* and *Globe and Mail* ran articles and photos and we were put on the cover of *Monday Morning* magazine, which ran photos and interviews over two issues.

These events gave me confidence that I could be a filmmaker. I had been accepted by two universities for engineering. Against my parents' wishes, I applied and was accepted for the inaugural year of York University's Film Program. I was a mere film student, but a lot of doors opened because of the awards in Europe. James and I got a commission from the International Red Cross to make a documentary. I also landed a job at Theatre Passe Muraille during one of their most creative periods, designing projections for their landmark theatre production *Dukhobours.*

I was in attendance at the first meeting of the Toronto Filmmakers Co-op at Rochdale College. This was the first film co-op in Canada, which later morphed into the Liaison of Independent Filmmakers of Toronto (LIFT). Wildly anarchistic, they designated me, in absentia, to be the co-op's first chair. The thinking was: Keith is Chinese, therefore he should be our chair because it would be like Chairman Mao, who is also Chinese. It was a good-humoured 'fuck you' to those outsiders who demanded such things as a chair in the first place. This was typical of Rochdale, which was often the first stop for young American draft resisters fleeing the Vietnam War. Here, being Asian was not a negative. If anything, it had a kind of strange cachet. Rochdale College was filled with fresh ideas and an urgent energy. I taught courses in filmmaking there for the co-op. Immersed in all the stuff surrounding Rochdale, the incredible experimental free university, I had just turned twenty.

Around this time I bought a second-hand Bolex camera with one fixed lens. In the spring of 1972 I took this camera up to a farm 'commune' started by some friends of friends at a really remote place called Buck Lake. I was totally entranced with the place and the essential idea of creating a community that lived in harmony with nature. Completely off the grid, the log-walled building had no electricity and was a one-mile walk through heavy woods to the nearest road. Born of the 'Back to the Land' movement prominent in popular culture of the time, Buck Lake's inhabitants were a mixed group of men and women. The oldest and de facto leader was a twenty-six-year-old French Canadian boilermaker, Thomas Broulliette.

I was not quite twenty-one and had one year to go in my BFA program at York. Totally against my parents' wishes, I dropped out of university and moved permanently to Buck Lake to shoot a film. I remained there for about five years, hitchhiking to the city more frequently, however, toward the end of this period, especially to buy film and processing.

One time while in Toronto, I happened to be introduced to Michael Snow at the Canadian Filmmakers Distribution Centre. Michael and his partner, Joyce Wieland, had just arrived in Toronto after more or less fleeing New York. I had seen Snow's films in university and greatly admired them. Michael asked me if I would be in his new experimental film, *Rameau's Nephew.* The scene was simple. I was to be one of a bunch of people riding a TTC bus. At one point Michael struggled to set up his camera tripod in the bus's narrow aisle. I got out of my seat and helped him out. After that, he asked me to work on *Rameau's Nephew* as a cinematographer, shooting his epic four-hour film.

Through the '70s, I shot other works with Michael Snow, including an installation piece, *Two Sides to Every Story*; a book of still photographs, *Cover to Cover*; and another film, *Presents.* He and Joyce were both very kind, and I would sometimes hang out at their house after the work was done. Michael was always supportive in a strict, no-nonsense way. An internationally famous artist and arguably the foremost experimental filmmaker in the country, he seemed to take pains to avoid pretentiousness and would introduce himself to my friends as 'Mike.' One time we were driving somewhere and he asked how the new film I was shooting at Buck Lake was going. I told him the footage was shit, which was just the way we talked. He then gave me some advice that I will always hold dear. He said, 'You just have to keep looking at it until you start to see something in it you like.' I still wonder if this comment illuminated how Mike's early masterworks were conceived, like *Wavelength* and *New York Eye and Ear Control,* each built entirely around one specific camera movement.

I shot my film at Buck Lake over 1973 into 1974. I wanted to have a film that was beyond mere documentation, more a meditation on filmmaking and nature. During this time I discovered two Chinese classic texts that were readily available at bookstores, *Dao De Jing* and *I Jing*. I carried these two volumes with me in all my travels and read them almost every day. Without electricity or electronic information media, one starts to develop a really different perspective on things. In this time the Zen concept of chopping wood and carrying water took on a literal meaning.

I would hitchhike back to Toronto whenever I needed film or processing, and that's when I would reconnect. Michael Ondaatje was making a documentary on the Theatre Passe Muraille production of *The Farm Show* and he asked me to record sound on it. Created by a collective of actors who went out to live within the small farming community in southwestern Ontario and then created a play from their experiences, *The Farm Show* had been immediately recognized as a landmark in Canadian theatre. Now the theatre company was taking it back to the community to show it to the farmers, and this was the subject of the documentary. Working with Michael Ondaatje, in combination with artistic director Paul Thompson, proved profoundly influential. To this day, the whole Theatre Passe Muraille experience forms the kernel of my screenplay writing process.

Inevitably, the commune fabric at Buck Lake began to fray. I had read a book on the First Nations tipi. Partly as a way of getting out of the cabin to clear my head, I decided to build one for myself. Using money from recording sound on *The Farm Show,* I bought canvas at Gwartzman's Artist Supplies and sewed the cover on my mother's sewing machine. The resulting structure was eighteen feet across. I lived in that amazing shelter through five seasons. The tipi was cold in winter, but with a fire going, was always sheltered and secure. I found that cold is relative. At Buck Lake in winter, we periodically cleansed ourselves by sitting in a small wood-heated plywood outbuilding and then jumping through a hole chopped in the ice.

Towards the end of my time at Buck Lake, as people drifted apart and away, I was sometimes left alone to shoot my film. The longest period I ever went without seeing or speaking to another human being was ten days. Through these periods of isolation I began to understand how I was affected by the thoughts of other people through social pressure, wanting to be liked by others, for instance. My time at Buck Lake also was a way of understanding myself, becoming aware of the inner core of my being.

Reading the classic Chinese texts while living with basic technology gave a feeling of connecting with the ancient Chinese writers. The *Dao De Jing* made me really want to learn tai chi. I hitchhiked back to Chinatown and I spoke to an uncle, James Lore, a well-respected kung fu master. Uncle Jimmy invited me to learn kung fu at his club, Jing Mo, but I had already made up my mind and was determined to learn tai chi, so he sent

Robert Brouillette, photograph of tipi at dawn (1974).

me to his friend Master Moy Lin Shin, with whom he shared his space at 10 Hagerman Street. I still practice tai chi to this day.

Everything Everywhere Again Alive was finished in spring of 1975. At 72 minutes it was my first feature-length film and my first film that was not a collaboration with James Anderson. It had taken me three years from start to finish. I moved back to Toronto where I finished the post production at the Film Co-op. *Everything Everywhere Again Alive* premiered at the Pacific Cinematheque in Vancouver later that year.

Most of my work was done within a small circle of people in the arts and indie scene where I felt I had some autonomy. However, to make ends meet I had to take on low-paying jobs under a temporary staffing agency, through which I would be sent out with other poor souls to clean up construction sites or unload crates from tractor trailers. It was back-breaking work, but the worst thing about it was the big bite the agency took out of our paycheques at the end of the day.

At this time, the film industry wasn't as built up as it is today and individual productions would advertise in the trades for their crew. I read that Claude Jutra, the great Quebecois director, was making his first English-language film. I had seen a lot of the early work he had done at the National Film Board. Jutra's film *Mon Oncle Antoine* had been an incredible experience. It had defined the notion of a Canadian national cinema for me as a young adult. The production underway was to be a filmed version of Margaret Atwood's CanLit classic *Surfacing*. I really wanted to work on this film.

I arrived at the busy *Surfacing* production office as a DGC (Directors' Guild of Canada) trainee assistant director. I'm about five foot six in height and then weighed under 120 pounds. The production manager behind the desk sized me up and told me to follow him outside. He took me to where a canoe was lying on the ground beside a truck. He told me to put the canoe on the top of the truck and lash it on. It was obviously a test and, judging by his face, he didn't think I was going to be able to do it. Somewhere deep inside, my heart leapt with joy. At Buck Lake I had used a canoe every day and had a J-stroke that was the envy of many cottagers. I quickly manoeuvred that canoe to the top of the truck and lashed it on securely using proper knots. I know the PM was impressed because after I was signed on, I heard a driver, a member of the Teamsters, say, 'How come you hired . . .' and the PM answered, 'Because he's the best candidate for the job.'

Being a third AD was hard work and long hours but I really loved it, loved being on the set and being part of the big film crew. It was so different from shooting indie films. On the remote location, I felt totally at home. A lot of the *Surfacing* exteriors were on water. As I mentioned, I was good with boats and canoes. On the first day of shooting, Claude Jutra chose my boat from which to direct. It was an unbelievable honour and a great opportunity to watch a master Canadian director at work. I didn't speak much with Jutra, but one day when he had a moment, he asked me what I wanted to do, what my goals were in the industry. At the time I had been doing a lot of cinematography. I had shot Joyce Wieland's rehearsal videos for her film *The Far Shore*, for which Richard Leiterman won a Best Cinematography Genie. Leiterman was shooting *Surfacing* and was working a few steps away. I had been half-considering cinematography as a career. I looked over at Leiterman for a moment while I thought about the question, then I looked at Jutra and said, 'I want to be a director.' Jutra had his script on a guitar strap that he wore across his shoulder. He took his script and put the strap over my shoulder and said, 'Your job is to call the actors when they are needed and to stand beside me and give me my script when I ask for it.' So I got to stand beside Jutra while he worked. It was like a dream.

I remember once we were shooting a little connecting scene. I called the actors on the set, they did the run-throughs and then we started rolling film. After 'action' was called, I looked over at where Jutra had been standing, but he wasn't there. I thought to myself, 'Should I, or shouldn't I?' Then I took a few steps and stood in Claude Jutra's spot. I wasn't really sure why Jutra had moved, but it was obviously a good chance for me to get the feeling of directing, so I took the opportunity gladly. At the end of the day I asked Mr. Jutra how he thought the shooting day had gone. Jutra replied cryptically, 'You were a little slow.' I think he had deliberately moved so I could have the feeling of directing, but I don't know for sure.

In those days Canadian feature film sets could be a little rough. All the keys, the DGC members and other professional departments were highly professional; however, the drivers were all teamsters and they didn't care all that much about cinema. One driver in particular took a strong dislike to me and refused to take any instructions from me. It got so bad that when I needed the drivers to do something, I had to ask someone else who would then ask him. This man cursed me loudly and often, usually to appreciative laughter. I remember he bragged he would 'make [my] nose flatter than it already [was].' But he took extraordinary pains not to utter the 'ch' word. The *Surfacing* unit was billeted in small motels not far from the park where we were shooting. At night this man would drink and rant about me. It got so bad that one morning the owner of the motel where I was billeted came down to the location to find me. He clamped his hand on my shoulder and advised me to stay away from that driver that day. Apparently, he had been saying particularly terrible things about me the night before.

It's pretty difficult to stay away from somebody you're working with. The production office and other ADs were all supportive, but the teamsters could shut down the set if they chose and they were already grumbling with their deal. It was painful for everyone and I felt I didn't have any choice but to resign from the picture.

Five years later, in 1984, I ran into Claude Jutra again at a reception at the Toronto International Film Festival. My experimental film *Everything Everywhere Again Alive* had been programmed as part of the retrospective of Canadian cinema in celebration of TIFF's tenth anniversary. Of course Jutra's *Mon Oncle Antoine* was programmed and had been voted the foremost Canadian film of all time.

Right after *Surfacing,* Jutra made a second film in English, *By Design.* In the film are a few scenes that take place in the home of a Chinese Canadian family. There's no reference in the story or reason for these characters to be Asians. It was an early example of so-called colour-blind casting. When I saw Jutra at the TIFF party, I told him I had seen *By Design* and liked it, especially since there were Chinese Canadians portrayed in a realistic way. Claude Jutra pressed two fingers just above my heart and said, 'I did that for you.' I don't know whether this was true or not, but he obviously knew what I had been going through on the set of *Surfacing.*

My experiences on the set of *Surfacing* had been profoundly upsetting and only reinforced my belief that the non-indie film industry was morally suspect. On the other hand, my encounter with Jutra had inspired me to want to direct narrative films. I saw a notice that York University was offering a graduate degree in film and I decided to apply. Post-graduate cinema studies would be an antidote to the bitter summer of 1979.

However, I had dropped out after completing three years of the four-year BFA degree. I found the number of an old professor in the phone book. He remembered me from six years before. All of my grades in film were A's, so he encouraged me to apply. Joyce Wieland wrote me a nice letter and I had to have a meeting with the dean of Fine Arts, who conceded that my six years of experience working in the film industry would be equivalent to the few missing undergrad courses. I was accepted into the program, fating me to explain at every job interview ever afterwards how it is I happen to have an MFA but no bachelor's degree. The MFA course at York was really great, a chance to study cinema formally once again. I worked as a teaching assistant and even brought home some much-needed income. I graduated in 1981, age twenty-nine, but feeling much older and more serious.

While at York, I read a collection of short stories by Alice Munro. There was one story I felt particularly emotionally connected with. After graduation I thought it would make a good short film subject. I spoke to

Alice Munro's literary agent in New York, who said I should go ahead and apply without taking an option on the story. The agent said the story was one of the first ones Alice Munro had written and was not exactly a hot property. She added that if anyone else inquired, she would ask them to choose another story. At this time nobody was thinking of CanLit as a source of film stories. I applied for and received my first large Canada Council grant to make this film.

Shortly after that, in my endless search for freelance work, I happened to call the NFB in Toronto and spoke to a producer there. He said he didn't have any work for me, but as I was hanging up, he asked, 'Are you the same Keith Lock who we are in competition for over the rights to the Alice Munro story?' I was totally in shock after I hung up the phone. I spoke to two good friends who worked at the NFB who told me not to worry, that this was not even officially on the production board and the producer in question was a really nice guy. Reassured, I called him back and made an appointment with him. Over the phone he sounded reasonable and I went into the meeting feeling hopeful.

When I walked into his small office, he seemed much less open. I can say only that I walked out of that meeting feeling totally disrespected and humiliated. Having a super 8 film listed on my CV made me an amateur in his eyes. At one point he even had his feet up on his desk, muttering, 'No way.'

Alice Munro happened to be giving a reading at the Harbourfront authors' festival. I phoned her and introduced myself. She'd heard about the situation and agreed to have lunch to discuss my film bid. The lunch was at Harbourfront. When I arrived, it was an amazing scene. The big dining hall was filled with famous authors who were calling out to each other and table-hopping. On the way to Alice Munro's table, I ran into Michael Ondaatje and I chatted and joked a bit with him before I introduced myself to Alice Munro. This really helped break the ice and I ended up having a wonderful, free-flowing conversation in which we shared insights into the creative process and country living. As we parted she warned me that she left all her business decisions to her literary agent, but said she would tell her agent she had met me and liked me, and that she thought I would make a good film.

The NFB producer audaciously claimed that he wasn't really in competition with me because my bid had already failed by the time he expressed his interest in the story. However, he made a mistake in giving precise dates. My meeting with Alice Munro in which we discussed my bid was after his dates, and I was able to show that this part of his account was false. However, it would soon all become moot. Munro's agent inevitably went with the NFB, and they went on to produce their film. Although my position was more of an ethical than a legal one, many people heard about it and were supportive. Roy Moore, the screenwriter of *Riel* and *Black Christmas,* sent me a script, *The Highway* by John Bonenfant, which had similar elements to the Alice Munro story. With the blessing of the Canada Council, I went on to make that film instead.

The Highway received a Golden Sheaf nomination for Best Short Drama at the Yorkton Short Film Festival, and I was invited to be on a panel. Coincidentally, the NFB film was also nominated for the same prize. Their director was speaking on the same panel as I was. One day the phone rang. When I picked up the receiver I was surprised to hear the voice of the NFB producer. He begged me not to say anything at the panel about what had happened. I don't even remember what I replied. Hearing his voice again really disturbed me. It brought up really bad feelings I'd first learned to feel in childhood. I didn't want to confront him and have to publicly rehash all this old stuff. Besides, being an indie filmmaker, I couldn't afford airfare to Yorkton. I wanted to move on to something a little more positive and I did not attend the panel.

During the making of *The Highway,* I saw Wayne Wang's *Chan Is Missing,* which was set in San Francisco's Chinatown. It made me want to do something in my Chinatown. I got my chance when Paul de Silva asked me to write and direct the Chinatown episode in his CBC Toronto documentary series, *Neighbourhoods.*

Making the episode, 'Chinatown,' was like a homecoming. People in Chinatown all knew my parents and remembered me as a little kid growing up. My father was quite well respected and had been one of the founders of the Mon Sheong Home for the Aged on D'Arcy Street. During the sixties, many survivors of the bachelor society, being without family, had been reduced to begging on the street to survive. My father and a few business people decided to do something about it. With donated land and very little money, they built the Mon Sheong Home for the Aged, the first old-age home of its kind.

When I went there to shoot some footage for 'Chinatown,' everyone seemed excited that one of their own was directing. A former railway worker, whose house had been expropriated to build the new city hall, grabbed me by my arm and pulled me close. In a voice full of emotion, he said, 'Tell them the truth!' I didn't think much of it at the time but his words often come back to me now.

However, I was to learn that telling the truth can sometimes be unsettling in nice little TV docs about Chinatown. No film about Chinatown can really be complete without mentioning food, and I was introduced to master chef Yip, who agreed to create something for the camera. I suggested dim sum, but he disdained such pedestrian morsels. He promised to make me a dish that would not be boring. Chef Yip took a live fish, gutted and scaled it, wrapped its head in a wet towel and plunged its body into a wok full of boiling oil. He then poured a measure of whisky into the gills of the uncooked fish head, put it on a platter and poured a delicious looking white sauce over the lower part of its body. The cooked fish's head began twitching. This was Lively Mouth Carp. We filmed a table of diners digging delightedly into the fish with chopsticks. All the while, its head and mouth twitched and moved in a most lifelike manner. It certainly wasn't a boring dish. Master Chef Yip described it as a true test of a chef's ability.

After my episode aired, I got called into a meeting with the producer and executive producer. Looking very serious, they showed me some letters they had received from people about Lively Mouth Carp. One particular letter started with the words 'Do you know what's going on in Chinatown?' and then went on into a huge amount of detail describing the dish. This person was organizing a protest and was planning to hold a demonstration in front of the restaurant. Gravely, the producers instructed me to go personally to the restaurant and warn the owners of what was about to go down.

I fully expected the owners to react with fear. I prepared myself for the possibility they could become angry with me for bringing this upon them. Certainly, the image of a mob marching on their restaurant would have thrown many Chinese restaurant owners into a panic. Vigilante incidents remained all too real in the minds of the older Low Wah Kew. However, this was 1983 and the owners were of a new generation of restaurateur from Hong Kong. They didn't show the least bit of concern. They said, 'We know. We have already talked to our lawyers and we have done nothing wrong.' Such confidence in the system surprised me, and I was extremely relieved. Chinatown was rapidly changing and definitely for the better. No protest demonstration ever did materialize. However, a lingering trauma had been created in the minds of the series producers. I don't think they will ever be able to forget 'The Fish.'

For the filming of 'Chinatown' I had been assigned a CBC crew and it had been hard to operate without attracting a lot of attention. I remember, while we were shooting at Jing Mo Kung Fu club, spotting Uncle Jimmy come around a corner. Seeing our crew, he instinctively snapped into a 'ready' stance. I wanted to film again in Chinatown, but this time it would be a drama using an all-Asian cast and crew.

I wrote a half-hour script about visa students from Hong Kong living in Toronto. The Ontario Arts Council gave me some funds to shoot it. Today, Asians working together on a film is commonplace in Canada, but in 1986 it had never been done before. *A Brighter Moon* turned out to be an amazing artistic experience for all of us. Looking back, I see that I was very fortunate to work with actors William Koon, Ken Yan, May Wong and Jean Yoon; co-producer Francis Ayock; and cinematographer Naohiko 'Kuri' Kurita. In spite of any differences, we all seemed to be working together with a complete unity of purpose. *A Brighter Moon* premiered at the Tenth New York Asian American Film Festival and at the end of the film the packed theatre leapt to its feet, applauding. However, a Canadian reviewer whose purpose was to promote Canadian short films, and who almost never wrote bad reviews, panned *A Brighter Moon,* saying it had been written by a committee.

Rena Kravagna at the CBC bought *A Brighter Moon* for her series, *Canadian Reflections.* That meant I had to have the film certified as Canadian content by the CRTC. The man I spoke to at the CRTC asked me to read the cast and crew list to him over the phone. After I did, he said, 'In this case, none of the cast and crew would be Canadians.' I responded with a condensed lecture on multiculturalism. Flustered but game, he then asked me to give him the names again, 'starting with their Christian names.' I actually felt sorry for him and didn't comment further.

Our sound recordist, Cathy Morin, the sole non-Asian in the unit, was especially proud of her work on *A Brighter Moon.* Since the broadcast on *Canadian Reflections* made it eligible for the Gemini Awards, she really wanted to me to submit her work for consideration. As a producer, I was convinced it would be like throwing the entry fee into the garbage. However, she wouldn't take no for an answer and we ended up agreeing to split the fee.

A Brighter Moon was submitted and I completely forgot about the whole thing until I got a call from a woman at the Canadian Film and Television Academy. She told me to be at the Sutton Place Hotel for an announcement. I honestly didn't have a clue what she was talking about until after I hung up and I remembered our Gemini entry. At the Sutton Place, it was announced that *A Brighter Moon* was nominated in the Best Short Drama category. At the time I had so little regard for the 'commercial' industry that I was as interested in the food and drink available at the side table as I was in the nomination.

It didn't really sink in until later when I read the brochure more closely and realized our film, made on a modest Ontario Arts Council grant, was considered one of the three best short dramas on Canadian TV that year. We didn't win, but as they say, it's an honour just to be nominated, and I dined out on it for several years afterwards.

However, it still bothered me that the NFB had shown so little respect for me as a filmmaker. The NFB was an important player and as a freelancer I was always looking for a gig. Shortly after finishing *A Brighter Moon,* I decided to give them a ring and show them my work. My call was put through to John Spotton. As soon as I told him who was calling, he said. 'Keith, stay on the line. Don't hang up!' Being partly of the 'model minority' generation, I found myself apologizing for all the trouble and I asked him if he would have time to look at my new film. Agreeably, John Spotton replied, 'After what we did to you?' We made an appointment to meet.

I arrived at the NFB and waited, my film can tucked under my arm. John Spotton poked his head out of his office, scanned the otherwise empty room and went back into his office. After a few more minutes went by, he poked his head out again and said, 'I'm looking for Keith Lock. Has anybody here seen Keith Lock?' Still the only one present, I said, 'I'm Keith Lock.' The fact that I was Asian seemed to make Spotton even warmer in his welcome. He ushered me into his office and called in some other people. We all went down to the screening room and sat in the dark, watching the film together.

Keith Lock, still from *A Brighter Moon* (1986).

ROYAL BANK
650
LEE DUCK
HAND
LAUNDRY
& CLEANERS

STILLS

PART III

Mieko Ouchi, still from *Shepherd's Pie and Sushi* (1997).

Anne Marie Nakagawa, still from *Between: Living in the Hyphen* (2005).

Karin Lee, still from *Comrade Dad* (2005).

Caroline Mangosing, photograph of Romeo Candido on the set of *Rolling Longaniza* (2005).

Aeschylus Poulos, postcard for *I Pie (A Love Story)*, dir. Nobu Adilman (2001).

Helen Lee, still from *The Art of Woo* (2001).

QUEER HONGCOUVER AND OTHER FICTIONS

WAYNE YUNG & NGUYEN TAN HOANG

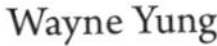

Wayne Yung

Nguyen Tan Hoang

I first met Wayne Yung in June 1995 at the San Francisco International Lesbian and Gay Film Festival. Wayne was there with his very first video, Peter Fucking Wayne Fucking Peter *(1994); I also presented my first video,* 7 Steps to Sticky Heaven *(1995). I remember meeting Wayne at a festival brunch in the Castro, where we got into a heated exchange about the different cultural and racial politics in Asian communities in Vancouver and San Francisco. A further tension arose for me after I saw Wayne's video. Both of our videos dealt with gay Asian male sexual subjectivity and interracial (Asian-white) relationships—but in markedly different ways. As someone who was basking in my recent politicization around 'sticky rice politics' (*7 Steps *giddily celebrates Asian men dating other Asian men), Wayne's romantic depiction of a relationship with a white boyfriend—though infused with self-determination and hot sex—simply rubbed me the wrong way. Though our videos engage similar social, sexual and artistic concerns, our engagements diverge in many ways. However, the difference in our approaches to a resistant, queer Asian art production that I had first found so polarizing has turned out to be a generative link between our respective practices. Since that first meeting, I have become an avid fan of Wayne Yung. Always on the lookout for his latest productions whenever they come to town, I have appreciated their humour, honesty, sexiness and political commitment, not to mention their formal virtuosity.*

This conversation began with a physical meeting on New Year's Eve 2006 in Berlin, Germany, and resumed several months later, virtually, via instant messaging, email and finally a live telephone conversation from Cologne, Germany, to San Jose, California. Wayne's move from Vancouver, where he was based for many years, to Germany, where he has lived since 2001, inspired us to take stock of ideas about community and the representational politics of race and sexuality that have strongly informed both of our work.
—N. T. H.

NGUYEN TAN HOANG: I wonder if you could talk about the role of 'community' in your work. To begin with, let's consider two rubrics: (1) the art/video community, and (2) the queer/Asian community. How have these two senses of community, artistic and cultural, figured in the production of your work? What is unique about the Canadian/Vancouver artistic and cultural milieus?

WAYNE YUNG: My career as a video artist began at Vancouver's Video In Studios (VI), an artist-run centre that offers low-cost access to equipment and training, and functions as a central gathering place for alternative art exhibition and distribution. These government-funded ARCs are a major reason why Canadian artists can be so productive. VI was my 'birthplace' as a video-maker, forming the centre point of the artist community where I found most of my friends (queer and straight, Asian and otherwise).

Growing up in Edmonton, it wasn't until 1994, when I moved to Vancouver, that I first found queer Asian friends. They soon became my collaborators, my subject matter and my audience. I got involved with GAVA (Gay Asians of the Vancouver Area), where a tension was already emerging between two competing agendas: a social service one (coming-out group, immigrant counselling, AIDS education) and a leisure one (parties, bar nights). Eventually GAVA dissolved and the ex-members dispersed to other groups. I later did some work with the Asian AIDS group, but eventually stopped going altogether.

Vancouver also has a vibrant, wider Asian Canadian cultural scene, but in the end, I would say that my 'home community' is actually the gay scene, as opposed to the Asian scene. Although there is certainly racism in gay scenes, it's much easier to deal with than the conservatism and homophobia encountered in some Asian scenes.

NTH: We have talked about the various manifestations of community in your work: the crew you worked closely with at VI, conversations with and feedback from gay Asian friends, the inclusion of Asian bodies/images in the videos themselves. You also mentioned that the intended audience for your work was a 'gay Asian' one—although you admitted such an audience was at times projected or theoretical, existing in the abstract. I find this last point very interesting, the suggestion that a gay Asian community is actively forged through the production, exhibition and reception of a video; that for those of us who must straddle multiple communities—Asian, gay, immigrant, artist, people with HIV/AIDS—'community' is not something that can be easily assumed as an essential, pre-existing entity. Rather, it's something that's consciously created, contested, partial and always in process. I think Benedict Anderson's idea of an 'imagined community' is helpful here: his notion that mere coexistence in physical proximity does not necessarily constitute community, and also his attention to print media as the means by which community became imagined and imaginable[1]—a concept that we can extend to include experimental queer Asian videomaking.

WY: In Vancouver, I did have a physical community of Asian friends, both queer and straight, artist and activist. What bound us together was a certain sensibility, a particular attitude toward being both Asian and Canadian, which was strongly marked by camp and ironic humour, recognizing that purely 'positive representations' of Asian Canadians were boring, unrealistic and often counterproductive. (It can become a straitjacket if you're not allowed to show your 'unacceptable' side.) I depicted these attitudes in my videos, especially in *Lotus Sisters* (1996) and *The Queen's Cantonese* (1998), but in such an overblown way that it looks like Vancouver is completely dominated by radically queer Asians, which it certainly isn't. It's more like a 'serving suggestion,' where the glossy photo looks much more appetizing than the real thing, or a fantasy of how I wish Vancouver really was.

I would also agree that I'm also part of this 'imagined community' of queer Asian film- and video-makers. There can't be more than thirty of us in the entire world, including those who make just one piece and then disappear. Gay film festivals usually put us in the same program every year, which is how we often first meet, and then we stay in touch via email and infrequent visits. My secret fantasy is to get all of us in the same room: that would be a fabulous party!

NTH: What I find really fantastic about your videos is a desire for community, yet there is also a reinvention of communities that complicates conventional identity categories. Do you feel like you have a responsibility to one community—gay, Asian and/or gay Asian—that is your projected audience?

WY: Sometimes at Asian cultural events it seems like the agenda is to convince white people to accept us as normal and respectable. For example, a female programmer at one Asian American film festival told me privately that some of her straight male colleagues objected to the inclusion of my video, *The Queen's Cantonese.* Many Asian American men feel emasculated by mainstream US culture, and images of non-macho gay Asians represent a further threat by sending out the 'wrong message' of what Asian men are like. But I'm actually not that interested in what white or heterosexual audiences think of my images. If you have to choose a target audience, and every director has to make this choice, why should you always privilege the white or heterosexual one? My central audience has always been this postulated gay Asian community. If whites and heterosexuals also happen to enjoy the work, then that's just an added bonus.

Sometimes gay Asian audience members also criticize my videos, saying that I 'misrepresent' gay Asians, in that my experience doesn't represent their experience. My response has always been 'Well, go get a camera and make your own video!' I can't represent all of us; nobody can. My goal is simply to add one more onscreen example of what a gay Asian could be like, with the hope that other people will provide other (even contradictory) examples. When I attended my screenings in Hong Kong, Seoul and Paris, I often got the feeling that the local gay Asian audience didn't feel any particular connection to my Vancouver-based stories; they might as well have been watching a video about African gays in Zimbabwe. It's only in North America that I got this feeling of 'recognition,' that the audience knows what I'm talking about because they've been there too.

NTH: I do sense a transnational yearning in your work, one that translates across various gay Asian contexts outside North America. I believe there are continuities between gay Asian male cultures in North America, gay Asian diasporic communities, and those in Asia. If nothing else, there is the recognition and affirmation of seeing same-sex desire articulated by Asian male bodies and voices onscreen. For example, a gay film from China *does* resonate for me as an Asian American even if I don't grasp all of the cultural specificities; it is different from watching a gay-themed film from an African culture.

WY: In *My German Boyfriend* (2004), I fly away to Berlin just to fulfill my fantasies; this bespeaks a certain amount of socioeconomic privilege that may be a bit fantastic to a gay Filipino in Manila. For a gay Taiwanese who spent his entire life watching Chinese faces on TV, there's nothing particularly urgent about the simple act of representing an Asian man onscreen. In *Search Engine* (1999), I trace my feelings of unsexiness to being Asian in Canada, but how does this relate to a Japanese person in Tokyo, where all the sexy people are also Japanese? I once described this unsexy feeling to a Korean who grew up in Germany, and he said it was completely alien to him: he never felt unsexy, because he'd never had a shortage of offers.

The very category of 'gay Asian' is largely limited to the Western world and can't really be applied to gays living in Asia itself, where the word 'Asian' doesn't conjure much sense of commonality or community. A gay Korean in Seoul doesn't necessarily feel related to a gay Indonesian in Jakarta; so why should he feel related to a gay Chinese Canadian in Vancouver?

I once spent five months living in Hong Kong, where I realized that a major defining experience of being a Westerner is the time we spend living alone. Most Asians (in fact, most humans) live with their parents until marriage, constantly ruled by the social expectations of others, without ever really having the time and space to try living out their private fantasies; this is a huge chasm that separates a typical gay life in the West from one in Asia.

NTH: In Bangkok, interactions between Thais and other Asians are very much mediated by class differentials, which lends support to your argument. For example, there is no natural coalition between gay Thai locals and gay Singaporean weekenders under the rubric of 'gay Asian' brotherhood.

That said, there is also a very visible aspect of gay life in Bangkok that mirrors the old-white-rice-queen/young-Asian-potato-queen relationships one still finds in North America. In addition, a possible translation of North American sticky rice politics—although they wouldn't characterize it in such terms—can be found in circumstances where middle-class gay Thais prefer to date East Asians, because to be seen with white men in public would mark them as low-class sex workers. So that is one example where video work made with a gay Asian North American social and political agenda might resonate with a gay audience in Bangkok. I'm not saying that these phenomena are directly transported from one location to another, just that there are fruitful continuities, crude translations, weak resonances. I think that the increasing forces of globalization—economic, cultural, political, social—complicate any absolute division between the West and the rest. But returning to the West for now, I wonder if you can speak more about the central theme regarding the intersection of race and homosexuality. How did this emerge as a central concern in your work?

WY: It was first in 1994 (after coming in contact with Vancouver's gay Asian scene) that I was introduced to Richard Fung's landmark 1991 essay, 'Looking for My Penis: The Eroticized Asian in Gay Video Porn.'[2] His analysis of the (mis)representation of Asian men in gay white video porn inspired me to address these issues in my own art practice. I took up for myself the goal of expanding the range of images featuring gay Asian men, using the pleasures and complications of my own sexual and romantic experiences as a starting point.

In the mid-'90s, various gay Asians were promoting the idea that white/Asian relationships were intrinsically 'incorrect' (marked by racism, self-hate, colonialism, exoticism, etc.), and that the only 'correct' relationships were Asian/Asian (marked by equality and mutual empathy). This topic was well explored by your own 1995 video *7 Steps to Sticky Heaven,* which was the first I saw addressing this subject.

Why was this issue coming up in the '90s? I think part of it might have been a demographic wave. It was only in the early '90s that the population of gay Asians in Vancouver reached a critical mass, allowing for the formation of gay Asian community groups like GAVA where these discussions could take place. These groups included many men (like myself) in their early to mid-twenties, who had recently come of age and were becoming increasingly aware of the role of racism in their sex lives, leading to an activist politicization. The demographics were different in my hometown of Edmonton, where there weren't yet enough of us to form a community group.

Another factor was the influence of neighbouring groups (especially young dykes and American gay black activists) that were becoming increasingly critical of bourgeois gay white men's privileged position, who were seen as being uncritical of their own sexism, classism and racism. Many gay Asian activists were inspired by a line from Marlon Riggs's 1989 film *Tongues Untied,* which said that black men loving black men is a revolutionary act. This became a strategy for men of colour to find political solidarity and strength with each other, in the face of gay white male complacency and complicity in regards to racist structures. It had become obvious that racism was an issue only for people of colour, and that most gay white men were not interested in doing the work to combat racism: it was our problem, not theirs.

NTH: To what extent was your treatment of these issues a 'transcription' of discussions taking place in gay Asian spaces and to what extent was it a passionate intervention into those discussions?

WY: I wrote *The Queen's Cantonese* in collaboration with fellow gay Asian video artist Winston Xin, with whom I had many debates about the agenda of this project, in particular about the valorization of 'sticky rice' (Asian men loving Asian men). I found it was a bit dishonest, seeing as both of us had been happy dating white men, but in the end, I came to understand that the project wasn't necessarily about me or my own particular experiences: it was more of an idealized portrait of this 'Canto-centric' Vancouver, albeit one that only existed as a 'politically interesting' fantasy.

Peter Fucking Wayne Fucking Peter was a much more personal project, describing the various and contradictory power dynamics between me and my older, white, HIV+ boyfriend. Gay Asian viewers have rarely discussed this video with me; I suspect it makes some uncomfortable, as if I was being too candid, airing our dirty secrets in public. For some, it might also underline the 'disconnect' that happens when one's public activist agenda doesn't necessarily match one's private sex life. It was a lesson I learned from Vancouver artist Persimmon Blackbridge, who once described how her early, idealized depictions of egalitarian lesbian sex seemed unrealistic, almost floating in outer space, and unconnected to the messy realities of what was really happening in her bedroom.

At the time, I wasn't finding any positive images of white/Asian gay relationships at all; in fact, they tended to be cast in a negative light. In watching the late Kirby Hsu's 1994 tape *GOM,* I heard this oft-repeated idea: my rice queen done me wrong, but everything's better now that I've turned sticky. This analysis didn't speak to me of my own personal experience: although race and racism have certainly been factors in my love life, they haven't prevented me from having fulfilling relationships. I actually take a certain pleasure in discussing and negotiating these interracial power dynamics, and often explore them in my videos.

NTH: Well, there is one argument that maintains that, since lesbians and gay men are attracted to others of the same gender, we tend to eroticize other kinds of differences, such as race, ethnicity, class, region, culture, nation and so on. Does that line of argument shed any light on the treatment of interracial sex in your work?

WY: In *My German Boyfriend,* I play a Chinese Canadian who fantasizes about finding the perfect German lover but who is confronted in return by German stereotypes about Asians. According to the script, I finally fall for a Kurd who grew up in Berlin; this is the politically correct 'happy ending,' but in fact, as I reveal in the second 'making of' part, I actually fell for one of my white German actors. So again there's this mismatch between the political agenda of the script and what really happens behind the scenes.

NTH: I hear a tension in what you're saying here, and it's between your commitment to articulating a political agenda and the unforeseen consequence of that agenda. In *Field Guide to Western Wildflowers* (2000), you recruit various white men to kiss you, a Chinese man, onscreen; the premise of the video rests on this novel sight of interracial intimacy, but the 'agenda' turns out to be that Asianness doesn't really matter. You're committed to making Asian bodies visible, yet in that very gesture of making visible, you want to overcome the necessity of that move. So why does the representation of Asian bodies and voices continue to be important for you? What kind of work does the inclusion of (your) Asian body/voice accomplish, beyond a basic move of 'filling in the absences' in mainstream media?

WY: As a teenager, I took several acting classes and found that I enjoyed performing; at the same time, I quickly realized that I had no future in acting, because there was little room for Asian male actors on North American screens. It was only later that I became conscious of what a deep effect this lack of Asian male images had on me and my self-perception. Presenting Asian male images onscreen has not only been a corrective for this absence, but also a way for me to work through my own personal experience of it. However, it's not just a private therapy: I've also had some gratifying feedback from other Asian men who say they've had similar impressions and were glad to see someone talking openly about them.

Although I do still occasionally address issues of race and racism, I also believe it's important to show Asian faces onscreen in situations that are *not* about race and racism. So in *Miss Popularity* (2006), I discuss the issue of polyamory, without mentioning race and racism. The images are mostly found footage showing white American teenagers of the 1950s; in fact, you don't see any Asians until the very last scene, where you see me kissing a white guy. Until then, the viewer could have easily assumed that the narrator was white, and it wasn't actually necessary for me to show any Asian faces at all, since the story could have just as well ended with two white men kissing. However, the inclusion of Asian faces is still an important, consciously defiant political choice; I hate the fact that many directors still use all-white casts without considering other possibilities, thus perpetuating the racist underrepresentation of non-whites onscreen.

NTH: Can you talk more specifically about what some of the relevant issues are when it comes to Asian Canadian vs. Asian American media representation?

WY: The dynamics of racial representation are of course marked by the context of the surrounding society. I think the American situation is much more marked by racial ghettoization and open confrontation, while the Canadian model tends toward trying to negotiate a peaceful compromise. American media is mostly privately controlled and market-oriented, and

Wayne Yung, still from *Miss Popularity* (2006).

seems much less hesitant to exploit racial stereotypes in order to sell tickets and get a laugh. Meanwhile, the Canadian media scene was for many years dominated by the publicly funded CBC, which tends to toe the line on Canada's official multiculturalism policy, introduced in 1971. Certainly there's racism at the CBC too, but it tends to be the unintentional, liberal type, and not a blatantly arrogant one.

In comparing the position of Asian Americans vs. Asian Canadians, I think a major difference is that there are more blacks and Latinos in the US than in Canada. When measured against these groups, Asian Americans are seen as a 'lesser threat,' or even co-opted as a 'model minority' in alliance with the dominant whites. In Vancouver, Asian Canadians are the biggest visible minority and therefore constitute the 'biggest threat' to white hegemony; this tension was especially felt in the early '90s as large numbers of Hong Kongers emigrated to Vancouver before the 1997 handover, buying property and building so-called 'monster houses.' However, I think this particular tension has since died down; nowadays, Asian Canadians seem to be a well integrated part of Vancouver's sociocultural landscape.

NTH: I wonder if we can bring the gay issue into this discussion of racial representation. How do queer people of colour figure in gay Canadian media, both mainstream and alternative media?

WY: When I first started consuming Canadian gay mainstream media (I'm thinking particularly of gay newspapers), it was difficult to find any evidence that gay Asian men existed at all, especially in the visual language of advertising: gay bars, parties and consumer products were all promoted using images of white male models. Often the only sign that gay Asians existed was in the classified personals ads; I spent a couple of years clipping out these ads, later using them in my 1999 video *Search Engine.*

In the alternative gay media scene, the presence of people of colour was much stronger. For example, Vancouver's Out on Screen festival invited me to join their programming committee in 1995, as part of a pro-active strategy to increase diversity at the organizational level. I decided to organize their first gay Asian video program, which drew a large gay Asian audience that had not been specifically addressed by the festival until then. This happened in the years when Out on Screen was beginning to shift from being more alternative (including various political/activist programs that hardly anyone attended) to a more mainstream position.

These days, I think gay Asians are fairly well represented in Canadian gay media, both mainstream and alternative. My impression is that Asians are less present in the US gay media: I only know of three or four gay male Asian directors in the US, as opposed to at least five in Canada, despite the fact that the US population is about ten times the size of Canada's. (When you extrapolate these figures, there should be at least fifty gay Asian American directors!) It seems like it's easier for people of colour to produce media in Canada than in the US; this may have to do with the much greater availability of government arts funding in Canada. However, in the age of cheap camcorders and YouTube, people now have much more opportunity to make and distribute their own media without any other assistance.

NTH: Getting up to speed, how has the move to Germany transformed your perspectives on what community means, especially what a 'gay Asian community' looks like from your new location?

WY: I certainly miss the sense of community I felt in Vancouver. It's been difficult for me to find the motivation to make videos here when I feel like I'm just 'talking to myself.' I feel almost no affinity with the few gay Asians I've found here; most grew up in Asia, and don't have the same priorities or sense of political agency that I do, so I keep in touch with

Wayne Yung, still from *Search Engine* (1999).

'my community' via email and infrequent visits. They're scattered around the world, with just a few here in Europe, and none in Germany.

NTH: If this is the case, where do you go from here? How do you intend to make work that is socially/politically important to you if you have lost these community ties in a physical sense?

WY: Since leaving my Canadian career behind, I've been trying to develop a German one, but now I suspect I need to reconnect to Canada, and try to develop an international career that would be equally valid in both countries. Beyond the question of location is the bigger question of subject matter: I do feel like I've already said everything I wanted to say about being gay and Asian, with *Miss Popularity* representing my first tentative step away from making 'identity tapes.' Having just finished a two-year postgraduate film studies program in Cologne, it feels like a new phase is now beginning for me, as I continue to find my way as a gay Chinese Canadian artist living in Germany.

1. Benedict Anderson, *Imagined Communities: Reflections on the Origin and Spread of Nationalism* (New York: Verso, 1991).

2. Richard Fung, 'Looking for My Penis: The Eroticized Asian in Gay Video Porn,' in *How do I look?: Queer Film and Video,* ed. Bad Object-Choices (Seattle: Bay Press, 1991), 145–60.

BLACK MAGIC BUDDHISM

JULIA KWAN & IRIS YUDAI

For the purposes of the following conversation, director Julia Kwan and radio producer Iris Yudai became modern-day pen pals. Their correspondence took place via email, so each question and each answer was punctuated by hitting the Send button. The catalyst for the conversation was Julia Kwan's feature-length debut, Eve and the Fire Horse. *The film centres around Eve, a curious and imaginative nine-year-old, who struggles to reconcile conflicting notions of Buddhism, Catholicism and superstition. The film won the Special Jury Prize in the World Dramatic category of the Sundance Film Festival.*

IRIS YUDAI: I'm really drawn to the theme of magical thinking that infuses *Eve and the Fire Horse.* It brought to mind the superstitions of my own culture. For example, Filipinos of a certain generation say rice is the first thing you bring into a new house. They get very upset if you cut the ribbon of a wedding gift with a pair of scissors. They also consider it bad luck to stack dirty plates at the dinner table. I might laugh about these odd rules, but I still abide by them. Can you talk a bit about your own ambivalence around what you call 'Black Magic Buddhism'?

JULIA KWAN: I love your examples of Filipino superstition. I always feel like there was, at one time, some logical reasoning behind these 'superstitions,' but it got lost through the generations. It's funny you say you still abide by them, because I find myself filled with a wave of guilt and anxiety every time I disobey them. My mom still asks me not to wash my hair a few days before and after the Chinese New Year. I've never been able to abide by this one, but I always feel terrible the second the water hits my hair, like I'm washing away all my luck for the new year!

The term 'Black Magic Buddhism' came from this Buddhist monk I met on a bus years ago. I told him how my parents' type of Buddhism was so entwined with luck and superstition and he coined that term. Unfortunately, meditation and compassion weren't part of the equation for my parents' religion. Growing up this way, though, I was exposed to this kind of lateral/magical thinking. You know, linking two separate events that really don't have anything to do with one another. For example, in the film, Eve ties her mother's miscarriage to her mother chopping down the apple tree. This kind of thinking really fuelled my imagination as a child and made me think that anything was possible.

IY: I'm a romantic, so I worry that magical thinking will be swallowed up by today's ocean of instant information. Where do superstition and imagination fit in this era of Google, Facebook and text-messaging?

JK: Yes, information is so much more accessible than ever before. Everything is available at the tips of your fingers, and you don't even have to leave your house. Personally, I miss going to the library, filing through the Rolodex (remember the Dewey Decimal System?) and searching through the aisles of books. I liked the ritual of it—I felt engaged in the process and connected somehow.

I think that superstition and imagination do get lost through this new way of communicating through instant-messaging and text-messaging. We're all more 'connected' and accessible than ever before, but at the same time, more isolated. Communicating through an apparatus like a computer or Blackberry is more distancing, and not an organic experience. Imagine carrying on the 'oral' tradition and storytelling via instant-messaging! The experience is so much less intimate and engaging. There's something to be said for one-on-one human interaction. I feel like we've lost something in this new process.

IY: Technology is such a big part of filmmaking today. How do you preserve that connection to the story, that sense of intimacy and wonder, when you're directing?

JK: Well, I graduated from film studies in 1993, so this age of digital technology is relatively new to me. I had to be educated on the whole digital intermediate process. At one point, I was talking about animating this newspaper shot on the 'animation stand' and everyone looked at me like I was nuts! That stand probably belongs in a museum now! Luckily, the digital technology really lent itself to the magical realist aspect of my film. I can't imagine how I would have done the images of the singing goldfish or the horse drowning without this technology ten years ago.

In terms of preserving that sense of intimacy and wonder, I really tried to hold that feeling of childhood wonder throughout the entire production. Unfortunately, we lose that capability for magical thinking as adults and I really wanted to tap into that mindset since the film is seen through the perspective of a nine-year-old girl. I found music was a great trigger for that. I was listening to music I loved as a child (e.g., Supertramp, America, ELO, Elton John, ABBA, Anne Murray) and it helped create a kind of mood for me. It opened the floodgates to all my childhood angst, joys, anxiety, dreams, and I was able to use that when I was directing.

IY: And yet you didn't rely on that music to evoke the '70s. The look of the film is so particular to the time, right down to the macramé wall hanging in Sally's living room, but the music is much more timeless. Why is that?

JK: It was a creative choice to not rely on a lot of pop music to evoke the time. I definitely didn't want to make a period piece that was all about the cool soundtrack. For me, the music was less about 1970s nostalgia and more about creating a sense of childhood wonder. I think the composers, Mychael Danna and Rob Simonsen, did a brilliant job with the score. We did manage to licence three pieces of music from the '70s: 'Magic' by Pilot, 'Beautiful People' by Melanie and a tune from *Godspell.* Creatively and budget-wise, I think it was just the right number of songs to evoke the decade without hitting the audiences over the head with it.

IY: That reminds me of something I read recently. It was in the liner notes for the soundtrack to *You and Me and Everyone We Know.* The director, Miranda July, said she had a theory when she was little. She thought you should draw a picture using all the colors except yellow, and then add the yellow at the end, because yellow had the magical ability to bring the picture to life. She believes Mike Andrews's score is the yellow for her film.[1] What's the relationship between the score and the rest of the film, for you?

JK: What a lovely way to describe her score. I loved that film. I always feel that the score is the final element that transports you into another realm. It triggers the emotional landscape of each scene. I wanted my score to have this childlike, almost biblical simplicity, with minimal live instruments and no synthesized music. I wanted the music to convey a playful, wondrous and ethereal quality. I didn't have the musical language to describe what I wanted to Mychael and Rob, so I described each scene in terms of the emotions I wanted to evoke. I wish I had thought to use colours!

IY: That's got to be one of the biggest challenges of directing: conveying ideas that live in your head to so many different people so they can carry out your vision. Not just the composers but the producers, actors, lighting director, camera crew, everyone! How do you do that, especially with a film that is so personal?

JK: I think the first thing is that your collaborators understand the artistic sensibility of the film as well the themes and the emotions. Then, it's finding the right language to convey your ideas to that person, whether it be through visuals, music or just plain discussion. For example, Nic, my DOP, and I watched films like *The Ratcatcher* and we spent hours walking through the sets and discussing shots. Working with Mary Ann, my production designer, it was just a lot of talking and reminiscing because she lived in a Chinese Canadian household and grew up in the '70s. She knew exactly what each setting should look like and she was a great resource for me in terms of the Chinese Canadian customs. She came up with the wonderful details like how they used to bundle up the offerings to the gods. It's a wonderfully collaborative experience, but at the end, the onus is on you, the director, to protect the story because everyone is focused on his/her role.

IY: And then there are the actors. I've heard a few references to the 'love letter' you wrote to Vivian Wu when you were trying to persuade her to take on the role of May Lin. What exactly did you say to her?

JK: Actually, it was Vivian who referred to it as being like a 'love letter,' and I started to use her description because I found it amusing. I basically appealed to her through our connection as 'fire horses' and expressed my admiration for the kinds of roles she has chosen to play—strong-willed, independent women who have the spirit of the fire horse. Vivian was touched by my words and she felt an emotional connection to May Lin, the character she plays in the film.

IY: I think I heard you describe yourself on CBC Radio as not first-generation Canadian or second, but one-and-a-half. How does that perspective make its way into your work?

JK: When I was interviewed by Roger Ebert, we spent a lot of the time talking about our admiration for Ang Lee. Ebert said that all of Lee's films are seen from an outsider's perspective because that is his perspective as a Chinese person living in America, and he is treated like an outsider when he comes back to China. Being a one-and-a-half generation Chinese Canadian, you have one foot in and one foot out and no strong sense of belonging. I understand that outsider's perspective because that's mine as well and that perspective permeates my film.

IY: *Maclean's* magazine said *Eve and the Fire Horse* 'suggests a new brand of fusion cinema.'[2] What does that mean to you?

JK: Brian Johnson uses that term to describe my film and Deepa Mehta's. He makes our films sound exciting, like a new kind of cuisine! Actually, I like the word 'fusion,' because the word accurately reflects the true nature of the Canadian experience. My film skirts two worlds and is in both English and Cantonese. People have such homogeneous notions of identity, but my film is both Canadian and Chinese.

IY: One of my favourite things about *Eve and the Fire Horse* is the way it captures so many permutations and nuances of family relationships. You get right up close to the bond between sisters, between father and daughter, between cousins, between husband and wife, and so much is revealed in small moments. Some of the scenes are almost like short stories within the larger film. What inspired you to approach family in this way?

JK: It's funny you would describe the scenes as short stories because after I wrote the first draft, I actually wrote the film again as a series of short stories. Then I rewrote the second draft based on the short stories. I've always loved the short story format and the hard part was trying to find the connecting threads and themes to make it a cohesive whole. I also think that a child's experience is quite episodic so I wanted to reflect that.

IY: What kind of conversations do you have with your family about your films, both during the writing and filming and after screening?

Julia Kwan, still from *Eve and the Fire Horse* (2005).

JK: My family weren't involved at all during the making of this film because I really just wanted the film to be filtered through my memories and imagination. My work and my family I keep very separately in my life, mostly because the parents don't really understand what I do. My parents are the type of Chinese parents who equate money with success, so they've always been resigned to my choice to be an artist. When I told them I was studying (film) writing at Ryerson, my mother thought I was studying calligraphy! I think they really started to understand when they came to the premiere screening at the Vancouver Film Festival. They didn't really understand the film, but they were proud of me. They saw it as important work for the Chinese community. My dad actually cried after the screening. It was very moving.

1. Miranda July, liner notes, *You and Me and Everyone We Know: Soundtrack,* composer Michael Andrews (Everloving Records, 2005).

2. Brian Johnson, 'Jesus Meets the Buddha in Chinatown.' *Maclean's* 119.5 (2006): 50.

CINEMATIC IMAG(IN)INGS OF THE JAPANESE CANADIAN INTERNMENT[1]

MONIKA KIN GAGNON

In her short interview in the film documentary *Keepers of the Frame* (1999), Karen Ishizuka, of the Japanese American National Museum (JANM) in Los Angeles, speaks to the importance of home movies as a form of social history, and then illustrates her observations with clips from two films by Robert Nakamura based on archival film footage: *Moving Memories* (1993) and *Something Strong Within: Home Movies from American's Concentration Camps* (1994). In this film about the history of film preservation and restoration, Nakamura's compilation films and Ishizuka's brief comments bring out what Karin Higa has called the 'strange dichotomies that characterize the [Japanese American] incarceration.'[2] One manifestation of these 'strange dichotomies' was the legal prohibition of ownership and use of photographic and film equipment by Japanese American World War II internees, which has been historically counterpointed by the surreptitious (as well as sanctioned) cinematic and photographic archives that have survived to vividly represent it.

In World War II Japanese Canadian internment camps, still and film cameras were similarly prohibited by legal order, presumably for fear of espionage, also giving rise to paradoxical image archives that were both official and furtive, and that invoked analogous problematics of representation concerning surveillance, questions of authorship, and the subjection and subjectivization of those internees represented. Kirsten Emiko McAllister's recent work on personal photographs from several Japanese Canadian photo archives suggests that the so-called prohibitions were not strictly enforced or observed, and, like the 'strange dichotomies' of which Higa writes, that they point toward more complex and negotiated imaging practices than the rule of law upheld. In speaking with two former internees, McAllister discovers that 'in addition to internees who ignored the ban and kept their cameras, the government permitted a number of Japanese Canadian professional photographers to bring their equipment into the camps.'[3] She also writes: 'Researchers, myself included, have found very little documentation on the restrictions regarding photography in the camps to date. . . . After 1943, the restrictions apparently became lax and adolescents began openly taking snapshots of their friends and social events with brownie cameras and mailing the film out of the camps to be processed.'[4]

These observations call attention to the complicity and the gap between cinematic and photographic practices, to the rule of law, and to the extent to which none of these categories are able to confer definitive truth on the images of the internment(s). This paper introduces four National Film Board films on the subject of the Japanese Canadian internment, created over sixty-five years, between 1945 and 2001, to consider the social, discursive and textual considerations that come into view when analyzing images produced during and about this vexed political period. These four films could not, in many ways, be more different from one another in their treatments of the broad history of the internment. They demonstrate how a singular cultural institution, such as the National Film Board of Canada, is able to retain seemingly contradictory representations of a major socio-political event like the internment within their library and archive. While there is a rich body of work that consists of more experimental films and videos concerning the internment and Japanese Canadian identity, my intention here is to point to some changing and constant emphases across a wide historical range of films created for a broad spectatorship. Together, they offer a way of examining historical information about the internment and juxtapose how so-called historical 'facts' are constructed and represented. Yet they also bring attention to media modalities and the specificity of their representations as archives of a traumatic event. In *How Societies Remember,* Paul Connerton distinguishes practices of memory making as inscriptive (constituted through information storage and retrieval devices such as print, photographs, cinema, sound media and computers), and incorporative (involving body postures, gestures, facial expressions, body movement, storytelling and oral histories, dances, ceremony and other ritual forms).[5] In its indexical capacity, cinema can perform both, or at least be suggestive of the kinds of embodiment that incorporative memory making enables.

Who and what appear in these images? How were these images intended to be used, and how do they continue to circulate today? Who were and are the spectators and viewers of these films? Such questions bring attention to the site of the images' making, the content within them, and their contexts of viewing and distribution. At a preliminary level, such considerations are meant to problematize any notion of documentary reality in representations of the Japanese Canadian internment, and, following Peter X. Feng, underline how cinema is 'a technology not of reality but of fantasy: rather than depict the way things are, it shows us the way things could be.'[6] I will begin with the propaganda film *Of Japanese Descent: An*

Interim Report, produced by the Canadian Department of Labour in 1945 (the government department that managed Japanese Canadians through the internment); go on to consider *Enemy Alien* (1975), a film that is critical of the government's actions and treatment of Japanese Canadians during the internment; and then conclude with two films produced by Japanese Canadian directors: Michael Fukushima's *Minoru: Memory of Exile* (1993) and Linda Ohama's *Obachan's Garden* (2001). Reading these films longitudinally offers insight into the kind of Japanese Canadian identity that is being sustained over this period of time. Even, or perhaps especially, when historical events are being represented, notions of and claims to truth must be interrogated. And this is no less, or it may be especially, the case with the documentary genre: from propagandistic to experimental documentaries, these films may reveal more about the circumstances of their creation than any certainty concerning the internment itself.

A capsule history of the internment tells that in the days following the bombing of Pearl Harbor on December 7, 1941, Japanese-language newspapers in Vancouver were closed down and fishing boats impounded, immediately affecting some 1,800 Japanese Canadian fishermen. The Canadian government justified these actions as 'precautionary measures,' and it was initially believed that no further actions would follow. In early 1942, Order in Council 365 ordered the removal of male Japanese nationals between eighteen and forty-five years old who were living within the designated 100-mile protected area along the BC coast, stating 'All enemy aliens of the ages of 18 to 45 years, inclusive, shall leave the protected area herein before referred to on or before the first day of April, 1942,' and 'That no enemy Alien shall have in his possession or use, while in such protected area, any camera, radio transmitter, radio shortwave receiving set, firearm, ammunition or explosive.'[7] Although it was thought that Canadians of Japanese ancestry would not need to fear such treatment, on February 24, 1942, Order in Council PC 1486 was passed, authorizing the removal of all persons of Japanese racial origin from the 100-mile protected area, empowering the Royal Canadian Mounted Police (RCMP) to search homes and businesses without warrant, to enforce a dusk-to-dawn curfew for Japanese Canadians, and to confiscate all cars, radios, cameras and firearms, in addition to the boats that had already been seized.

In expanding its reach from Japanese nationals to naturalized and Canadian-born Japanese Canadians, Order 1486 uses a language of racialization, and one perceives the construction of the 'enemy alien' that is a threat to the Canadian nation, including second-generation Japanese Canadian *nisei,* who were Canadian-born. On March 4, 1942, the BC Security Commission was empowered to carry out the expulsion of 'all persons of Japanese origin' from the 100-mile range of the coast, and a 'Custodian of Enemy Property' was to administer and 'hold in trust' the properties and belongings of those who were being displaced.[8] (Later sales of this property were justified as paying for the food, clothes and basic housing of those being held and incarcerated.) Thousands of Japanese Canadians were taken into custody, often with less than twenty-four-hours' warning, and their property seized. Numerous personal accounts of this deportation exist, as Japanese Canadians were first gathered into the stables of the Pacific National Exhibition (PNE) buildings in Vancouver under appalling conditions, and families were then broken up and individuals shipped off to a variety of hastily prepared internment centres throughout the interior of British Columbia.

Violations of citizenship and human rights were justified through an institutionalized racism, to which cinematic representations certainly contributed. One key point of contention has been the terminology used to describe the subjection of Japanese Canadians. The elusive language had partly to do with Japanese Canadian constitutional rights and the legal designations that were made during wartime. As Ann Sunahara points out in her book, *The Politics of Racism,* 'legally . . . the *nisei* could not be interned. They were Canadian citizens and internment under the Geneva convention is a legal act applicable only to aliens. . . .'[9] The shifting quality of this vocabulary is evident in all representations of the internment, and notably stark in the cinematic examples under discussion here, evincing the changing discourses and the contested legal nature of actions undertaken by the Canadian government. This language struggles to precisely name the interned: were they 'evacuees,' 'prisoners,' 'internees,' 'Japanese,' 'Japanese Canadians,' 'enemy aliens' or 'Japs'? These terms continue to be the subject of qualification, as Roy Miki has comprehensively summarized in his description of the euphemistic use of 'evacuation':

> For the government, constructing euphemisms was an effective mechanism to whitewash its actions. Euphemisms helped to translate the inherent racism of its policies for Japanese Canadians into the

> language of bureaucratic efficiency. This way of neutralizing the abuse of power generated a complex of terms that rendered 'normal'—in the eyes of the Canadian public—its brutal implications.[10]

In the term's cinematic equivalents, one can also identify shifting languages, a function of the changing legalities that the internment required for legitimation in the larger public sphere. 'Evacuation,' as Miki argues, has come to identify all phases of the internment experience, while 'dispossession, deportation, dispersal and assimilation'[11] more accurately characterize its different phases. Miki also details how 'evacuation' has become uncritically adopted even by Japanese Canadians themselves, for instance, in Ken Adachi's often-cited book, *The Enemy That Never Was*: a testament to the normalizing effect of the descriptor. Across several essays that are experimental in literary form, Miki captures the linguistic violence of these namings, as well as the discursive multiplicity with which the histories are maintained: that is, how 'evacuation,' as a term, establishes itself across popular, legal and cultural representations.[12] Had Japanese Canadians been 'interned,' rather than 'evacuated' (the latter implying removal and relocation undertaken in the evacuees' interests), their rights would have come under the protection of internal law. Instead, Japanese Canadians were 'detained at the pleasure of the Minister of Justice,'[13] thereby stripped of their rights with no possibility of appeal, and furthermore forced to pay for their own incarceration.

Of Japanese Descent was a propaganda film produced by the federal Department of Labour in 1945. Its choppy, static camerawork, often like snapshots, reveals it to be a rote exercise, a bleak, constructed documentation of the internment camps. An officious male voice-over mechanically narrates the film and rationalizes the images of subjection before the spectator. His words forcibly cast a positive light on the violence of displacement and incarceration that was happening at the moment of the film's making. Smiling children pose cheerfully for the camera, and they are depicted playing and swimming; sweeping vistas of mountains and lakes betray the remoteness and harshness of these environments and the impossibility of escape; industrious men and women build and maintain makeshift, hastily built homes for their own incarceration: all contributing to a representation of the internment as a leisurely vacation rather than the violation of human rights that it was. This film represents the internment experience in a positive, neutralizing manner that erases its violence. The narrator emphasizes: 'It should be made clear that Japanese residents living in these towns are not living in internment camps,' as if the deportation and camps somehow arose organically or voluntarily, instead of being imposed. As in David E. James's account of the amateur archival home movies in Nakamura's compilation film *Something Strong Within,* created by Japanese Americans from within US concentration camps: 'All everyday personal activity here both manifests and conceals massive public implications. These home movies were made by people who had been expelled from their homes; they document their recreation of a home in a racist prison.'[14] Similarly, *Of Japanese Descent* constructs an image of compliant, productive Japanese Canadians, happy to build and to live in their own prisons.

Enemy Alien, directed by Jeanette Lerman some thirty years later, in 1975, also undertakes a broad telling of the history of the Japanese Canadian internment, but now with greater hindsight and critical evaluation. There is a detectable shift from the socio-political details of the community's collective fate to considerations of individual experiences and the personal impact of incarceration. The film uses a traditional documentary style that begins at the site of a previous internment camp at New Denver, BC, where some internees continued to live after the war, including Mrs. Horiuchi, who is pictured gardening in front of her house. A male voice-over narrates the film, composed of historical newsreel footage, animated still archival photographs and archival documents, all of which move through a chronological historical narrative. But unlike the earlier propaganda film—which attempts to neutralize the Japanese community's displacement and incarceration by referring to the 'evacuation' and to idyllic 'towns' inhabited by contented Japanese Canadians—*Enemy Alien* situates the internment within a broader Japanese Canadian history, beginning with the arrival of Manzo Nagano in 1877. The film further historically contextualizes the contested immigration policy and BC race riots in 1907, introducing structural racism as an essential dimension that enabled the internment to occur as it did. It describes the humiliation of individuals and the community, in contrast to the enjoyable, extended vacation depicted in the earlier film. Racist newspaper headlines flesh out the dominant discourses of the period, and the film elaborates the complexity and politics of intergenerational and interpersonal relationships within the camps.

Acknowledging the human-rights violations of the war has been a complicated and often controversial process.[15] During the internment itself, Japanese Canadians were already beginning to organize themselves, although such political activities also resulted in the incarcerations of prisoners of war if they were deemed too vocal or political. Beginning in the 1970s, increased lobbying and political organization resulted in a movement demanding redress from the Canadian government for civil-rights abuses and illegal confiscation of property. The redress movement resulted in an official public apology by the Canadian federal government, as well as extensive financial restitution in 1988. However, the redress movement was also widely divisive within the Japanese Canadian community, particularly across generations, reflecting the extent of the trauma and fracturing that had been inflicted on the community as a whole.[16]

Eighteen years after Lerman's *Enemy Alien, Minoru: Memory of Exile* (1993) was created by Japanese Canadian filmmaker Michael Fukushima. *Minoru* employs various voices, images and perspectives to render the internment's afterlife and subsequent resonances as a stage in its history. Fukushima uses classical animation techniques, portraying himself as a young boy, combined with archival photographs and newspapers, to retell the memories of Fukushima's father, Minoru, in a complicated and conflicted story. Created following the post-redress period, the film revisits and explores the narrow options that were made available to internees after the war. Fukushima's father chooses the option of repatriation to Japan, which had been extended also to Canadian-born Japanese Canadians who had never been to Japan. *Minoru* demonstrates a notable shift from the so-called objective narrators' voices in the earlier films in its use of Fukushima's father's first-person oral testimony. In this way, *Minoru* undertakes a filmic representation from within the Japanese Canadian community directly affected by the internment, rather than from a perspective outside it. Fukushima's film concludes with a description of the official redress of Japanese Canadians in 1988, and how his mother had died one year before this watershed event.

Writing about *Minoru,* McAllister bemoans the pre-redress dependency on realist representations of history, and notes how the film's 'mix of animation and biography challenges the institutional strictures established for objective historical texts: of what constitutes a legitimate representation of "the real."'[17] In *Obachan's Garden* (2001), Japanese Canadian filmmaker,

Linda Ohama, takes such challenges even further, in a hybrid documentary about her remarkable grandmother, Asayo Murakami, who celebrated her hundredth birthday in the year the film was made. In the same vein as Jun Xing's characterization of the hybrid styles characteristic of films by Asian American women (including Janice Tanaka, Trinh T. Minh-ha, Rea Tajiri and others), *Obachan's Garden* engages a combination of aesthetic strategies of representation. Xing writes: 'Although [these minority filmmakers] share some discursive ground with the avant-garde tradition, the films and videos . . . use alternative narrative techniques and cut across the constricting boundaries of the political, experimental, and documentary genres.[18] *Obachan's Garden* uses a first-person narrative voice-over, archival newsreel footage, home movies, photographs and dramatization, as well as interviews with and appearances by various family members, including Ohama's *obachan* (meaning grandmother in Japanese) and her own daughter, Caitlin. Even with its multiple genres and complex temporal use of flashbacks, dramatic reconstruction and fantasy, the film remains remarkably coherent in its chronology and crystal-clear reflection on historical events. Yet interestingly, like *Enemy Alien* and *Minoru, Obachan's Garden* is focused on and structured around individual subjects and their experiences. These events include her grandmother's departure from Hiroshima when she was twenty-three years old in 1924 and her arrival in Steveston, a Japanese Canadian fishing community in BC, as well as her family's displacement to a Manitoba sugar-beet farm during the internment. At the centre of the film is Obachan's upcoming hundredth birthday, and the disclosure of the traumatic reason why she left Japan.

In *Obachan's Garden,* the flower garden plays a central role as refuge. In a poignant scene anticipating their deportment to the camps, Asayo gives her friend Yasu some seeds from her garden, to plant 'wherever we go.' While Obachan's garden in this film is a flower garden, it is worth noting that gardens played a variety of roles within the internment camps. They were used as sustenance gardens to grow fresh vegetables (including those used in Japanese cuisine) and to supplement the paltry food rations provided by the government. In the context of the Japanese American internment, the development of sustenance gardens as a form of 'food protest' in the camps is described by Jane Dusselier:

> By 1943, over 10,000 acres of idle land in and around the perimeter of the camps produced daikon, strawberries, corn, watermelon, spinach and napa cabbage. Many internees took advantage of land immediately surrounding living quarters by planting and harvesting vegetables and fruits. Even though the energy and care devoted to these crops far outstripped the results, small plots on the side and in front of barracks were common features of camp landscape.[19]

In *Of Japanese Descent,* there are numerous images showing the 'beautification' of the camps with flower gardens and the growing of vegetables in sustenance gardens, identifiable as greens, tomatoes and squash. Here, the gardens and vegetables signal both a willing productivity by the internees to cultivate the soil on their own behalf, as well as their commitment to a long-term incarceration necessary for the garden's seasonal growth—consistent with the film's characterization of contented, productive Japanese Canadian citizens who accept their incarceration. In the opening images of *Enemy Alien,* Mrs. Horiuchi is situated in her garden in New Denver, site of a now-transformed internment camp, cutting purple lupins, a scene that then dissolves into archival footage of fighter planes and a description of Pearl Harbor. The gardens, although unique in each of the films, suggest a conjuncture between the work of cultivating the land and memory work that may be particular to the Japanese Canadian experience. Might the cultivation of physical terrain, which evokes the convergence and divergence of 'nature' and 'culture,' jostle memory and impact history in ways that other idioms for recollection do not?

1. An early version of this paper was originally presented as the Day of Remembrance Address at the Asian American Studies Institute at the University of Connecticut on February 19, 2005. The Day of Remembrance recalls US President Roosevelt's Executive Order 9066, executed on February 19, 1942, which authorized the incarceration of 120,000 Japanese Americans living on the west coast. Thank you to Dr. Roger Buckley for extending the invitation to visit the institute, and to Fe Delos-Santos for hosting my visit with such generosity.

2. Karin Higa, 'Toyo Miyatake and "Our World,"' in *Only Skin Deep: Changing Visions of the American Self,* eds. Coco Fusco and Brian Wallis (New York: Harry N. Abrams and International Centre of Photography, 2003), 338.

3. Kirsten Emiko McAllister, 'A Story of Escape: Family Photographs from Japanese Canadian Internment Camps,' in *Locating Memory: Photographic Acts,* eds. Annette Kuhn and Kirsten McAllister (London and New York: Bergham Books, 2006), 153.

4. Kirsten Emiko McAllister, 'Photographs of a Japanese Canadian Internment Camp: Mourning Loss and Invoking a Future,' in *Visual Studies*, 21.2 (October 2006): 133–156.

5. Paul Connerton, *How Societies Remember* (New York: Cambridge University Press, 1989).

6. Peter X. Feng, 'Introduction,' in *Identities in Motion: Asian American Film and Video* (Durham, NC: Duke University Press, 2002), 2.

7. Roy Miki and Cassandra Kobayashi, *Justice in Our Time: The Japanese Canadian Redress Settlement* (Winnipeg and Vancouver: National Association of Japanese Canadians and Talonbooks, 1994), 22.

8. Miki and Kobayashi, 24.

9. Ann Gomer Sunahara, *The Politics of Racism: The Uprooting of Japanese Canadians during the Second World War* (Toronto: J. Lorimer, 1981).

10. Roy Miki, *Redress: Inside the Japanese Canadian Call for Justice* (Vancouver: Raincoast Books, 2004), 51.

11. Miki, 50.

12. See Roy Miki's 'Can I see your ID? Writing in the "race" codes that bind,' *West Coast Line* 31.3 (1997); and *Broken Entries: Race, Subjectivity, Writing* (Toronto: Mercury Press, 1998), especially 15–28.

13. Quoted in Miki and Kobayashi, 24.

14. David E. James, *The Most Typical Avant-garde: History and Geography of Minor Cinemas in Los Angeles* (Berkeley: University of California Press, 2005), 161.

15. See Miki, *Redress.*

16. In addition to individual financial compensation for surviving internees, a portion of redress monies were designated to form an anti-racism organization called the Canadian Race Relations Foundation, which works to promote and support anti-racism activities. See their website: http://www.crr.ca/

17. Kirsten Emiko McAllister, 'Narrating Japanese Canadians In and Out of the Nation: A Critique of Realist Forms of Representations,' in *Canadian Journal of Communication* (Online), 24(1): 10.

18. Jun Xing, 'Hybrid Cinema by Asian American Women,' in *Countervisions: Asian American Film Criticism*, eds. Darrell Y. Hamamoto and Sandra Liu (Philadephia: Temple University Press, 2002), 187; see also Jun Xing, *Asian America through the Lens* (New York: Rowman and Littlefield, 1998).

19. Jane Dusselier, 'Does food make place? Food protest in American concentration camps,' in *Food and Foodways* 10 (2002): 155.

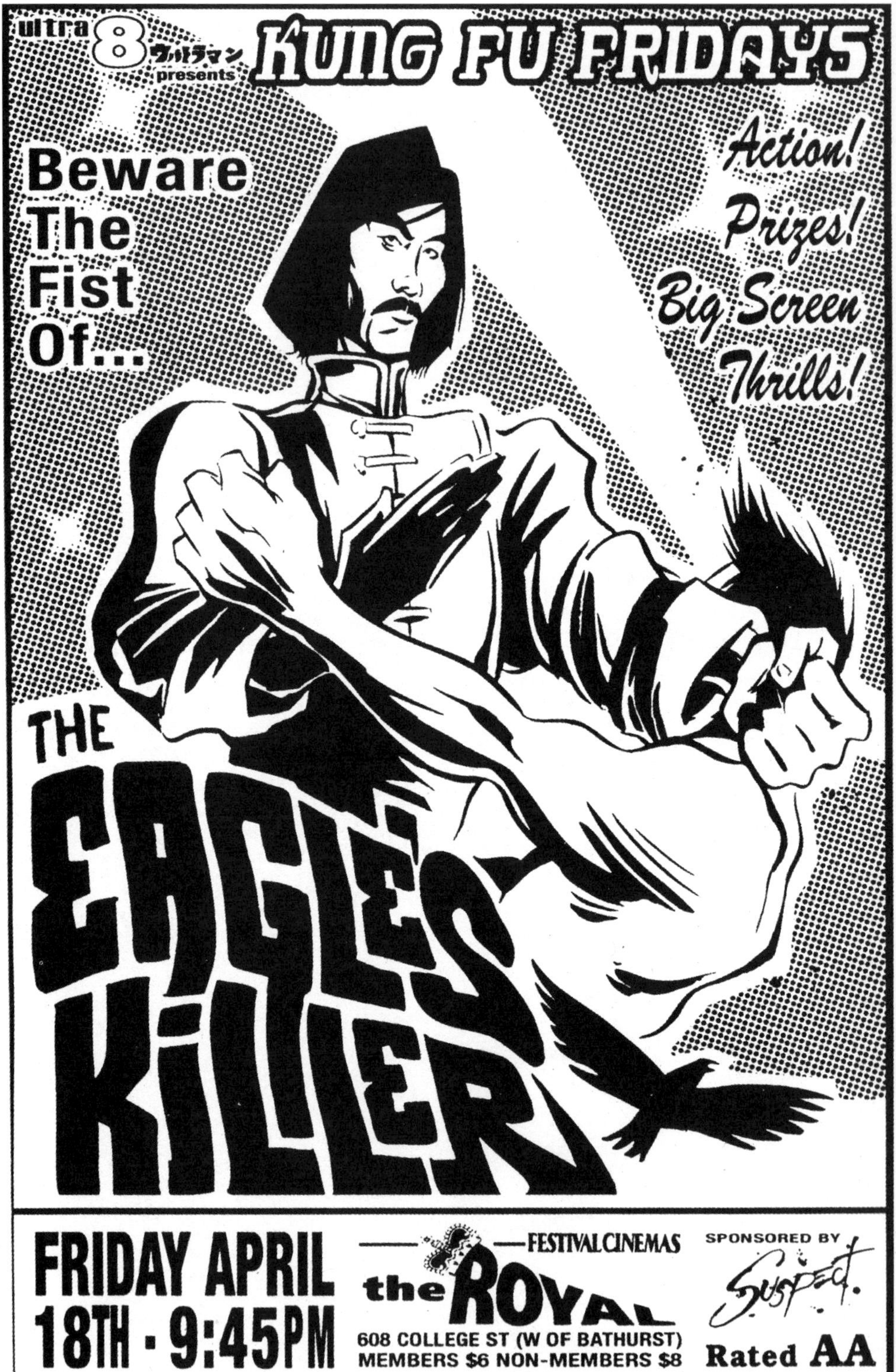
ultra 8 ウルトラマン presents
KUNG FU FRIDAYS
Beware The Fist Of...
Action! Prizes! Big Screen Thrills!
THE EAGLE'S KILLER
FRIDAY APRIL 18TH - 9:45PM
FESTIVAL CINEMAS
the ROYAL
608 COLLEGE ST (W OF BATHURST)
MEMBERS $6 NON-MEMBERS $8
SPONSORED BY
Suspect.
Rated AA
www.ultra8.ca

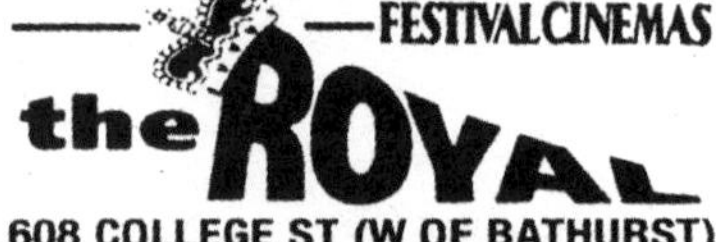

CHINATOWN TOMB RAIDER: REFLECTIONS ON KUNG FU FRIDAYS

RECORDED, EXCERPTED

COLIN GEDDES, JASON ANDERSON & PHIL TSUI

Not long after founding his fanzine Asian Eye, *Colin Geddes began screening prints of martial-arts classics and contemporary Hong Kong action films in various Toronto cinemas in 1996. Eventually dubbed Kung Fu Fridays, the series would run until 2006, by which time Geddes had also assumed the post of Midnight Madness programmer for the Toronto International Film Festival (TIFF). Film critic Jason Anderson and Reel Asian board member Philip Tsui joined Geddes to discuss his efforts at fostering a wider appreciation for Asian genre cinema among cinephiles and thrill-seekers alike.*

COLIN GEDDES: My interest in Hong Kong and Asian cinema started around 1980 when *Shogun* was on TV and it was the first boom of ninjas and samurais. Around that time I was being picked on at school by a bully, so my dad and I took judo together. To fuel that interest, we started renting ninja films, but in the country, there wasn't much selection. I bought a martial-arts-movies magazine and now when I look back at it, there are these iconographic images that I digested as a kid but never really understood.

Growing up just outside of Kingston, we had maybe three TV stations on a clear night, so I didn't grow up seeing *Lone Wolf and Cub* or *Ultraman* on TV, any of the stuff that kids living closer to the border, Toronto or Windsor area grew up with.

JASON ANDERSON: That was the same when I was a kid. We were renting VCRs as opposed to even owning them yet. Some of the earliest stuff that I saw on video was the Bruce Lee films. That '70s Bruce Lee craze was still around.

CG: Well, part of the experience of catching up and watching the stuff was a re-release of *Enter the Dragon* with Bruce Lee on a double bill with Jackie Chan's *The Big Brawl.* I saw *Big Brawl,* but didn't really know who Jackie Chan was. It was overshadowed by *Enter the Dragon,* a cool James Bond-esque action flick. That planted the seeds, I guess. Once I came to Toronto for a summer with my parents and we went to Chinatown; I had a boxed drink for the first time and bought some Chinese comic books that, because of the radical action-packed design, really blew me away. When I moved to Toronto, there was a process of catching up on different cult films, but not getting into the Asian stuff at that point. Toronto used to have a cult film-zine community: *Trash Compactor, Kill Baby, Subterranea, Tame, Panicos,* and around 1988 to '92 I hung out with these zine guys. I wanted to do a zine on my own, primarily because I was going to school for graphic design and wanted a portfolio piece. One guy knew everything about spaghetti westerns, one guy knew Italian slasher films. I knew little bits, but not enough to be an expert.

PHIL TSUI: You had to specialize.

CG: Exactly. I was trying to figure out the thesis of the magazine, then I saw *A Chinese Ghost Story* and Tsui Hark's *Swordsman* at TIFF in 1990. I realized I could go to Chinatown and rent this stuff on VHS and ninety percent of titles were subtitled. That was a huge journey: being the only white guy in a Chinese video store, realizing that I couldn't ask for it by the English name because the translation is something completely different. An example is *The Killer,* which translates as 'A Pair of Blood-Splattered Heroes.' If I went in there asking for 'A Pair of Blood-Splattered Heroes,' I might have been able to get somewhere, but asking for 'The Killer' . . .

JA: Now, with the internet, you can get that data in seconds. Back in the day, you had to troll for whatever sources you could find, because how are you even finding titles?

PT: At the video store, did you ask for titles or did you just point them out by looking and pointing at the boxes?

CG: That's what I'd have to do. I'd just point, or they'd recommend something, and I'd slowly work through it. It was literally a big jigsaw puzzle—filling in the gaps, and writing little synopses of the films.

JA: So, I'm curious. When was *The Killer*? Is that really the breakthrough film for Hong Kong in the West?

CG: That was one of the first breakthrough cycles. You originally had the kung fu boom, but the main discovery of what was going on in the '80s in Hong Kong would have been *The Killer,* as that was the first one to play in art-house cinemas. I remember hearing that when they showed *A Better*

Tomorrow at TIFF, there was almost a riot afterwards with people wanting to see the last reel again because it was just so incredible.

PT: *A Better Tomorrow* was actually a cultural milestone in Canada. I remember after that came out you would see a proliferation of Asian youths wearing trench coats in high schools in Calgary. If Chow Yun Fat's trench coat made it from a screen in Hong Kong to backwater western Canada, it probably made an impact in major cultural centres as well.

JA: It's also interesting because it was more of an era for American action cinema. So there was an opening because it wasn't as though you were getting that calibre of films from North America.

CG: At the time I was doing the zine, I was getting jaded with American cinema, and even European fantasy, action or horror cinema. Suddenly this secret cinema opened up that no one knew about. When I first moved to Toronto, there were around five or six Chinatown cinemas. There even used to be one up on College Street that would show Shaw Brother films. The only way you could find out what was playing in the cinemas was if you knew where they were and walked by, or found a newspaper and could see one of the ads. There was a guy at my college who was Chinese and when he found out that I was into this, he took me to see a double bill at the Far East Cinema of a film with Andy Lau and Tony Leung called *Who Do You Think You're Fooling?*, a wacky comedy by the director who did *Untold Story* and *From the Queen to the Chief Executive*. That was my first big-screen experience. You would pay six dollars, see two films and the snack bar was amazing. Shrimp chips, cuttlefish, dried mangoes, coconut milk—all this great food. I started looking to see what was playing and I'd drag my friends to these films, telling them, 'Okay, we're going to be the only white guys, but trust me, it's going to be so worth it.' And I'd see films that a couple of months later would show up at TIFF. The Royal Cinema used to be the Golden Princess, and that's where I saw *A Chinese Ghost Story 3* and John Woo's *Once a Thief*. One of the great things about doing a zine is that you don't have to be an expert. You just start writing and you'll find people who'll be interested. And so I did my first two zines of *Asian Eye*. The first one had an interview with John Woo, way before Woo came to North America. I had biography sections on Tsui Hark and

Ringo Lam. I might have been one of the first people in the English press to compare *Reservoir Dogs* to *City on Fire.*

JA: This was all pre-internet. So how did you research this?

CG: I found information from other zines from Europe; there were only one or two zines on the subject in North America. I'd go to the Cinematheque Ontario Film Reference Library for film festival guides, particularly Hong Kong film festival guides that had biographies in English. That was an eye-opening experience—being able to find filmographies of directors and actors. I would trade information with people who would order my zine from North America, from Europe—really trying to share these films with other people. Based on my newfound knowledge of Hong Kong cinema, I got a job working at Golden Classics Cinema, a short-lived repertory cinema in Toronto that screened Asian films to a Western audience. It was kind of a strange experiment that didn't last that long.

JA: But that *Rumble in the Bronx* night was classic...

CG: We opened with the premiere of the Chinese version, with English subtitles, of Jackie Chan's *Rumble in the Bronx,* to a packed house. We ran retrospectives of Jackie Chan, Kurosawa, Naruse, Chinese classics from the 1930s...

JA: And the *Sex and Zen* series.

CG: When the cinema closed, I figured out that Chinatown distributors had 35mm prints of Hong Kong films, and I had their numbers and everything. I actually came into the possession of a print from a closed Chinatown cinema, Jackie Chan's *Snake in the Eagle's Shadow.* This was the first breakthrough film that Chan had done, directed by Yuen Wo Ping in 1979. I figured I'd book a theatre and hold a screening. Toronto has a rundown porn theatre called the Metro with a small theatre inside, called the Riviera. I could rent that cinema for around $200 for a whole night on a weekend, which was a steal. So I booked the cinema, made some flyers, went street postering and sold advance tickets at Suspect Video. This was in...

JA: ’96 . . .

CG: Yeah, February 1996. I had sold out the place, but the day before the film started, I pulled out the film, looked at it, and realized that the film was in Cantonese with no English subtitles. I had printed up a zine, more of a playbill, with pictures from the film and a bio of Jackie Chan in case you didn’t know who he was. As I introduced the film, to about two hundred people, I told them, ‘Okay, the good news is you’re here for a Jackie Chan film. The bad news is there are no subtitles, but it’s a Jackie Chan film, so plot is secondary . . . you’re not going to need to know who is saying what.’ I gave out sheets with pictures of the various characters and said, ‘There’s a fat kung fu student who’s always picking on Jackie Chan. Anytime you see this guy, yell out “piggy.” Every time you see the old drunken master, who’s actually played by Yuen Wo Ping’s father, call out “Sifu.” And there’s this bad *gweilo* villain who’s a priest carrying a cross with a dagger inside. Anytime you see him, shout out “Hallelujah!”’

JA: So you made it an interactive *Rocky Horror* type thing!?

CG: Yeah! As soon as people started doing that, it didn’t matter that there weren’t any English subtitles, and everyone had a great time.

JA: One thing—this was during an era when most of the first-run Chinese theatres are going belly up, too. So is this a period where you’re finding stuff becoming available? Because you’ve got all these prints sitting in various depots in the city that aren’t really going anywhere.

CG: At that point, downtown, there was the Far East, the Mandarin, and then you could go to Golden Harvest up in the ’burbs. The theatres were still there, but they never advertised to English-language audiences.

PT: But video was really killing off these theatres at this time. Much like we get DVDs today before the actual release. At that time, you could get a lot of these films on video before they actually screened in these Chinese theatres.

CG: Yeah, but the audience that I was going after was different. Maybe less than a quarter of them were Chinese, and if they were Chinese, they were

Canadian-born Chinese with their skateboards. They were going back and looking at the stuff that they grew up with. The second one that I did was *Full Contact,* starring Chow Yun Fat, and I rented a print from the distributor in Vancouver, paid for it to come out on the bus, and I did two shows, again selling out. We actually had a guy in the audience who was an extra in one of the Thailand bar scenes. The director, Ringo Lam, was in Toronto shooting a Jean-Claude Van Damme film. I did an interview with him and invited him to the screening, but he was really shy and asked, 'Well, what would I say?' He was kind of baffled that these white guys were clamouring for his stuff.

JA: That was one of the movies that turned me on to Hong Kong action cinema too. I mean, it hasn't dated as well as I might have hoped, but at that time it was mind-blowing.

CG: Yeah, with those great point-of-view bullet shots, which were later reappropriated in Mario Van Peebles's *Posse.* But again, it was a great show, in this space that people weren't used to going to. To have a lineup outside a porn theatre was the coolest thing. Everyone was going into this secret spot that everyone walked by and talked about going into, but it was a really weird space as well. I'd have to go in and freshen the place up and light incense to get rid of that stale . . .

PT: Jizz smell . . .

JA: It's actually not the smell of jizz—it's sadness . . .

CG: (*Laughing.*) And in the cinema there were these surreal pictures of Mary Poppins, Laurel and Hardy, Charlie Chaplin—sadness! The big thing I'd like to boast about was the poster I did for this run. On the top, it said 'Chow Yun Fat is God.' One night a couple of years later, I was coming home from a bar, and they were taking out all the old wooden telephone poles from along Bathurst Street. A flatbed truck went by with a stack of telephone poles and there, ripped, was a shred of my poster. All you could see was 'Chow Yun Fat is God.' My heart was just beating when I saw that.

PT: It was in the '80s that the Hong Kong film industry switched from making kung fu movies to the gangster films that seemed to be really in vogue in the '90s. What do you make of that?

CG: That was just an updating of themes. John Woo, for example, was taking the themes of swordplay films and literature that he loved, and replacing swords with guns, but it was just updating the ideals. But yeah, there were just so many Chow Yun Fat/John Woo gangster look-alike films and productions that came out.

JA: It's interesting too, that you had a title for your series at this point: 'Hong Kong Film Explosion...

CG: ...Number 3'. I returned to kung fu with *Master Killer,* also known as *The 36th Chamber of Shaolin.*

JA: Which really is the Rosetta Stone of martial arts films...

CG: This film I did for two nights, four shows, and it was a huge success. Personally it was a big success because we had Quentin Tarantino show up. He was in town because his girlfriend at the time, Mira Sorvino, was shooting *Mimic* in Toronto. He stopped by Suspect Video and they gave him free tickets to the screening. They phoned me up and told me that, and at first I thought they were pulling my leg 'cause I was frantically getting the show ready. Well, for the first show, suddenly Tarantino comes into the smelly porn theatre with this girl—we didn't know it was Mira Sorvino—and sat down. There was this buzz in the audience: 'Quentin, Quentin...' We showed some trailers and a couple of cartoons: Tony Walsh's *Rat Boy, He's Just a Rat* cartoons. And you could hear Tarantino's laugh above everything. As the screening was going on, I was in the lobby thinking maybe there will be a mob scene afterwards, but it was a typical Toronto audience: completely polite, no one got in his space. Someone won some kung fu posters I'd given away in the beginning, went over to Tarantino and gave him the prize, saying 'I think you might like these better than I would.' Tarantino came out and the first thing I said to him was, 'I apologize for the funky smell in the theatre.' He replied, 'Don't apologize. This is how I remember seeing these films, in hot, smelly theatres.' Then

I thanked him for coming out and he said, 'Oh no, thank you!' Then I realized that, for once, I wasn't seeing his films, he was seeing my film. We started talking about Hong Kong films, our love and passion for this film, and stuff that he had on 16mm in his collection. There was a picture taken of the two of us in the lobby of the porn theatre, which ran in the *Toronto Star.* Behind us, you can see double-ended dildos and inflatable dolls. There was this weird souvenir shop...

JA: It was actually not as weird as the hot dog stand...

CG: Oh, the hot dog stand's disturbing. In 2001, when I was in Cannes, Tarantino was also in Cannes. And I was able to track him down. He was staying at a hotel and I phoned him up, and we started talking and right away: 'You're the motherfucker who brought that print from Texas.' I'm thinking, 'Wow! He just called me a motherfucker in kind of an affectionate way.' One of the neat aspects of *Master Killer* is that the lead actor, Gordon Liu, was later cast as Pai Mei, the kung fu priest with the long white beard in *Kill Bill Volume 2.* So I'd like to think that I reinforced the casting for *Kill Bill Volume 2*...

I moved the series to the Royal Cinema around '99, when I also went to Hong Kong for the first time. The first screening at the Royal was *Martial Arts of Shaolin* starring Jet Li, the third film he ever did, and *Crippled Avengers.* And it was great to be able to go back to the Royal...Well, not back to the Royal, but to the space that used to be the Golden Princess, a former Chinatown theatre. The audience didn't really know its history, but there we were, showing these images from Hong Kong on the screen.

PT: There's a beautiful irony to that.

CG: I printed up these really nice flyers to post on the street to advertise the series. Kagan McLeod did the art work. When I was working at Suspect Video, one day I got a phone call from a woman from the 'burbs asking to buy some really obscure kung fu films, like *Mystery of Chess Boxing* and *8-Diagram Pole Fighter,* for her son's birthday. So I got these titles for her son, a shy kid who'd come in and talk to me about kung fu films. One day he said, 'I've got a comic. Do you guys sell comics on consignment?' And he pulled out this comic he'd self-published called *Infinite Kung Fu.* The images and art work in it were incredible. He'd grown up watching these kung fu films and pulled all these elements into his own art style. I got to know Kagan really well over the years, and he was able to do custom posters for the films.

PT: So, over the years, what would you say the influence of Kung Fu Fridays has been? In terms of nourishing not just an audience that can appreciate the genre, but other artists.

CG: I guess the influence comes from how I was presenting films that for a long time had a bad name because they were improperly presented. People would see them on TV, dubbed into English; they'd see a scope film cropped into a horrible pan-and-scan where you just see guys' noses. One of the prime reasons to see kung fu films projected is to see them in scope, because you've got a duelling image of one guy on the right, one guy on the left. The directors really played with the ratios of cinemascope. So to be able to see these films with more than three people, hearing laughter, hearing cheers, hearing gasps, and also seeing the films in their native language with English subtitles really changed the way that a lot of people saw them. Also, it was some kind of alternative, cool cultural oasis. A lot of the times—and I don't want this to sound the wrong way—it didn't really matter quite what I showed. You watch something with an audience, and it boosts it up from a two-star-rated film to a five because it's a completely different experience. You can watch a film that's not a classic, maybe a little clunky, but the audience brings it to life.

JA: And do you think there was a process of educating the audience as well, that you were pushing them toward further and further obscurities?

CG: Yeah, I'd be able to experiment and throw some different stuff at them. We showed two films by King Hu, who did *Touch of Zen*—the director who inspired Ang Lee to make *Crouching Tiger, Hidden Dragon.* I showed *Haunted Cop Shop,* a comedy with vampires in a police station written by Wong Kar Wai. It made an audience curious and eager to try different stuff, and I always pointed out that we were presenting the work properly. Like if you knew someone who's only had a diet of boiled instant ramen, and you give them a proper Chinese meal for the first time, they'll come back for more. This audience would take a chance and see something else that might not be kung fu but would be art-house esoteric Asian stuff. And they'd also be able to get the cues when they go and see *Crouching Tiger, Hidden Dragon.* It would give them a broader understanding of the genre.

PT: So what kind of factors went into your mind when deciding what to show?

CG: Well, at this point, most of it was, what prints did I have on my own, in my collection? What prints I knew I could get from other private collectors. And we'd do swaps. I'd often show stuff that I hadn't seen, or at least hadn't seen on the big screen. There were a couple of chances that I took. There was one film I ended up showing called *Big Boss 2,* which I thought was a fun sequel to the Bruce Lee film, but there was a misprint on the label and it was actually a Taiwanese crime film from the early '80s.

PT: And you didn't know it until you'd screened it?

CG: Yeah. I told the audience, 'This film stars Lo Lei. And it's got crocodiles in it. And it's got black magic in it.' The film starts and they're going after drug dealers. 'Noooo!!!!!' But it was cheesy fun, and the audience stuck with it.

PT: And they were richly rewarded.

CG: Another example of kind of educating the audience: I was able to bring Sammo Hung to Toronto for TIFF, for the kung fu film *SPL* starring Donnie Yen, and we had a sold-out show at midnight, 1200 seats. When Sammo Hung walked on stage for the introduction, he got a standing ovation. I'd like to think that he got it because I helped to educate the audience about who this fat man was. This guy is a genius choreographer, director, producer, actor. He would probably have been so surprised and delighted to know that a quarter of that audience had seen *Enter the Fat Dragon* on the big screen.

JA: One thing that's really clear in all this is the reverence for the Hong Kong pop culture. When you think of it, people were able to appreciate it in a whole-hearted, interested way, not with the kind of irony that infected so much '90s culture.

CG: Anytime I see someone who does a kung fu parody where it's about bad kung fu, poorly dubbed, I feel that's the easiest joke to do and that it's culturally disrespectful.

JA: Was there a point when you were getting closer to folding the series? What was your burnout factor?

CG: Well, around February 2006 I was looking at how much longer I could do this. I was running out of sources for prints, playing stuff again for the second, maybe the third time, but I was still able to get an audience... I had a huge board at my studio office that had the series mapped out for the next two years. At this point I'd moved from the Royal to the Revue Cinema out of necessity because the Royal was becoming more of a venue for rentals. But when it was announced that the Royal and the Revue were going to be closed and sold in June 2006, I was given a month's notice. Ironically, the last Kung Fu Fridays screening took place on June 23, the same date that it had started at the Royal, with one of the same films. It was great; we had a sold-out show, we showed a great film, audience members came and brought gifts. It was really quite touching. And my mom and my sister came in for the screening and didn't tell me. People asked if I was going to move it somewhere else, but I looked back and realized I'd been doing it for ten years. I decided that this was the way I'd end it. I wanted to move on and do other things, not just kung fu. I still think about doing a once-a-year return.

JA: What's the best thing about closing out Kung Fu Fridays? Being able to create an audience of educated viewers?

CG: For me, it was the joy of being able to share an alternative to the pasteurization of the mainstream. Everything is being co-opted right now. There's less and less different fare to go out and see when it comes to cinema. Just to be able to offer a beacon on a Friday night twice a month where one could go and be guaranteed a fun time. It was also about making it an event, where you see four trailers for coming attractions of films that will never be coming to a theatre near you; you celebrate this old, wild genre; and then you do a raffle. Even if you didn't like the film, you had fun with trailers and you walked away with a prize. So that was the biggest joy, being able to give people something different in this time when there's less and less variety.

PT: But whether it was intentional or not, in another sense you did become not just an educator, but a tastemaker. And when people do see some mainstream films now—from *Kill Bill* to *Grindhouse*—they would probably not be able to get half the references had they not been educated by the films that you've shown.

CG: And it all came just from a love of these films. It's very organic, but it's interesting, too, because I'm a white guy. I grew up in rural Ontario with no influences from Asian friends; even when I got into these films in Toronto, I didn't have many Asian friends. Yes, I'm liking these films because they are exotic, but I'm also rescuing the films and posters from a culture that didn't really seem to care about protecting these things. I've described myself as the Chinatown Tomb Raider: finding old movie prints and posters from the garbage and holding on to them and archiving them, and then finding out, 'Wow. There's not an existing print of this film even in Hong Kong. They don't even have copies of this paper material in Hong Kong.'

PT: I think that's what really struck me when I first met you. I'd grown up in the '80s with other Asian Canadians, and these movies were a familiar part of our cultural vocabulary. And, like you said, it was being forgotten. Hong Kong culture had grown out of it and seen it as something that they wanted to grow out of. When I met you I thought, here's a guy who is passionate about this stuff. He just happens to be white, and to know more about the genre than any person has a right to know.

LA CHINOISE; OR, THE 'OTHER'

SCENES FROM A LONG, UNFOLDING SCROLL OF A LIFE THAT SOME CALL KARMIC, TRANSNATIONAL OR NOMADIC, WHICH INVOLVES THE ART OF DRINKING TEA AND ÇAY, FILMMAKING, MOTHERHOOD, THE FULL MOON IN PARIS AND ELSEWHERE, LOVE, MENTORS AND OTHER ANGELS ON MY PATH

MARY STEPHEN

. . . The longest subtitle in the world: I apologize for my long-windedness.

Is it a matter of indecision—of having too much on my mind, and not enough time and discipline to sieve these thoughts into some reasonable structure? Has it to do with age, or laziness?

Time, it has to do with time. There's so much, once unleashed, that one wants to share.

Let's focus. The keyword is TEA . . . tea, *çay* . . . *ÇAY* . . .

It's the *fil conducteur,* the silken thread linking the moon to the earth where our childhood legends wind up. (Somewhere there was a cowherding boy and a lonely lady in the moon and their love was tied with a silken thread . . .)

I am writing this in a newly adopted city, an old old place that is new to me. I have been here since January 17, 2007, exactly, not even a week after another birthday that I did not celebrate. Since that date, I have spent literally half of my life in Istanbul, to which I came without true advance warning or mental preparation. Sometimes commitments have to be dealt with only at the last minute, simply because something essential has not yet fallen into place. Before arriving here, I would not have had the dénouement to my Eric Rohmer tea stories, stories I had promised would figure in this piece of writing (which I promised I would write a year ago). I would not have known of the existence of the interminable ritual of *çay*—Turkish tea, brought incessantly in this *wooloo*-looking glass on a tiny silver plate (a *wooloo* being a Chinese gourd carried by especially powerful Taoist monks in our favourite legends).

To start my *çay* musings:

A 'witnessing' or 'investigatory' mission is organized in Turkey for Turkish and Kurdish intellectuals visiting Kurdish sites destroyed by the Turkish army during the many incursions in the region. Breakfast is served at the hotel. The Turkish participants drink coffee. The Kurdish ones drink tea. When asked why they don't all go for coffee to adapt to their 'host' country, they answer, 'It took us fifty years to go from soup to tea (the Kurdish villagers used to drink soup at breakfast). Now grant us another fifty to go from tea to coffee.'

This story was told by a laughing man with green eyes, ones I used to call 'eyes the colour of jazz' in some faded poem somewhere about somebody else, but would here describe as 'eyes the colour of the call to prayers at dawn and dusk, when the swallows fly across the Bosphorus sky, and Galata Bridge fishermen are not yet up to their tricks.'

It was in the context of an informal lunch on the University of Bosphorus campus. We had been invited by those responsible for the independent Film Centre to be interviewed for an unorthodox collaboration: a Chinese-Canadian-French film editor long associated exclusively with the works of one of the last of the French masters of the filmic Word, and an independent young Kurdish director in Turkey who hates Paris and has spent time in wildly incongruous places like Japan, Argentina and a Turkish prison.

The laughing man is telling the soup-to-*çay* story because he is laughing at himself for having changed his mind, switching from ordering his habitual cup of tea, which he confesses is central to his earthly existence, to Turkish coffee along with the rest of us, perhaps an unconscious or kind step to bridge the cultural gap between him and me.

And I suddenly thought, it is only fitting that it's here, in this golden light surrounded by gentle pink blossoms, which I momentarily imagined to be hibiscus from the Hong Kong hillside, where I would wrap up the train of thoughts that have led from tea-drinking thirty years back, as a young Chinese Canadian film student newly arrived from Montreal in Eric Rohmer's Parisian office, to the mature woman now drinking Turkish coffee in the shade. Feeling the energy and the calm of the moment, feeling ageless, feeling buoyant, feeling—in the flow of the wildly unfamiliar sounds of a completely unknown language—the very stranger totally at home with her 'stranger-ness' and the strangeness of the situation. There, above the Bosphorus waters' dancing diamonds, in the euphoria of creation and the right and fertile combination of experience + dreamy poetry (mine) and idealism + youthful dynamism (his). Where have the years gone?

Then, the romantic French language enveloped me around cups and cups of tea, brewed every afternoon by Rohmer, who fashioned a sort of mini-salon out of his young actor friends and technicians. I was the little 'Chinese flower' on the wall, a sort of *intrus,* the incongruous element in a totally French *paysage.* I had freshly disembarked from Montreal, after three years of Communication Arts at Loyola College—not yet Concordia University—and desperately wanted to escape the predominantly engineering-accountancy-sports-beer-sexual politics of a cold hard Canadian entourage. I wanted and needed dreams, images of dance and dancing men, poetry, the promise of some incredibly romantic and impossible love, the possibility of making films just like all the *Hiroshimas* and *India Songs*, as well as living intimate moments with the Juleses and the Jims and the Jeannes...

FLASH-FORWARD

In an Istanbul café, a visiting pal from Loyola days is saying, 'But you, you're a gypsy, aren't you? You like to be elsewhere, anywhere else, don't you? You'll never "settle down," you'll always be a nomad.' He says—having intuitively picked up some psychic information I was not to recognize myself till weeks later—'and there you go again, falling in love with this city, just like you did thirty years ago with Paris...no?'

Does one fall in love again after a lifetime of being in love with some other place? One does not fall in love again when Time sets the rules of love-falling. Or does it?

My introduction to life in the City of Lights was to be brutal. There was no romance in the Ile de la Cité police station where policemen took exception to my and my partner John's protesting the long wait and rude attitude towards immigrants applying for the *Carte de séjour* necessary to stay beyond three months. Having come from Canada, where this kind of rudeness was not overtly visible, we were not ready for this treatment. We were also not ready to live without enough money to live on, without work permits to earn some money, without any kind of help from any French person in the streets whom we had imagined to be so romantic and generous.

However, Paris was beautiful, and remains so today. There is not a single late night when I drive through quiet Parisian streets, cross the bridge from Rive Droite to Rive Gauche, that I don't stare at the Seine with its dancing lights and whisper aloud, 'You're so beautiful, and you're mine.'

Or am I yours?

Self and Other: for me, this is always a love relationship. Love has always been a necessary driving force, a self-induced state of drunkenness *à la* Anaïs Nin, inspiration and discipline...without love I can do nothing. Some people are wonderfully self-sufficient, completely in control of their lives and their art. I have always been a puddle of dreaminess. Some take an intellectual approach to problems, are able to analyze a situation intelligently and bring up examples and counter-examples and references to illustrate their point. I have always been reduced to mumbling, which is not exclusively the art of an Other who is not fluent in 'our' language.

The 'other' language, thirty years back, was French—learned from movies and books, from Truffaut to Resnais to Duras. To the French, the Other was me: La Chinoise.

I was once asked, 'Were you always La Chinoise, or did you only become one when you got to France?' In Canada, I was any Chinese immigrant from Hong Kong who landed through Vancouver with her family at fifteen. We went to Montreal Chinatown every Sunday just like everyone else and had dim sum. My worst identity problem would boil down to some run-in at a beer bash with 'unliberated' Chinese students who could not accept that I was dating white boys. I could not say that I was up against some heavy racist plot or that I felt lost in my new land.

It was therefore a shock, to the protected bourgeois girl that I was, that in a crowded Parisian métro at rush hour, a drunken French bum wagged his finger at me, calling me names for having 'taken jobs' away from his countrymen. I started to cry. No one budged. Suddenly, from the other side of the car, a black man leapt across the aisles and pushed the bum aside. I rushed out of the car weeping, and to this day regret not having thanked my gallant defender, who had acted in solidarity with/as another Other.

When I went to ask for a budget from already-veteran director Eric Rohmer, in order to do my own film *Ombres de soie,* I could not imagine that his secretary, of course doing her job and screening all petitions to the famous personality, would put a little star beside my name on the sheet of messages, with the notation: 'she's very cute.'

So that's how I got my foot in the door, at twenty-three.

You, with eyes the colour not of jazz but of prayers and which only today I discover are the colour of the green dancing Bosphorus. You in the rough rawness of your intelligence and your talent, in all the faults and unpolished uneasiness of a first film. You the stranger to the social graces and polite exchanges of 'higher' circles. If those eyes were not misty green, if those lashes were not reminiscent of some pretty legend from my childhood, would I have ever set foot inside your door?

Mary Stephen in *Labyrinthe,* dirs. Philippe Bridgeman, Alec MacLeod and Mary Stephen (1973).

Since that day, I have advised young students and even my own daughter not to get stuck in straitlaced theories and rigid social politics, not to hesitate before the door over the fact of a pretty face or what, to some, might be some other dubious asset. I think I've always been politically incorrect, but now age has finally allowed me to say whatever the hell I want. I admit that I got my foot in the door because Eric was intrigued to see how 'cute' this little Chinese flower, whom only his secretary had seen, could possibly be. But for the likes of Eric, and me, and others who have been through a lot in our professional and personal lives, a pretty face, or eyes the colour of jazz or the Bosphorus may get you in the door, but you won't get to stay if you can't prove yourself worthy of the trust and friendship.

And since that day I got through the door, in November 1976, Rohmer has never left my side, has been there at my bleakest moments, helping me spiritually, financially, professionally, emotionally, intellectually. I don't think all this can be attributed to the memory of a pretty face.

FLASH-BACK:

A long and exhausting time trying to get a co-production on with another country for a musical film I wanted to make, and introduced to one of the most creative, most powerful theatre and film producers of this genre, my pretty face got me in the door once more. It got me invitations to exclusive dinners at the townhouse where top models and rock geniuses were in the same room. Stupidly and innocently, I end up missing the last tube home and am offered the guest room upstairs. The Man's live-in official girlfriend is many time zones away, a pretty actress friend is in his bedroom, ready to play; I am in a narrow single bed upstairs, in a narrow T-shirt he's loaned me, when he comes up to ask, simply, 'Do you or don't you, Mary? You know, it's nothing complicated, it's just like accepting an after-dinner mint.'

I think stupidity protects you more than intelligence sometimes. I am stupid enough to say, 'I'm here for just one thing, to get my film on. I'm focused only on that and I can't concentrate if I get into anything else.' He does not insist. I fall asleep peacefully, leaving the others to play.

The next morning, we went for a long walk in the posh city park across from his house. A sincerity and familiarity had somehow emerged from last night's strange exchange.

He has spoken warmly and highly of me ever since, and I have also always spoken of him fondly, even in front of his enemies.

Sometime in 2006, I agreed, as I often do, to put my name on a letter of support for an independent first feature film by a young Kurdish director, Hüseyin Karabey, from Istanbul. It's nothing for me to write such a letter. If it can help someone, so much the better—even though I, in my hardness acquired over years of self-protection in the cold, cynical and closed Parisian 'society,' am always skeptical that my influence would help anybody. Sadly, most of the ventures to which I have contributed my name have never seen the light of day.

However, sometime in December, I was informed that the Turkish Ministry of Culture awarded funds at the eleventh hour, and that filming had actually started in Istanbul, Eastern Turkey, Iran and Iraq (Kurdistan). Would I agree, they asked, since the budget was tight, to come on an advisory basis, one week every month—*if* everything would be organized and prepared to my specifications? They seemed ready to do everything *my* way, so almost-certain that I'd decline.

'Sure, why not?' I said. January seemed far away at that time, and Istanbul? It was a strange and unlikely place in my mental and emotional map.

In between, I had accepted commitments in Paris for a Chinese documentary to be re-cut and a fine-cut for the long-awaited second feature by an award-winning director in China. Somehow, these commitments seemed logical—somewhere word had gotten out that Eric Rohmer's editor speaks Chinese, *is* Chinese for Chrissakes, and it became not only a matter of putting a name prestigious-by-association on a project, but also killing two birds with one stone and economizing on an interpreter for post-production.

I have had some unpleasant experiences working with Chinese directors, especially young ones. Interestingly enough, I have become in these cases a true bridge between East and West, Tradition and Modernity, the Old and the Super-New. The relationship with the young Chinese directors would always be complex: on the one hand, I was the Chinese sister, the 'family' member to whom they could vent their disdain of the Western culture; on the other, I was also the 'traitor,' the too-Occidentalized hybrid who had forgotten her 'native' culture.

In China, I always felt, somehow, a stranger; my Chinese culture came from the literature and art that I learned in Chinese secondary school in Hong Kong. My longing was for a China of the Tang Dynasty, my life was guided often by a kind of karmic/Taoist/Buddhist mish-mash mixed with strong ancestor worship (family members who had passed away are constantly making their presences strongly felt on my path, for example). I have no intimate relationship with money and material possessions, and I can't get myself organized enough to show my value through Dior eyeglasses, Gucci shoes or Louis Vuitton bags. China today with its new fast track, its youth-dominated culture all based on the here and now, all calibrated in dollars and Euros and yuans, seems very 'foreign' to me.

Who is the Other then, and to whom? The fact that I'm Chinese by blood doesn't prevent me from feeling alien when I'm walking on the streets of Beijing, when I have to watch how the 'natives' gulp their noodles or their buns before I can imitate them, to hide the fact that I'm not one of them.

The evening before flying to Istanbul, I had the jitters. It had been a long time since I had gone to a completely unknown place: a totally different culture, with people, maybe Muslims, bearing strange names and beards (the men at least). Should I wear long skirts, or trousers, or tie my hair back, or hide the fact that I am divorced, or...

What about the earthquakes? And being a single woman travelling alone?

(The last time I had asked similar questions was when I was going to Timbuktu, in the middle of the Malian sands. I had become lost with the rest of the crew during an exploratory journey for an African Poetry Caravan, in a village with no name, in the middle of somewhere without roads or even trails.)

> *'Remember the man who invented this caravan . . .' You with eyes the colour of jazz, the African jazz by a guy with a Muslim name, you are the only thread who pulls my camel forward in the desert with no name, in the sands with no end, you who had to speak in codes and dream in tongues, your more-or-less official message to the team was peppered with veiled and private love letters—one letter at a time—to the 'lady of the heart' you were in love with. No one was to know, but you wanted it shouted at the top of the dunes, somewhere at the start of a dawn, when prayers are still locked in sleep . . . You, writing in the middle of a serious instructional message: 'Remember . . . remember the man . . . remember me, remember me, my love, even when you are so far away, being completely the Other in a land of sands on which you would never in a million years have set foot. You who are afraid of the slightest jaunt to the Canadian countryside, you who don't even want to know how to spell "scorpion," you who have never been to Africa as an ordinary tourist, let alone as an adventuring pioneering route-opener: you are here anchored in my imaginary, visionary, necessary love. We are locked in our mutual need for this improbable, impossible love.'*

I was worried I wouldn't recognize the face of the director I saw only once, for twenty minutes, sitting on the floor of the young French producer's home, mumbling some compliments about my work. I am yet another sufferer of the tired joke about how all Chinese, or all Asians, look the same. I always have had trouble remembering Caucasian faces to begin with, and now I would have to distinguish this one man's bearded face from a multitude of others at the airport.

But the moment I caught his eyes, among the crowd waiting behind the barrier, and the way his body spoke, already lurching sideways and ahead to greet me, I knew it was him, I remembered that it was him, I had always known, for a long time already and forever, perhaps, that it was him. It was fine and it was right.

I was whisked, after a short rest, to a dinner with a group of Mediterranean documentary filmmakers. One of the first people I met in the group, from Israel, said to me, jokingly, 'Did they warn you that this is the Middle East? Did they warn you in Europe that it's scary over here?' I answered with a nonchalant wave of my hand, 'You think it'd stop me? Yes, sure, they warned me, but do I care?'

I didn't tell him, of course, of my last-minute doubts just the night before, of my hesitations, of driving the French co-producer crazy, of changing my dates again and again because I simply could not bring myself to come here, another unknown, a region that I wasn't sure about. I was scared, but none of them were to find out. Then he thanked me for having agreed to come to Turkey to work on this project, with a sincere humility that touched me deeply.

The next morning, I was taken to the office, a small two-roomer in a building that smelled of gas, on one of the hilly, picturesque streets next to Taksim Square. There, Hüseyin introduced me to his 'friends': 'friends' being the English word used in Turkey to refer to staff, collaborators, co-workers. Our editing room would be on the shady side of the suite, whereas the front room, overlooking the street, was flooded with sunlight.

And there it began: the interminable rounds of cups of *çay,* brought by smiling, unassuming young persons . . . the *çay* to end all my tea stories to this point.

And while Hüseyin assembled some red Ikea lamp for the newly refurbished office, talking to his colleagues in this strange tongue that resembled no other language I knew, while I was *totally* excluded from the conversation and the laughter, while I was *completely* the Other, I was strangely and unabashedly happy. I was not at home, I was an utter stranger, but I loved the unorthodox combination, the unlikely situation, the strangeness of it all. And when I laughed for one reason or another, when I pointed at something and made an appreciative noise, when I squeezed my eyes even more narrowly than usual to express a fondness, they laughed heartily, in unison, sharing the joy and appreciating my appreciation.

I was much happier, in that sun-drenched moment, than I was 'at home' in the middle of a lavish dinner in old Beijing.

CLIP:

Lee Marvin in *Paint Your Wagon*: 'I'm an ex-citizen of nowhere and sometimes I get homesick.'

In these nomadic moments, going from nowhere to nowhere, love is the only anchor, the only port, for a seasonal and seasoned wanderer like me.

How can anyone live up to the idealized version of the beloved, so often the theme in a Rohmer film? How can the poor lovely soul in some strange land, or that mythical hero in another tropical place live up to the colour of their eyes? At the same time, how have I lived, how can I live up to my myth: of the superwoman, the Lady of the Heart, the Queen of Snakes, the Mother, the Giver, the Expert Adviser and other incredible names? By my twenties, I had already heard that I was 'the kind of girl who scares men shitless.'

Tonight the petite fleur chinoise has her feelings à fleur de peau . . . comment dire . . . how should I say . . . feelings like brushing flower petals on the skin . . . raw and fragile . . .

Tonight at least I would get a crying spell off the ground. Tonight I leave the superwoman cloak in the dressing room and put on my ordinary clothes. Remember? I'm a woman in disguise. A flesh-and-blood woman of a certain number of years who has lived, lived fully, loved fully, and nothing has altered the fleur or the peau, either the rawness or the fragility.

Every fully lived experience is a risk, an experiment; at what age does one stop rushing headlong into choices that one knows from experience and from the advice one gives to others, are suspect and bound to hurt? How can I, at this time of my life, imagine living in creative unison and co-habitational harmony with an Other twenty-four hours a day, in a language I cannot even begin to decipher, with the best of my knowledge of alphabets and pictograms? How can I soothe heartache, and whisper away insecurities and blow on the boo-boos to make them better, while not taking the precaution of a Kleenex or a band-aid for myself? However much my heart might have been cautioned about possible sudden changes of climate, I walk a rope strung in mid-air, without a safety net below me.

Again. And me allegedly older and wiser—how can I be so stupid?

And yet I am the responsible one. I am the bridge between his, their hopes and the civilized organized world of Europe and America. I am the messenger bringing his, their talents to the cynics who decide the creative fate of people like them. I cannot be fragile. My tears would shock and disappoint those who see me as a superheroine. It's not fair to frighten them, I must remember.

It's lonely up here, in the moon. As I knew from the Chinese legend, long ago, when I was a child. For the sake of love, in all its forms, we'd tread the thin line again, brave the moon's cold loneliness, become the ever sturdy bridge over troubled waters. 'I will lay me down.' The ever-mothering, the ever-flowering.

Looking a débonair forty at the age of fifty-six, Eric Rohmer squired me around Paris when I was twenty. He would show me the architectural differences between 1900s and 1920s buildings, or bring me to the old ramparts of a Paris still called Lutécia, or tell me the story of the tiny square where men were hanged in the seventeenth century. When asked why I was the only person to command such attention and devotion, he answered, 'Mary is the only person I know who drinks more tea than I do.'

Now, I've found a city in which everybody drinks more tea than I do.

Full Moon in Paris, a pretty Rohmer picture. Over Timbuktu, the full moon was a round disc, on top of the dunes and the reeds. Whether I'm La Chinoise in Africa or France or Istanbul, I am seeing the same moon with others who share the same fascination.

In my film on Breyten Breytenbach's paintings and poetry, *Vision from the Edge,* I laced the soundtrack with multiple layers of his poems in different languages, and a conversation in which he, Buddhist and Eastern at heart, spoke about communicating from 'my heart to your heart,' as in Zen philosophy. 'As a Chinese,' he said, 'you should understand.'

After being away for almost forty years, I'm as Chinese and Eastern as I can ever hope to be. That was the *cri de cœur* when my young Kurdish director and I decided to finalize our collaboration. He explained that though it was true that they had a lack of professional film editors here, it was a gamble to work with an editor from the West. But, 'from the first week you were here,' he said, 'I sensed that you were a stubborn, committed person; that once you'd said yes, you'd see it through to the end no matter what.' For him, the most reassuring thing: 'You are totally Eastern.'

Mary Stephen, poster for *Vision from the Edge: Breyten Breytenbach Painting the Lines* (1998).

Eastern. East-West, South-North . . .

Rohmer used to refer to 'Eastern discretion,' the quietness he considered part of 'my' culture. Little did he know that at the time, I was more Canadian than Chinese; all my values and my behavioural patterns shaped by an adolescence spent with Canadian youths. I was the hard-hitting, hard-swearing, liberated young Canadian woman, a carapace I'd constructed to survive the very abrupt, very brutal, very sexually aggressive Canadian youth culture. I had had a difficult time, in those years, nurturing the dreamy, poetic, literary, artistic, romantic, soft other self in me that was synonymous with 'pushover.'

At this point in my life, after so many years of *çay*-drinking, older but no wiser, I try to come to terms with time passing, time passed, many calls for prayers, a multitude of eyes the colour of jazz and other musiques. I try to make that *vécu* a plus rather than a minus, an added element of attractiveness rather than a point one forfeits to the young and beautiful *poupées* who walk surely, easily on the street: a déjà vu of oneself, after all.

But the real privilege of age is finally becoming the age one wants to be, the age one feels to be, at any given moment. The Chinese 'me' demands the right to be respected at my age, the Canadian 'me' allows me to discuss my age openly, the French 'me' takes for granted that a woman is a gift of love at any age. The newly Turkish 'me' learns that if I get astonished looks here it's not for the cosmetic effect of my Asian skin, but for the fact that I have three beautiful grown children at the same time that I am a capable professional woman.

In Africa, although I had never been in a rural culture before, true native of Hong Kong high-rises that I am, I found a common ground, a place of togetherness, in the way that Ancestors and Spirits were said to be everywhere: in the baobabs, in the sands, in the whisper of the wind, in the glimmer of a river stone. Like many other times in my life, like an actress searching for the key to her role in her own life experience, I found the Elders, the Transmitters of Tales, the Ancestors. They helped me through this unlikely experience: in the Ancestors' sphere there is no North-South-East-West. All the Elders and the Ancestors occupy one big wooden shelter somewhere up in the sky, and they share one common language.

One of the stories I like to tell in France is that we—Asians or Chinese: I am always so poetically imprecise, knowing it's a trait the French love—respect age so much that one is not permitted to consume opium until he or she reaches the honourable age of sixty. (I have told this line so often that I have come to believe it this myself. Someone else can tell me if it is, in fact, true.)

Over three decades of tea-drinking in Rohmer's office, and three months of *çay*-sharing here in this at once familiar and strange city, I have seen that the full moon has the same sheen in Paris and Istanbul: the rabbit and the lonely Chinese lady of legend don't care if the moon is French or Turkish or even Kurdish. My angels have come and gone in the forms of mentors and lovers. Perhaps not yet eligible to smoke opium, I may have become another's angel.

You, who say to anyone who asks or cares to hear, how lucky you are that I've come into your life. You of those eyes that are sometimes sad and lost at moments in which I want to throw cultural correctness to the wind and hold you in my arms, to tell you in my language that life cherishes you. You most of all should know it has nothing to do with luck.

Mary Stephen, self-portrait (2005).

Karmic—what we say in the East, the very faraway and long-ago East—Karma: we owe each other something from another life. We owe each other loyalty, mutual encouragement, love and nourishment, imagination and dreams. We could have been mother and son, father and daughter, brother and sister, emperor and concubine, goddess and slave, lovers in other lives.

In others' lives. Karma. Mandala. Much has been given to me, hands have been stretched out, paths have been smoothed for me. In repayment of my debts to those who came before me, I extend my hands to you.

But this time, in due time, I may be the first to depart.

Tamam?

Istanbul, May 22nd, 2007.

REEL ASIAN, THEN AND NOW

ANITA LEE & CAMERON BAILEY

Toronto once had only one film festival, instead of over sixty. But starting in the late 1980s, a new politics of identity led directly to the creation of several new festivals, often organized around a specific ethnicity, orientation or artistic practice. As if possessed of prenatal wisdom, the Toronto Reel Asian International Film Festival waited out the fray to be born in 1997.

But the critical questions of the late '80s and early '90s still shaped Reel Asian, even as its own evolution helped push the debates forward. Anita Lee and Cameron Bailey are two veterans of those years. In conversation, they compare then and now, aesthetics and politics, black and Asian.

CAMERON BAILEY: Why Reel Asian? What was the inspiration, and what was the need?

ANITA LEE: I made my first short film (*Translating Grace*) in 1994 and was invited to Asian film festivals in New York, San Francisco and Chicago, where I experienced such a powerful sense of community. With one of the largest Asian populations outside of Asia, Canada still didn't have an Asian film festival, so I decided Toronto should be the place. I also sensed a new wave emerging in Asian diasporic filmmaking. There was a bumper crop of feature films that year, including Chris Chan's *Yellow,* Justin Lin and Quentin Lee's *Shopping for Fangs* and Rea Tajiri's *Strawberry Fields,* that treated identity politics with a youthful irreverence. That was exciting.

When was (the Toronto International Film Festival program) Planet Africa conceived? What inspired you?

CB: I first went to Burkina Faso in 1991 for the Pan-African Film Festival, called FESPACO. I saw a lot of films in open-air cinemas with bats flying overhead that week, but what I really remember is the sense of a tribe gathering. People came from all over the African world, including the Caribbean, the US, Europe, even an African film specialist from Japan. That was inspiring, and when the chance came to start a section at the Toronto Film Festival to bring more African films to Toronto, that week in Ouagadougou was always my model.

Also, I think we both remember Toronto going through the 'culture wars' in the late '80s and early '90s, when race and access were constant sources of debates. What was the landscape by the mid-'90s when you started Reel Asian, and what had you learned from those wars?

AL: I think the 'culture wars' had exhausted everyone. I was the executive director of the Canadian Filmmakers Distribution Centre and on the board of the Images Festival in the early '90s, so I had entered the 'wars' in their last phase. Race and access had polarized the film and video community so severely that true communication was impossible. There were some identity-based media groups like Black Film and Video Network and Full Screen still barely existing, but they were understaffed, underfunded and struggling with internal political strife. By 1996, when I wanted to start Reel Asian, I needed to convince artists from the community that it would be built on a completely different vision. For example, in order to convince Helen Lee and Keith Lock to join the board, I think I actually had to promise no internal politics or drawn-out meetings and that the organization would be a kind of an anti-organization that would be small and light on its feet. I mean, the words 'non-profit organization' and 'board meeting' were so not sexy, it wasn't funny!

CB: I found the culture wars both exhausting and exhilarating. There was definitely a power that we gained by organizing into groups like Full Screen and the Black Film and Video Network. We could call meetings with the arts councils, film funding agencies and other gatekeepers and they would have to come to the table. They'd have to at least listen to our concerns, even if we often got that very Canadian first response: 'We hear you. Calm down. We'll commission a study.'

I completely understand why so many people fighting the culture wars got tired of it. But I wish there'd been a clear victory instead of the cold war that followed. Anti-racism work got turned into 'diversity' programs, which meant we stopped talking about real racism in the film industry, even if it was still there. But I got tired like everybody else; after a while you don't want to walk out the door defending and defining your 'identity' every morning.

How did you come to define the 'Asian' in Reel Asian? Why not South Asia, for instance?

AL: Another thing I learned from the culture wars was how difficult it was to find common ground, so I wanted to define as small and specific a cultural space as possible. The key people of Reel Asian were all of East Asian descent so we decided that we should do what we knew best. Also, there was still Desh Pardesh then, which presented a South Asian film and video program; we didn't want to infringe. We started as a festival that programmed only Asian North American work and eventually became international.

But defining the 'Asian' in Reel Asian has been a continuous discussion from the beginning and evolves from year to year. One year, a programmer actually wanted to list all the countries that were included in our definition, and it became impossible to draw the line.

CB: And how hard was it to bring Asia together with the Asian diaspora? It strikes me that the films often have very different concerns and styles.

AL: Keeping a balance and continuing to highlight films from the Asian diaspora was the greatest challenge. As Asian films grew increasingly more popular here, we were faced with a wealth of Asian films we could show as compared to films from the diaspora. Asian filmmakers working in their native contexts had greater access and philosophical freedom to explore the world at large. Filmmakers from the disapora were often working in the margins and their work struggled with identity politics at some level. Ironically, Asian films were more accessible even for Asian Canadians than films from the diaspora, which were often more experimental or personal in nature.

CB: How conscious were your decisions about what direction Reel Asian should take aesthetically?

AL: Very conscious. Of course, the programming has evolved and expanded over the years, but there's always been a core focus on showcasing independent visions with an aesthetic edge, working outside of the mainstream. One of the founding objectives of the festival was also to provide a forum for Asian Canadian filmmakers.

It's been a tricky balance, though. If we were just box-office-driven, we could have easily focused more on international features, especially with the huge popularity now of films from South Korea, for example. But the Reel Asian board, which has always been pivotal in driving the overall programming vision, has been committed to creating a balance and a certain independent spirit, although that's such a broad term now it can mean almost anything.

CB: How much did you think about audience at the beginning?

AL: Embarrassingly little! Because I had experienced my first Asian film festivals in the US not as an audience member but as a guest filmmaker, I think my reasons for starting Reel Asian were completely one-sided. I focused more in the first year on bringing directors to the festival than on marketing the films to an audience. But fortunately there was an audience, a combination of an urban arts crowd, university students and young Asians. The audience has grown to include more industry people, a larger Asian audience outside the urban core, and a general festival-going audience, Asian and non-Asian, but filmmakers and young urban Asians in arts and entertainment remain our loyal supporters.

CB: There's been talk of a Korean woman mafia in the early years of Reel Asian. Can you put those rumours to rest?

AL: The rumours are absolutely true and we've tried our hardest to hold out but have finally been toppled by Deanna Wong, our first Chinese executive director! But it is interesting that all the other executive directors of the fest have been Korean women, including Caroline Sin, Sally Lee, Jane Kim and Shelly Hong, who worked with Caroline and me, and Grace Bai, currently our acting executive director. But I don't know what that means except we're tough and bossy. I think even more interesting is the fact that it's been all women! I'm sure there is something around Asian men having less freedom to explore non-traditional careers, but then maybe Asian women are just more rebellious.

Well, you have some very close Asian women friends and now you're engaged to one! What do you think?

CB: I can't even begin to comment.

More seriously, how do you go about building and maintaining a common Reel Asian community when there are so many differences in national origin, language, 'Canadianness,' class, gender, sexuality and all the rest?

AL: That's a tough question and requires a very complex answer to do it justice, but on a very simple level, I've found that the whole attitude toward identity has changed somewhat with the new generation of hybrid Asians. The culture wars have been fought and although the victory is not clear, as you said earlier, it's produced a more open climate that's given permission for irreverence, humour, dissension and difference within the community. There's greater tolerance and we can laugh at our own stereotypes.

CB: You must have had to answer the 'identity politics' question many times over the history of Reel Asian. Do people still question the need for an Asian film festival?

AL: I'm asked that question in an interview every year.

CB: How is that question different when it comes from Asians versus non-Asians?

AL: The non-Asian question is 'Why do we need one?' The Asian question used to be 'Will we always need one? Are we there yet?' But now I feel the question has vanished for most Asians. It's now more: 'Why wouldn't we celebrate if we can?'

CB: What moments are you proudest of?

AL: Often the small things: watching executive directors make their opening remarks, spotting a Reel Asian Award proudly mentioned on an emerging filmmaker's DVD, standing in a corner at an opening night gala and taking in a sea of young Asians partying. And our tenth anniversary festival really stood out for me. Maybe because I knew I was stepping off as chair of the board, but I felt a great sense of closure and an even greater sense of another beginning with an energy and a voice of its own.

CB: And at what point did you start thinking legacy? How long should Reel Asian last, and how did you go about planning for its future?

AL: Legacy. That sounds so grand. I think I was thinking much more pragmatically. I knew it was time for me to leave. On a personal level, I'd become a mom and a full-time producer at the National Film Board, and juggling it all was becoming impossible. But furthermore, I knew it would be best for Reel Asian. I've had enough experience with institutions big and small to know the dangers of a fixed leadership. I think cultural organizations in particular need fresh blood on a continuous basis and a full change of guard at key turning points to stay relevant. But I wanted to leave a well-built house with a full pantry. My husband's father died when he was only fifty-three. He had eleven kids, my husband being the tenth. One day his father built a shed in the back of the house and started to store tons of food. Then when the shed was full, he said he was ready to go, had a heart attack soon after and died. At the risk of sounding melodramatic, it was more that kind of planning. I wanted to leave Reel Asian with a sound infrastructure, stable operational funding and, most importantly, a group of committed people who owned it.

And how long should it last? That's a good question and I really don't have an answer. I think if you had asked me that ten years ago, I would've said when we've achieved our goals, and no longer needing to exist would be our greatest marker of success. But now it's not so singular. Now I actually think the 'Asian' in Reel Asian is not essentially about being Asian. It has an identity of its own. And maybe it should last as long as it can change and evolve.

SNAPSHOTS

NICOLE CHUNG

We hide ourselves instead of showing ourselves. And when we show ourselves, we're still hiding, hiding our defencelessness so we can stay safe.

Life is always ending. Every day we grow old. So before we're gone, use your camera. No one else will be here to tell your truth after you're gone—the hurt, the disappointments, the joy—tell everything, because after the world will be a little emptier without you.

Every day, someone puts another label on you, another mask, and to get through your day, you let it happen… so take that camera and use it. The truth brings us back to who we are. Show us how that kiss felt, how much you want them, how your heart breaks.

Your camera, your idea, your craft, and the collaborations—all these things will eventually fail you at some point or another. Start over. Tell us a story.

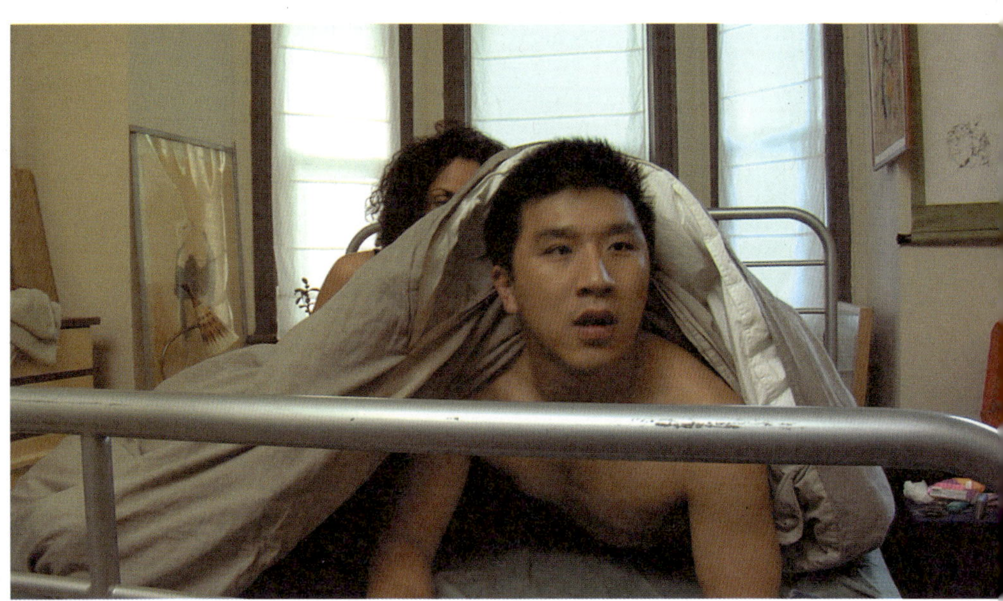

You might look at these pictures and think, that's not me! That's not a Chinese-Native Amerindian-Portuguese-Spanish-Dutch-Caribbean-Gaylord on screen! Actually, that's probably not what you think—what do you think?

Create your own truth. Don't feel guilty—revenge can be a virtue. How many of us have been mortified at the way other people have told our story?

It's not a crime to make something that people want to watch. It's also not a crime to make something people choose not to watch.

Don't hope that you will make a big film one day. If you live in hope, you will die in despair. Find your friends and borrow a camera. Don't regret something you failed to try. The world won't regret it—they don't know you.

If you love dogs, be 'the Dog Whisperer.' Don't try to be Stan Brakhage! If Cesar Milan tried to be someone who painted on celluloid, he would still be living on the street.

Find your way to your own home.

STILLS

PART IV

Wayne Yung, stills from *Field Guide to Western Wildflowers* (2000).

Wayne Yung, stills from *The Queen's Cantonese* (1998).

Michael Fukushima, still from *Minoru: Memory of Exile* (1992).

Linda Ohama, still from *Obachan's Garden* (2001).

Julia Kwan, still from *Eve and the Fire Horse* (2005).

RESOURCES

CONTRIBUTORS

NOBU ADILMAN is a Toronto-based artist who works with film, television and music. His most recent projects include making a food show entitled *Food Jammers* and the CBC-produced dramatic comedy *Shooting Stars*. More information can be found at www.nobu.ca and www.foodjammers.com.

JASON ANDERSON is a Toronto arts writer whose film criticism appears regularly in *Eye Weekly*, the *Globe and Mail* and *Cinema Scope*. His music columns for *Swerve* magazine in Calgary won a Western Magazine Award in 2006. He is also the author of the novel, *Showbiz*, and plays keyboards in the Two Koreas.

LEON AUREUS is an actor, writer and producer, and the founding artistic director of the fu-GEN Asian Canadian Theatre Company. Selected other theatre experience includes UNI Theatre's *Wild about Wilde* and *The Orange Fish*, and Tapestry New Opera Works' *The Iron Road*. His short film *Friends Like These*, which he wrote, directed and produced, premiered and was nominated for Best Canadian Short at the ReelWorld Film Festival in Toronto (2002).

CAMERON BAILEY is a writer, broadcaster and film programmer. For twelve years he has selected films for the Toronto International Film Festival, where he founded its Planet Africa section. Since 1988 he has reviewed film and video for Toronto's *Now* magazine and then CBC Radio One. His 2004 short, *Hotel Saudade*, made its US premiere at the Museum of Modern Art.

ROMEO CANDIDO is a Canadian-born Filipino; he grew up in Ontario and is now living in Manila. He has worked in theatre, music, documentary, short films, music videos, dance, performance art, television, radio dramas and feature films. To view his complete works, visit www.youtube.com/rofile?user=romeocandido. To listen to podcasts of his original music, visit romeocandido.podomatic.com.

ELAINE CHANG is a writer and professional culture vulture. Her publications include creative work and essays on Asian North American self-representation, film and popular culture, and feminist and postcolonial theory. She received the University of Guelph Central Student Association Award for Teaching Excellence in 2004.

LILY CHO is an Assistant Professor of English at the University of Western Ontario. Her research interests include work on diaspora, postcolonial studies, cultural studies, food culture, citizenship and affect. She is currently completing a book-length study of diaspora and Chinese restaurants in small-town Canada. Her publications include essays in *Essays in Canadian Writing* 85 (2006) and *Topia* 17 (2007).

NICOLE CHUNG is a Toronto-based artist of varied descent (Chinese-Guyanese-Spanish-Dutch-Amerindian). In 2006 she received the Best Canadian Female Short Award at the Inside Out Festival in Toronto. Her work has screened, among other places, at the Images Festival of Film and Video, Frameline San Francisco, the New York and Brazil MIX, and Toronto Reel Asian.

DAVID ENG is a Toronto-based director, actor, musician, writer and producer, and he has assumed all five roles on several of his film projects. His films have screened at many Canadian film festivals, including Reel Asian, the Worldwide Short Film Festival, ReelWorld and the NSI Film Festival. He is a member of the fu-GEN Asian Canadian Theatre Company, chair of the Screenwriters Committee at the Arts and Letters Club in Toronto, and the founder/moderator of the Toronto Screenwriters Network website.

ANN MARIE FLEMING is an artist and independent Canadian filmmaker (writer/producer/director/animator) who works in a variety of different genres (animation, experimental, documentary and dramatic), and whose work often deals with themes of family, history and memory. Born in Okinawa, of Chinese/Australian/Austrian descent, Fleming currently makes Vancouver her home.

RICHARD FUNG is a Trinidad-born, Toronto-based videomaker and cultural critic. A winner of the Bell Canada Award for video art and a Toronto Arts Award for media art, he teaches at the Ontario College of Art and Design.

MONIKA KIN GAGNON is the author of *Other Conundrums: Race, Culture and Canadian Art* (2000) and, with Richard Fung, *13 Conversations about Art and Cultural Race Politics* (2002) and *Territoires et Trajectoires* (2006). She is working on two archival projects on 1960s film, *Archiving R-69 and Imagining the Future: The Canadian Films of Expo 67*. She is Associate Professor in Communication Studies at Concordia University.

COLIN GEDDES is a film archivist, curator, journalist and consultant best known for programming the popular Midnight Madness selection at the Toronto International Film Festival. He also organized the long-running Kung Fu Fridays film series, showcasing martial arts and cult films from Asia. In 2003, he started Ultra 8 Pictures, an independent theatrical distribution company. For more information, visit www.ultra8pictures.ca.

KWOI GIN is 'Made in Hong Kong' and culturally disoriented in the Americas. This 'model diasporic' has lost close friends, survived poverty, attended art school, read some books, ran the streets and lensed the world. His fortune-cookie predictions include retiring a gentleman of leisure with a mah-jong parlour in a paradise somewhere in the diaspora with decent Chinese food, and devoting himself to the art of meditative probability after celluloid art becomes obsolete.

MIKE HOOLBOOM is a prolific, award-winning, Toronto-based filmmaker, writer and curator whose feature and short films have screened internationally at the Berlinale, the Toronto International Film Festival and many other venues and festivals. His written works include *Inside the Pleasure Dome: Fringe Film in Canada, Plague Years* and numerous essays. He is also working on the website, www.fringeonline.ca.

ALICE MING WAI JIM is an art historian, curator and writer. From 2003 to 2006, she was curator of the Vancouver International Centre for Contemporary Asian Art (Centre A) in Vancouver, where she organized numerous exhibitions of Asian Canadian and diasporic artists. Jim is currently Assistant Professor of Contemporary Art in the Department of Art History at Concordia University, where she teaches media art, curatorial studies and contemporary Asian and Asian Canadian art.

CHEUK KWAN grew up in Singapore, Hong Kong and Japan. After earning his masters degree in engineering in the US, he immigrated to Canada in 1976. In 1981, he co-founded *The Asianadian,* a magazine dedicated to the promotion of Asian Canadian arts, culture and politics. His first five films, *Song of the Exile, On the Islands, Three Continents, Latin Passions* and *Beyond Frontiers* are based on his *Chinese Restaurants* documentary series, and bring together his personal experiences, love of travel and appreciation of Chinese culture worldwide.

JULIA KWAN is a graduate of the Canadian Film Centre Director Program, where she made her award-winning short, *Three Sisters on Moon Lake.* She made her feature film debut with *Eve and the Fire Horse,* which had its world premiere at the Toronto International Film Festival and its international premiere at the Sundance Film Festival, where it won the Special Jury Prize for World Cinema. Kwan received the prestigious Claude Jutra Award for best first feature director and *Eve* garnered five nominations, including best supporting actor and actress, at the Genie Awards.

ANITA LEE is a producer at the National Film Board of Canada. Prior to joining the NFB in 2005, she was an independent producer for over ten years. She has worked with notable directors like Helen Lee and John Greyson, and her films have been nominated for Genie and Gemini awards in Canada and have screened at festivals worldwide. Lee is co-founder of the Toronto Reel Asian International Film Festival and served as chair of the board from 1997 to 2007.

HELEN LEE is an independent filmmaker whose films include *Sally's Beauty Spot, My Niagara, Prey, Subrosa* and *The Art of Woo.* She is a graduate of the University of Toronto, New York University, the Whitney Independent Study Program and the Canadian Film Centre. She was born in Seoul, where she currently resides.

KARIN LEE is a Vancouver-based media artist whose film and video works have been shown in cities around the world, including London, Toronto, Taipei, Leipzig and New York. Lee's works are about the effects of global displacement, the environment, feminism and the Chinese Diaspora in North America. Her family has lived in Canada for five generations.

KEITH LOCK holds an MFA from York University. A founding member of Toronto Filmmakers' Co-op, he has worked as Claude Jutra's assistant and Michael Snow's cinematographer. He has directed over twenty films and has received numerous awards. His film *A Brighter Moon* received a Gemini Award nomination for Best Short Drama. He has presented three films at the Toronto International Film Festival, including the experimental feature *Everything Everywhere Again Alive* and the dramatic feature *Small Pleasures.*

PAMILA MATHARU is a visual artist, educator and occasional curator. Her photo-based/media-art installations have been presented in galleries and her short films have screened in Los Angeles, Seattle, Turin and London, UK, as well as in Toronto, Ottawa and Sudbury. Born in Birmingham, UK, and raised in the Toronto regions of Rexdale, Concord and Willowdale, she currently lives in Parkdale. Currently in production is *Stains,* a short film about surviving suicide.

CHRISTINE MIGUEL has lived, laughed and loved film, television and music since she was a young girl listening to her dad's 8-track cassettes filled with Teresa Teng and Chinese opera while watching poorly dubbed kung fu films. A former entertainment editor for an Asian culture lifestyle magazine, and co-host for five years of an Asian pop radio show on CKLN 88.1 FM in Toronto, she has been featured on CBC Radio as one of the many voices in contemporary Asian culture. Currently she writes DVD reviews for Suite 101.com and produces POP 88 (www.POPcast88.com).

NGUYEN TAN HOANG is a Ph.D. candidate in Rhetoric/Film Studies at the University of California, Berkeley. His research interests include Asian American masculinity, queer experimental film and video, and the role of the racialized body in new media studies. His writings have appeared in *Porn Studies* (2004), *Vectors* (2006), GLQ (2007) and *positions* (forthcoming). He is also an experimental videomaker whose work has screened at the Museum of Modern Art, the Pompidou Centre, Anthology Film Archives and Pacific Film Archive, as well as numerous film festivals in the US and overseas.

MIDI ONODERA is an award-winning, Toronto-based filmmaker who has been directing, producing and writing films for over twenty-five years. She has over twenty-five independent short films to her credit; as well as her theatrical feature film, *Skin Deep.* In 2005, Midi completed a feature-length video shot in Japan, entitled *I have no memory of my direction.* She has just finished making a video a day for 365 days. Her films have been critically recognized and included in numerous exhibitions and screenings internationally.

MIEKO OUCHI is an Edmonton-based actor, writer and director who works in theatre, film and television. Her award-winning films, *Shepherd's Pie and Sushi, By this Parting, Samurai Swing* and *Minor Keys,* have played thirty festivals internationally and aired on CBC, Bravo! and W.

ALICE SHIH is a Toronto-based film journalist and a Reel Asian board member. She is a regular contributor to *CineAction* and *POV.* Her film criticism can also be heard on Fairchild Radio, the national Chinese radio broadcaster in Canada. She specializes in world films, especially films from Asia, the Asian Diaspora and Canada. She is also a filmmaker, writer and story editor.

MINA SHUM was born in Hong Kong. The award-winning writer/director has made three feature films, *Double Happiness; Drive, She Said* and *Long Life, Happiness and Prosperity,* as well as numerous short films, documentaries and installations.

MARY STEPHEN emigrated with her family from Hong Kong to Montreal and studied film-making at the Loyola College. She moved to Paris, France, in 1978 with an exchange Masters program and dropped out of to make her first feature and to begin a collaboration with French director Eric Rohmer: first as an assistant editor (under the woman who edited *Breathless,* Cécile Decugis), then, as it remains today, as his principal editor and co-composer. All the while she has made her own films, both narrative and documentary. She is currently editing *Gitmek* with Kurdish director, Hüseyin Karabey.

HO TAM was born in Hong Kong, educated in Toronto and at Bard College (Whitney Independent Study Program), and currently teaches at the University of Victoria. He works across diverse media and disciplines, including painting, video/film, photography, printmaking and public art, and has exhibited at the National Gallery, Walker Art Center, Pompidou Centre and the Museum of Modern Art. His feature film, *The Book of James,* received the Best Documentary Feature Award at the Tel Aviv LGBT Film Festival and the Outstanding Artistic Achievement Prize at OUTFEST, Los Angeles.

LORETTA TODD is an award-winning director, writer and producer who has been called 'one of Canada's smartest directors.' She is known for her powerful, visual storytelling and provocative writings. Todd is Métis/Cree, originally from Northern Alberta.

KHANHTHUAN TRAN was born in Vietnam and came to Canada at the age of three. After receiving a BFA at the Nova Scotia College of Art and Design, he hitchhiked across Canada, stopping in Ottawa to work as a sushi chef and videographer. His film *Vietnam, 1997* won the Emerging Local Artist Award at the 2005 Reel Asian Film Festival, and a new project, *Good Luck Counting Sheep,* is currently in post-production.

PHILIP TSUI is a crime fighter in Toronto who loves movies.

PAUL WONG's video career spans some thirty years. His work has been shown in exhibitions and festivals around the world, including London, Paris and Hong Kong, and has screened extensively at the Museum of Modern Art. Wong was instrumental in the founding of two artist-run centres in Vancouver: Satellite Video Exchange (Video-In) in 1973 and On Edge in 1985. He received the Bell Canada Award for video art in 1992 and the CHUM-NFB Expression Award celebrating diversity in the arts in 2003. His work is included in the National Gallery, MOMA and other major permanent collections.

SU-ANNE YEO is the Programming Director for the Vancouver Asian Film Festival and a Ph.D. student in the School of Communication at Simon Fraser University. Her doctoral research focuses on Asian Canadian and Asian American film cultures in comparative perspective. She is conducting research on Asian Canadian film and video, including experimental documentaries and Asian Canadian social movements. Previously, she has worked for public broadcasters in British Columbia and in Singapore.

IRIS YUDAI is an avid writer, crafter and photographer. She has been producing radio for the CBC since 1993. Her work has taken her from dinosaur-excavation sites in Saskatchewan to rice terraces in the Philippines. Currently she is the executive producer of CBC Radio's weekend arts and culture program *Definitely Not the Opera.* Iris is a proud member of Mentoring Artists for Women's Art (MAWA), and a passionate booster of all things Winnipeg.

WAYNE YUNG was born in Edmonton in 1971 to a Chinese immigrant family. As a writer, performer and video artist, he has explored issues of race and identity from a queer Chinese Canadian perspective. A curator, educator and collaborator, his first video was released in 1994, and his work has since screened at festivals around the world. After living in Vancouver, Hong Kong, Berlin and Hamburg, he is now based in Cologne.

ARTISTS' WORKS

Selected Films, Videos, Television and Other Relevant Works and Roles

Information provided by contributing film/video makers and/or distributors. All reasonable attempts have been made to provide accurate information. Abbreviations for distributors, where available, are in parentheses after entries; please see Distributor Contact Information on pages 348–349 for full details. Film/video credits are for writing and direction unless otherwise noted.

NOBU ADILMAN

Producer/Co-writer. *Shooting Stars.* CBC, 2006.
Co-creator/Co-creative producer. *Food Jammers,* Seasons I, II (also Co-host). 2006.
Prix Fixe. 2003.
Yoga, Man (also Producer and Co-writer). 2002.
I Pie (A Love Story) (also Producer and Co-writer). 2001.
Principal Actor. *Parsley Days.* Dir. Andrea Dorfman. Independent Film.
Actor. *Goldirocks.* Dir. Paula Tiberius. Independent Film.
Series Regular. *Trailer Park Boys.* Showcase. (VT)
Co-host. *Smart Ask!* Seasons II, III. CBC.
Reporter. *Play.* CBC.
Co-host. *Zed.* CBC.
Co-writer/Lead Actor. *Blowback.* 2001.
Writer. 'Cold Squad—Pretty Fly For A Straight Guy.' CTV, 1999.
Writer. 'Emily of New Moon—Command Performance.' Salter Street Films, 1998.

CAMERON BAILEY

Hotel Saudade. 2004. 24:22. (VT)

ROMEO CANDIDO

Smokey Mountain. 2007.
Spark (also Composer and Principal Actor). 2007.
Ang Pamana: The Inheritance. 2006.
Call My Name (also Composer and Principal Actor). 2006.
Snowhere. (also Composer and Principal Actor). 2006.
Directing Children/Fool for Love (also Composer and Principal Actor). 2006.
Rolling Longaniza. 2005.
Brother-hood. 2004.
Ron, R.N. 2004.
KUYA Medley. 2003. (RA)
St. Jamestown. 2003.
Dancers! Pick Up Your Bamboos! 2002.
North American Boy (also Composer and Principal Actor). 2002
Meditations for the Restless (also Composer and Principal Actor). 2001.
Lolo's Child (also Composer and Principal Actor). 2000.

Selected Theatre Credits:
Composer/Sound Designer. *SINKIL.* Factory Theatre Production. 2006.
Director/Musical Director. *The Romance of Magno Rubio.* Canadian Theatre Centre Production. 2005.
Composer/Sound Designer. *Banana Boys.* Factory Theatre Production. 2004/2005.
Writer/Performer. *Eat Away at Me* (various). January–May 1997.
Performer. *Miss Saigon* (Original Cast Member of the Toronto Company). Princess of Wales Theatre Production. 1993–1995.
Writer/Director/Composer. *Ako Ito* (various). May–September 1995.

NICOLE CHUNG

Wilson Leaves Home. 2007.
Sweater People. 2005. (VT) (RA)
Dream Machine. 2002. 9:30. (VT)
Bridge Passage. 2001. 6:00. (VT)
Breakbabies. 2000. 5:00. (VT)
Minor Crime. 2000. 1:40. (VT)
telefunk 8. 1998. 20:00. (VT)
Space Jazz Eros. 1997. 3:00. (VT)

DAVID ENG

Lust in Translation (also Producer and Principal Actor). 2005. (RA)

Sasha & Freddie (also Producer, Composer and Principal Actor). 2005. (RA)
The Summer Job (also Producer).
Producer/Composer. *David and the Conglomerate.*
Attraction (also Producer and Composer).
The Good Mother (also Producer).
...loop de loop de loop (also Producer and Composer).
Те Украинские Девчонки (Those Ukraine Girls). (also Producer and Composer).
Writer/Uncredited Producer. *Shaolin Delivery Boy.*
Perfect Pitch (also Producer, Composer and Principal Actor).
Rising Star! (also Producer, Composer and Principal Actor).

For distribution and information:
Big Film Shorts
100 S. Sunrise Way #289
Palm Springs, California, USA 92262
T: 760.219.6269
www.bigfilmshorts.com

ANN MARIE FLEMING

Running. 2007.
M.O.O.D. (My Obscure Object of Desire). 2006. (NFB)
The French Guy. 2005.
Room 710. 2005.
Making the Magical Life of Long Tack Sam. 2003. (NFB)
Magical Life of Long Tack Sam. 2003. (NFB)
Aguas de Março. 2002.
Blue Skies. 2002.
Heart. 2002. 7:30. (MI)
Lip Service: A Mystery. 2001. 45:00. (MI)
Hysterical: The Musical. 2000.
Drumstix. 1998. 4:30. (MI)
The Day My Grandfather Spied on Vladimir Ashkenazy. 1998. 5:20. (VT)
AMF's TIRESIAS. 1998. 4:30. (MI)
Great Expectations (not what you're thinking). 1997. 1:20. (MI)
Automatic Writing. 1996.
Pleasure Film. 1995.
I Love My Work. 1994. 4:30. (MI)
My Boyfriend Gave Me Peaches. 1994. 1:30. (MI)
I Love My Work. 1994. 4:30. (MI)
Pleasure Film (Ahmed's Story). 1994. 6:00. (MI)
It's Me Again. 1993. 46:00. (MI)
Buckingham Palace. 1993. 7:00. (MI)
La Fabula della bella Familia auf du World. 1993.
So Far So. 1992. 2:10. (MI)
Pioneers of X-Ray Technology (A Film about Grandpa). 1991. 15:00. (MI)
New Shoes: An Interview in Exactly Five Minutes. 1990. 5:00. (MI)
New Shoes. 1990. 75:00. (MI)
You Take Care Now. 1989. 10:00. (Also available with French narration.) (MI)
Drumstix. 1989. 2:00. (MI)
Waving. 1987. 5:00. (MI)

RICHARD FUNG

Uncomfortable: The Art of Christopher Cozier. 2005. 48:00. (VT)
Learning To Be Fabulous (co-directed with Tim McCaskell). 2004. 3:00. (VT)
Islands. 2002. 9:00. (VT) (VD)
Sea in the Blood. 2000. 26:00. (VT) (VD)
School Fag (co-directed with Tim McCaskell). 1998. 17:00. (VT)
Dirty Laundry. 1996. 30:00. (VT) (VD) (CA)
Out of the Blue. 1991. 28:00. (VT)
Fighting Chance. 1990. 29:00. (VT) (VD)
My Mother's Place. 1990. 49:30. (VD)
Steam Clean. 1990. 3:00. (VD)
Safe Place: A Videotape for Refugee Rights in Canada (co-directed with Peter Steven). 1989. 32:00. (VT)
The Way to My Father's Village. 1988. 38:00. (VD)
Chinese Characters. 1986. 22:00. (VT) (VD)
Orientations: Lesbian and Gay Asian. 1984. 56:00. (TW) (VD) (VT)

Selected Video Art/Installation:
'Installation with F-16s and Apache Helicopters and Rock Doves' (international video art

interactive exhibition). The Video Night in Jumoku, Tokyo Municipal Museum of Art, Japan, September 2005; Wynick/Tuck Gallery, Toronto (Images Festival), April 2004; The Wall, Chiyuko Gallery, Tokyo, March 2004; Artists against the Occupation. MAI (Montréal arts interculturels), Montreal, 2003.

'Unspeakable State of Sliced Bread' (collaboration with Christopher Cozier). A Space, Toronto, January 2004; No Country is an Island, Raritan Valley Community College, New Jersey, 2005.

'Threshold' (text in collaboration with visual artist Allan de Souza). Highways Gallery, Santa Monica, 1997.

Selected Publications:

'Re-Making Home Movies,' in *Home Movies: Excavations into Historical and Cultural Memories.* Eds. Karen Ishizuka and Patricia Zimmermann. Berkeley and Los Angeles: University of California Press, forthcoming.

Territoires et trajectoires 14 : dialogues sur l'art et les constructions raciales, culturelles et identitaires (co-authored with Monika Kin Gagnon). Montreal: Artextes Editions, 2006.

13: Conversations on Art and Cultural Race Politics (co-authored with Monika Kin Gagnon). Montreal: Artextes Editions, 2002.

'After Essay—Questioning History, Questioning Art,' in *Aboriginal Representation in the Art Gallery.* Eds. Lynda Jessup and Shannon Bagg. Hull: Canadian Museum of Civilization, Mercury Series, 2002.

'Future Past: 60 Unit; Bruise,' in *Magnetic North.* Ed. Jenny Lyon. Minneapolis: Walker Art Center, 2000.

'At Home at A,' on-line anthology, The Getty, Los Angeles, 1998.

'Uncompromising Positions: Antiracism, Anticensorship and the Visual Arts,' in *Suggestive Poses: Artists and Critics Respond to Censorship.* Ed. Lorraine Johnson. Toronto: Riverbank Press, 1997.

'Making Changes,' in *Naming a Practice: Cultural Strategies for the Future.* Ed. Peter White. Banff Centre Press, 1996.

'Colouring the Screen: Four Strategies in Anti-racist Film and Video,' in *Video re/View.* Eds. Peggy Gale and Lisa Steele. Toronto: Art Metropole and V Tape, 1996.

'Burdens of Responsibility, Burdens of Representation,' in *Constructing Masculinity.* Eds. Maurice Berger, Brian Wallis, Simon Watson (Dia Center for the Arts). New York: Routledge, 1996.

'The Trouble with "Asians,"' in *Whole Segments.* Eds. Monica Dorenkamp and Richard Henke. New York: Routledge, 1994.

KWOI GIN

The Last Falsetto. 2007.
Dark Sun; Bright Shade. 1993. 57:00. (CFMDC)

Director of Photography:
Uprooted. 2007.
Big City Broker. 2007.
The Asian Expats. 2007.
5 × 90: The Wake. 2005.
Chinese Restaurants: Beyond Frontiers. 2005.
Chinese Restaurants: Latin Passions. 2005.
Chinese Restaurants: Three Continents. 2004.
Chinese Restaurants: On the Islands. 2004.
Edge Codes.com: The Art of Motion Picture Editing. 2004.
Chinese Restaurants: Song of the Exile. 2003.
Broken Roots. 2003.
21 Hard Days Nights. 2001.
The Show. 1997.
Dirty Laundry. 1996.
Automatic Writing. 1995.
These Shoes Weren't Made For Walking. 1995.

MIKE HOOLBOOM

Fascination. 2006. 70:00. (CFMDC)
Public Lighting. 2004. 76:00. (VT) (VD)
In the Dark. 2003. 8:04. (VT) (CFMDC) (VD)
Jack. 2002. 15:00. (CFMDC)
Tom. 2002. 75:00. (CFMDC) (VD)

Imitation of Life. 2001. 20:00. (VT) (VD)
Positiv. 1997. 10:00. (VT)
Letters from Home. 15:00. (CFMDC)
Hey Madonna. 1997. 9:00. (VT)
Stormy Weather. 1997. 18:00. (VT)
House of Pain. 1995. 50:00. (CFMDC)

CHEUK KWAN

Chinese Restaurants: Beyond Frontiers. 2005.
Chinese Restaurants: Latin Passions. 2005.
Chinese Restaurants: Three Continents. 2004.
Chinese Restaurants: On the Islands. 2004.
Chinese Restaurants: Song of the Exile. 2003.

For distribution and information:
Tissa Films
www.tissa.com

JULIA KWAN

Smile (also Producer). 2007.
Laundry (also Producer). 2007.
Eve and the Fire Horse. 2006. (MM)
Three Sisters on Moon Lake. 2001. (WMM) (CFC)
10,000 Delusions (also Producer). 1999.
Prized Possessions (also Producer). 1997.
Inflamed (also Producer). 1993.

For additional distribution and information:
Fire Horse Productions
firehorsemail@gmail.com

ANITA LEE

Translating Grace. 1996. 20:00. (TW)

HELEN LEE

The Art of Woo. 2001. 95:00. (Odeon Films/ Alliance International)
Subrosa. 2000. 22:00. (CFMDC) (WMM)
Prey. 1995. 26:00. (WMM) (CFC)
My Niagara (also Producer and Co-writer). 1992. 40:00. (CFMDC) (WMM)
Sally's Beauty Spot. 1990. 12:00. (CFMDC) (WMM)

Video Art/Installations:
Writer. 'Casing About: The Picture of Dorian Gray.' 2005. Collaborative Gallery Project. Commissioned by Kitchener-Waterloo Art Gallery (www.kwag.on.ca/user_files/images/File/casting_about_feb_4.pdf)
'Cleaving' (video installation). 2002. Commissioned by Werkleitz Biennale.
'Star' (video). 2001. 3:00. Commissioned by the Liaison of Independent Filmmakers of Toronto (LIFT).
Media Artist. *The Yoko Ono Project* (theatre piece). Workshop for Jean Yoon's play.
'M. NourbeSe Philip' (video). 1995. 3:30. Commissioned by Toronto Arts Awards.
'To Sir with Love' (also Writer and Editor). 1992. 3:00. Collaborative Video Project by Shu Lea Cheang.

KARIN LEE

Oysters and Chocolate. 2006. 6:00. (VO) (VT)
Comrade Dad (also Producer). 2005. 26:00. (MI) (TD)
Sunflower Children. 2004. 20:00. (TD)
Made In China: The Story of Adopted Chinese Children in Canada (co-directed with Shan Tam; also Writer). 2000. 47:00. (MI)
Canadian Steel, Chinese Grit (co-directed with Jan Walls, David Choi and Julia Ningyu Li). 1998. 48:00. (MI)
Songs of the Phoenix—Voices of Chinese Women. 1997. 11:00. (TD)
My Sweet Peony (also Producer). 1994. 30:00. (MI)
Producer. *Dragonlines.* 1989. 30:00.

For additional distribution and information:
Top Dollar Sisters Productions Inc.
leesistr@telus.net

KEITH LOCK (LOCK KEI-KONG)

Re-Gifted. 2006. 1:00.
The Dreaming House. 2005. 6:00. (CFMDC) (RA)
The Road Chosen: The Lem Wong Story. 1997. 25:00.

Tough Bananas. 1997. 25:00. (CFMDC)
Small Pleasures. 1993. 86:00. (CFMDC)
A Brighter Moon. 1986. 25:00.
Chinatown. 1984. 25:00.
The Highway. 1983. 25:00. (CFMDC)
Jeannie Goes Shopping. 1981. 23:00.
Going. 1976. 5:00.
Parade. 1977. 5:00.
Everything Everywhere Again Alive. 1975. 72:00. (CFMDC)
Work Bike and Eat. 1972. 40:00.
Arnold. 1971. (CFMDC)
Base Tranquility. 1970. 6:00. (CFMDC)
Touched. 1970. 8:00.
Flights of Frenzy. 1969. 6:00.

For additional distribution and information:
Wondrous Light Inc.
174 Fulton Avenue
Toronto, Ontario M4K 1Y3
T: 416.429.7399

PAMILA MATHARU

Stains. 2006. 5:00. (work-in-progress)
Fracture. 2003. 4:00. (VT)
Haphazard. 2003. 3:00. (VT)

Selected Artist-curated Projects:
'Come Up To My Room.' Gladstone Hotel's Alternative Design Event. 2004–07. Toronto.
Toronto Alternative Art Fair International. 2004/5. Toronto.
'13.' 2003. Inside/Out Film & Video Festival, Toronto.
'runLomorun.' 2003. York Quay Centre/Harbourfront Centre, Toronto.
'video_flo.' 2002. Ed Video Media Arts Centre, Guelph.
'DocuLomo: The Toronto SuperSampler Challenge.' 2000. Gallery TPW, Toronto.
'Flomo.' 2002. Images Festival of Independent Film and Video, Toronto.
'Dirty Laundry and Parting Thoughts.' 1998. SAVAC, Propeller Gallery, Toronto.
'Against the Wall' (with Rachel Kalpana). 1995. Desh Pardesh Festival, Gallery 401, Toronto.

NGUYEN TAN HOANG

A Horse, a Filipino, Two Women, a Soldier and Two Officers. 2005. 7:20. (VO)
K.I.P. 2002. 4:00. (VO)
PIRATED! 2000. 11:00. (VO) (LC)
Crimson. 2000. 4:00. (VO)
Cover Girl: A Gift from God. 2000. 18:00. (VO)
The Calling. 2000. 8:00. (VO) (LC)
Forever Bottom! 1999. 4:00. (VO) (LC) (FL)
Forever Linda! 1996. 12:00. (VO)
Maybe Never (But I'm Counting the Days). 1996. 15:00. (VO)
7 Steps to Sticky Heaven. 1996. 24:00. (VO)
Love Letters 1 & 2. 1995. 4:00. (VO)
Forever Jimmy! 1995. 6:00. (VO)

Publications:
'I Got This Way from Eating Rice: Gay Asian Documentary and the Re-Education of Desire,' in *positions: east asia cultures critique*. Transnationalism and Queer Chinese Politics Special Issue. Eds. Lisa Rofel and Petrus Liu, forthcoming.
'Tony Leung's "Gorgeous Ass": Asian Masculinity in Jean-Jacques Annaud's *The Lover* (1992),' in *TransAsian Screen Cultures*. Eds. Chris Berry and Zhen Zhang. Hong Kong: Hong Kong University Press, forthcoming.
'Theorizing Queer Temporalities (An Electronic Roundtable),' with Carolyn Dinshaw, Chris Nealon, Annamarie Jagose, Roderick Ferguson, Lee Edelman, Judith Halberstam and Carla Freccero. *GLQ* 13.2–3 (Winter 2007). Queer Temporality Special Issue. Ed. Elizabeth Freeman.
'Objects of Media Studies,' in *Vectors: Journal of Culture and Technology in a Dynamic Vernacular 2.1* (2006). Ephemera Issue. Ed. Amelie Hastie.
'The Resurrection of Brandon Lee: The Making of a Gay Asian American Porn Star,' in *Porn Studies*. Ed. Linda Williams. Durham: Duke University Press, 2004.

MIDI ONODERA

365 Short Videos. (also Producer). 2006. Each 00:30–1:00 in length. (OA)
I Have No Memory of My Direction (also Producer). 2005. 77:00. (CFMDC)
True Believer. 2005. 00:36. (OA)
Nobody Knows (also Producer). 2002. 3:15.
Alpha Girls (with Tanya Mars, Louise Lilifeldt & Kinga Araya; also Producer). 2001. (VT)
Slightseer (also Producer). 2001. 3:20. English with Braille titles. (VT)
Nobody Knows (also Producer). 2001. 3:15. (VT)
Simulacra (in collaboration with Blair MacKinnon & David Oppenheim; also Producer).
Basement Girl (also Producer). 2000. 12:00. (CFMDC) (WMM)
Over 130 videos for M.A.C Cosmetics (also Producer). 1996–2007.
Skin Deep. 1995. 85:00.
A Performance by Jack Smith. 1992. 5:00. (CFMDC)
David Cronenberg—Artist's Profile. 1990. 3:50.
Heartbreak Hoteru (Writer/Producer Chris Bruyere). Face To Face Productions/CBC. 30:00.
General Idea—Artist's Profile. 1989. 3:50.
The Displaced View (also Executive Producer). 1988. 52:00. (CFMDC)
Then/Now (Writer/Producer Paul DeSilva). Toronto Talkies Inc./CBC. 30:00.
Ten Cents a Dance (Parallax). 1985. 30:00. (CFMDC) (MI)
Made in Japan. 2:30.
The Dead Zone. 2:30.
Three Short Films. 1984–85. (CFMDC)
Ville Quelle Ville. 1984. 4:00.
Home Was Never Like This. 1983. 9:00. (CFMDC)
Idiot's Delight. 1983. 5:00. (CFMDC)
The Bird That Chirped on Bathurst. 1981. 3:30. (CFMDC)

For additional information:
midionodera.com (as of January 1, 2008)

MIEKO OUCHI

Assembly. 2007. 15:00.
Paper Cut. 2005. 1:00.
Minor Keys. 2004. 42:00/54:00. (NFB)
SAIKI: Regeneration. 2002. 45:00.
Call Me Irresponsible. 1999. 5:00.
Samurai Swing. 1999. 19:00.
By This Parting. 1998. 13:00.
Shepherd's Pie and Sushi (also Producer). 1997. 45:00. (NFB)

For additional distribution and information:
Mad Shadow Films Inc./Irresponsible Films Inc.
7437–106 Street
Edmonton, Alberta T6E 4W1
m_ouchi@telus.net

MINA SHUM

Long Life, Happiness and Prosperity (also Executive Producer and Co-writer). 2002. (OF)
Drive, She Said. 1997. (SP)
Thirsty (also Producer). 1997. 20:00.
Double Happiness. 1994. (SP) (NFB)
Hunger. 1993.
Me Mom and Mona (also Co-producer). 1993. (MI) (CFMDC)
Love In (also Producer). 1991.
Shortchanged (also Producer). 1990.
Picture Perfect (also Producer). 1989. (MI)
'You Are What You Eat' (3-room immersive video installation). 2002.

MARY STEPHEN

Poem from South Africa. 1998. 54:00. (CFMDC)
Vision from the Edge: Breyten Breytenbach Painting the Lines. 1998. 56:00. (CFMDC)
In Transit, In Transition. 1997/98. 55:00.
Justocoeur. 1982. 90:00.
Ombres de soie (Shades of Silk). 1978. 59:00.
A Very Easy Death. 1976. 10:00.
Pawaganak: The Great Canadian Puberty Rite. 1975. 20:00.
Labyrinthe. 1974. 5:00.
Independence. 1974. 10:00.

HO TAM

The Book of James. 2006. 74:00. (VT) (FL)
In the Dark. 2004. 6:00. (VT)
Still Lives (In the Americas). 2003. 20:00. (VT) (VO) (VP)
She Was Cuba. 2003. 16:25. (VT) (VO) (VP)
Miracles on 163rd Street. 2003. 25:00. (VT) (VP) (VO)
The Books of James (earlier short version). 2002. 16:30. (VT) (VD) (FL)
My Memories of Me. 2001. 3:00. (VT) (VP) (VO)
Ho Tam Compilation 2001. 2001. 45:00. (VO)
Bus No. 7. 2001. 3:00. (VT) (VP) (VO)
The Loop. 2001. 18:00. (VT) (VP) (VO)
Ave Maria. 2000. 7:20. (VT) (VP) (VO)
Fine China. 2000. 8:30. (VT) (VP) (VO)
Hair Cuts. 1999. 8:00. (VT) (VP) (VO)
Cop Strings. 1999. 6:00. (VT) (VP) (VO)
dos cartas/two letters. 1999. 4:00. (VT) (VP) (VO)
Washington Heights Untitled. 1999. 4:00. (VT) (VP) (VO)
Matinee Idol. 1999. 16:30. (VT) (VP) (VO)
Dear Sis. 1998. 4:20. (VT) (VP) (VO)
99 Men. 1998. 3:00. (VT) (VP) (VO)
Pocahontas: TransWorld Remix. 1998. 4:20. (VT) (VP) (VO)
La Salle Primary. 1998. 5:00. (VT) (VP) (VO)
Season of the Boys. 1997. 3:30. (VT) (VP) (VO)
The Yellow Pages. 1994. 7:40. (VT) (VP) (VO) (TW)

LORETTA TODD

Kainayssini Imanistaisiwa: The People Go On. 2003. 69:36. (NFB)
Today is a Good Day: Remembering Chief Dan George. 1998. 44:00. (MI) (EE)
Forgotten Warriors. 1997. 51:00. (VT) (NFB)
Hands of History. 1994. 51:43. (VT) (NFB)
The Learning Path. 1991. 57:00. (VT) (NFB)

KHANHTHUAN TRAN

Good Luck Counting Sheep. Short animation. 2007.
Vietnam, 1997. Short documentary. 2004. (RA)

For distribution and information:
Khanhthuan Tran
638 Bathurst St.
Toronto, Ontario M5S 2R1
T: 416.531.4807
khanhthuantran@yahoo.ca

PAUL WONG

EAT: *Mainstreet Dinner for the Homeless*. 2003. 4:00. (VT)
Smash. 2002. 55:00. (VT)
RE-ACT (cd rom). 2001. 20:00. (VT)
Trieste. 2001. 5:00. (VT)
Refugee Class of 2000. 2000. 4:00. (VT)
Class of 2000: Unite Against Racism. 2000. (VO)
Born Under Surveillance (co-directed with Chris MacKenzie). 1999. 1:30. (VT) (VO)
Miss Chinatown. 1997. 4:30. (VT)
Blending Milk & Water—Sex in the New World. 1996. 26:00. (VT) (VO)
Temple of My Familiar. 1995. 20:00. (VO)
So Are You. 1994. 28:00. (VT) (VO)
Adrienne Clarkson Presents Paul Wong: Videoperspective. 1994. 60:00. (VT)
Paul Wong: Video Clips. 1992. 60:00. (VO)
Chinaman's Peak: Walking the Mountain. 1992. 25:30. (VT) (VO) (VT)
Dave (co-directed with Joe Sarahan). 1991. 89:00. (VO)
F.L.V.: Feature Length Video. 1989. 60:00. (VO)
Ordinary Shadows, Chinese Shade. 1988. 89:00. (VT) (VO)
Ordinary Shadows/Chinese Shade [2/2]. 1988. 44:00. (VO)
Ordinary Shadows/Chinese Shade. 1988. 45:00. (VO)
Body Fluid. 1987. 22:00. (VT) (VO) (VT)
Homelands (co-directed with Joolz and Western Front Video). 1986. 7:00. (VO)

Confused: Sexual Views (28 installments of varying lengths; co-directed with Gary Bourgeous, Gina Daniels and Jeanette Reinhardt). 1984. (VO) (VT)
Prime Cuts (WF) (co-directed with Western Front Video). 1981. 20:00. (VO) (VT)
Prime Cuts (PW) (co-directed with Western Front Video). 1981. 20:00. (VT) (VO)
4. 1978–80. 45:00. (VO)
in ten sity. 1979. 23:00. (VO)
Seven Day Activity. 1978. 13:00. (VO)
Asteroid (co-directed with Steve Paxton). 1978. 19:00. (VO)
Murder Research (co-directed with Kenneth Fletcher). 1977. 17:00. (VO)
7 day Activity. 1977. 13:00. (VT)
Mainstreet Tapes. 1976. 30:00. (VO)
Rotunda (co-directed with Valerie Hammer). 1976. 8:00. (VO)
Rock Garden. 1976. 10:00. (VO)
Gutter (co-directed with Valerie Hammer). 1976. 8:00. (VO)
60 UNIT: BRUISE. 1976. 4:30. (VT) (VO)
New Era Marathon (co-directed with Gerry Gilbert and New Era Social Club). 1974. 90:00. (VO)
Earth Works in Harmony. 1974. 32:00. (VO)

Video Art/Installations:
'Hungry Ghosts' (5-channel video installation). 2003. 33:00. (VT)
'Facing History (Chink)' (video-photo project). 2000–02.
'Facing History (Jig-a-Boo)' (video-photo project). 2000–02.
'Support Modeling' (installation). 1977. 10:00. (VO)
'Amass' (composite; co-directed with Valerie Hammer). 1976. 18:00. (VO)
'Amass' (video installation) (co-directed with Valerie Hammer and Performance Warehouse). 1976. 30:00. (VO)
'Subway Loop' (installation). 1975. 11:00. (VO)

WAYNE YUNG

Asian Boyfriend. 2006. 1:00. (VO) (VT)
Miss Popularity. 2006. 6:20. (VO) (VT)
Shan Xia Di: Under the Mountain. 2004. 38:51. (VO) (VT)
Postcard to an Unknown Soldier. 2004. 4:27. (VO) (VT)
My German Boyfriend. 2004. 18:29. (VO) (VT)
1000 Cumshots. 2003. 1:00. (VO) (VT)
My Heart the Travel Agent. 2002. 1:30. (VO) (VT)
Chopstick Bloody Chopstick. 2001. 14:19. (VO) (VT)
The Photographer's Diary. 2001. 26:16. (VO) (VT)
Field Guide to Western Wildflowers. 2000. 5:37. (VO) (VT)
Davie Street Blues. 1999. 12:35. (VO) (VT)
Search Engine. 1999. 4:08. (VO) (VT)
Angel. 1998. 4:47. (VO) (VT)
The Queen's Cantonese. 1998. 32:41. (VO) (VT)
Surfer Dick. 1997. 3:20. (VO) (VT)
Lotus Sisters. 1996. 4:59. (VO) (VT)
One Night in Heaven. 1995. 5:56. (VO) (VT)
Peter Fucking Wayne Fucking Peter. 1994. 4:31. (VO) (VT)

DISTRIBUTOR CONTACT INFORMATION

ALLIANCE ATLANTIS ENTERTAINMENT (AA)
121 Bloor Street East
Toronto, Ontario M4W 3M5
T: 416.967.1174
www.allianceatlantis.com/entertainment

CANADIAN FILMMAKERS DISTRIBUTION CENTRE (CFMDC)
401 Richmond Street West, Suite 119
Toronto, Ontario M5V 3A8
T: 416.588.0725
F: 416.588.7956
cfmdc@cfmdc.org
www.cfmdc.org

CANADIAN FILM CENTRE DISTRIBUTION (CFC)
2489 Bayview Avenue
Toronto, Ontario M2L 1A8
T: 416.445.1446 X 323
F: 416.445.9481
www.cfcdistribution.com/catalogue.php

CENTER FOR ASIAN AMERICAN MEDIA (CA)
346 Ninth Street, 2nd Floor
San Francisco, California, USA 94103
T: 415.863.0814
F: 415.863.7428
naata@naatanet.org
www.asianamericanmedia.org/rf_cms/index.php

DOMINO FILM AND TELEVISION INTERNATIONAL LTD (DF)
4002 Grey Avenue
Montreal, Quebec H4A 3P1
T: 514.484.0446
F: 514.484.0468
www.dominofilm.ca

EAGLE EYE FILMS (EE)
301—1645 Comox Street
Vancouver, British Columbia V6G 1P4
F: 604.687.4990

FRAMELINE DISTRIBUTION (FL)
145 Ninth Street, #300
San Francisco, California, USA 94103
T: 415.703.8650
F: 415.861.1404
www.frameline.org/distribution

LIGHT CONE (PARIS) (LC)
12 rue des Vignoles
Paris, France 75020
T: 33.1.46.59.01.53
F: 33.1.46.59.03.12
lightcone@lightcone.org

MONGREL MEDIA (MM)
1028 Queen Street West
Toronto, Ontario M6J 1H6
T: 416.516.9775
F: 416.516.0651
TOLL-FREE: 888.607.3456
info@mongrelmedia.com

MOVING IMAGES DISTRIBUTION (MI)
402 West Pender Street, Suite 606
Vancouver, British Columbia V6B 1T6
T: 604.684.3014
F: 604.684.7165
mailbox@movingimages.bc.ca
www.movingimages.bc.ca

NATIONAL FILM BOARD OF CANADA (NFB)
Sales and Customer Service (D-10)
P.O. Box 6100, Station Centre-ville
Montreal, Quebec H3C 3H5
TOLL-FREE: 800.267.7710
www.nfb.ca

OUAT MEDIA (OA)

488 Wellington Street West, Suite 100
Toronto, Ontario M5V 1E3
T: 416.979.7380
F: 416.492.9539
www.ouatmedia.com

REEL ASIAN FILMS (RA)

Reel Asian Films Online
Toronto Reel Asian International Film Festival
401 Richmond Street West, Suite 309
Toronto, Ontario M5V 3A8
T: 416.703.9333
F: 416.703.9986
www.rafilms.ca

SEVILLE PICTURES (SP)

147 St-Paul Street West, Suite 200
Montreal, Quebec H2Y 1Z5
T: 514.841.1910
F: 514.841.8030
www.sevillepictures.com/tempo/anglais/index.php?m=1

THIRD WORLD NEWS REEL (TW)

545 Eighth Avenue, 10th Floor
New York, New York, USA 10018
T: 212.947.9277
F: 212.594.6417
www.thirdworldnewsreel.org

VIDEO DATA BANK (VD)

112 S. Michigan Avenue
Chicago, Illinois, USA 60603
T: 312.345.3550
F: 312.541.8073
www.vdb.org

VIDEO OUT INTERNATIONAL DISTRIBUTION (VO)

1965 Main Street
Vancouver, British Columbia V5T 3C1
T: 604.872.8449
F: 604.876.1185
www.videoout.neocodesoftware.com/videoout

VIDEO POOL (VP)

#300—100 Arthur Street
Winnipeg, Manitoba R3B 1H3
T: 204.949.9134
F: 204.942.1555
www.videopool.org

VTAPE (VT)

401 Richmond Street West, Suite 452
Toronto, Ontario M5V 3A8
T: 416.351.1317
F: 416.351.1509
info@vtape.org
www.vtape.org

WINNIPEG ART GALLERY (WAG)

300 Memorial Boulevard
Winnipeg, Manitoba R3C 1V1
T: 204.786.6641
F: 204.788.4998
INFORMATION LINE: 204.789.1760
inquiries@wag.mb.ca

WOMEN MAKE MOVIES (WMM)

462 Broadway, Suite 500WS
New York, New York, USA 10013
T: 212.925.0606
F: 212.925.2052
www.wmm.com

IMAGE AND PHOTO CREDITS

pp. 10–11: Kevin Lim, photograph of a Toronto Reel Asian International Film Festival screening (2006).

p. 24: Midi Onodera, still from *Ten Cents A Dance (Parallax)* (1985).

p. 26: Richard Fung, still from *Dirty Laundry* (1996).

p. 34: Midi Onodera, still from *Basement Girl* (2000).

p. 35: Richard Fung, still from *Sea in the Blood* (2000).

pp. 36–37: John Cressey, photograph of Mary Stephen with her Bolex camera (1973).

pp. 48–49: Kwoi Gin, still from *Latin Passion,* dir. Cheuk Kwan (2005).

p. 66: Midi Onodera, still from *Down the Garden Path* (2006).

p. 67: Midi Onodera, still from *Skin Deep* (1995).

pp. 68–69: Richard Fung, still from *Sea in the Blood* (2000).

p. 70: Richard Fung, still from *Dirty Laundry* (1996).

p. 71: Kwoi Gin, still from *Three Continents,* dir. Cheuk Kwan (2004).

pp. 72–73: Kwoi Gin, still from *Beyond Frontiers,* dir. Cheuk Kwan (2005).

pp. 74–75: Kwoi Gin, still from *Three Continents,* dir. Cheuk Kwan (2004).

p. 76: Kwoi Gin still from *On the Island,* dir. Cheuk Kwan (2004).

p. 76: Kwoi Gin, still from *Three Continents,* dir. Cheuk Kwan (2004).

p. 77: Kwoi Gin, still from *Latin Passion,* dir. Cheuk Kwan (2005).

p. 77: Kwoi Gin, still from *On the Island,* dir. Cheuk Kwan (2004).

p. 78: Ajay Noronha, photograph of Kwoi Gin and Cheuk Kwan behind the scenes of *Latin Passion* (2005).

p. 80: Mina Shum, personal photograph (2007).

p. 97: Mina Shum, personal photograph (2007).

p. 98: Khanhthuan Tran, still from *Good Luck Counting Sheep* (2007).

p. 103: Pamila Matharu, still from *Fracture* (2003).

p. 109: Khanhthuan Tran, still from *Vietnam, 1997* (2004).

pp. 112–113: Ann Marie Fleming, personal photograph (2006).

p. 126: Leanne Poon, photograph of Paul Wong surveying traffic (2007).

p. 133: Christine Miguel, self-portrait with Paul Wong (2007).

p. 134: Ho Tam, still from *The Yellow Pages* (1994).

p. 145: Ho Tam, still from *Ave Maria* (2000).

p. 148: Ann Marie Fleming, still from *You Take Care Now* (1989).

p. 149: Ann Marie Fleming, still from *The Magical Life of Long Tack Sam* (2003).

pp. 150–151: Jeff Petry, production still from *The French Guy,* dir. Ann Marie Fleming (2005).

p. 152: Paul Wong, stills from *Hungry Ghosts* (2003).

p. 153: Paul Wong, stills from *Facing History* (2000–2002).

p. 154–155: Paul Wong, still from *Chinaman's Peak: Walking the Mountain* (1992).

p. 156: Ho Tam, still from *My Memories of Me* (2001).

p. 157: Ho Tam, still from *The Book of James* (2006).

p. 158: Ho Tam, still from *99 Men* (1998).

p. 160: Stan Trac, photograph of David Eng (2005).

p. 160: Pierre Gautreau, photograph of Leon Aureus (2005).

p. 172: Linda Ohama, still from *Obachan's Garden* (2001). Courtesy of the National Film Board of Canada.

p. 180: Mieko Ouchi, still from *Shepherd's Pie and Sushi* (1997). Courtesy of the National Film Board of Canada.

p. 181: Mieko Ouchi, still from *Shepherd's Pie and Sushi* (1997). Courtesy of the National Film Board of Canada.

p. 186–187: Mike Tompkins, photograph of Nobu Adilman on the set of *Trailer Park Boys* (2004).

p. 188: Photograph of Nobu Adilman at CBC Vancouver, guest co-hosting episodes of *ZeD* (2003).

p. 188: Caroline Mangosing, photograph of Romeo Candido (2006).

pp. 198–199: Eric King, Mao against CCTV image composited at the Banff Centre for the Arts (2005).

p. 200: Photograph of Karin Lee and Loretta Todd (2007).

pp. 210–211: Helen Lee, still from *Prey* (1995).

p. 214: Helen Lee, still from *Sally's Beauty Spot* (1990).

p. 223: Helen Lee, still from *The Art of Woo* (2001).

pp. 224–225: Kalli Paakspuu, photograph of Keith Lock and crew (1977).

p. 230: Robert Brouillette, photograph of tipi at dawn (1974).

p. 239: Keith Lock, still from *A Brighter Moon* (1986).

p. 242: Mieko Ouchi, still from *Shepherd's Pie and Sushi* (1997). Courtesy of the National Film Board of Canada.

p. 243: Anne Marie Nakagawa, still from *Between: Living in the Hyphen* (2005). Courtesy of the National Film Board of Canada.

pp. 244–245: Karin Lee, still from *Comrade Dad* (2005).

p. 246: Caroline Mangosing, photograph of Romeo Candido on the set of *Rolling Longaniza* (2005).

p. 247: Aeschylus Poulos, postcard for *I Pie (A Love Story)*, dir. Nobu Adilman (2001).

pp. 248–249: Helen Lee, still from *The Art of Woo* (2001).

pp. 250–251: Wayne Yung, still from *My German Boyfriend* (2004).

p. 252: Frank Dürrach, photograph of Wayne Yung (2007).

p. 252: Nguyen Tan Hoang, self-portrait (2007).

p. 261: Wayne Yung, still from *Miss Popularity* (2006).

p. 263: Wayne Yung, still from *Search Engine* (1999).

p. 264: Julia Kwan, still from *Eve and the Fire Horse* (2005).

p. 271: Julia Kwan, still from *Eve and the Fire Horse* (2005).

pp. 272–273: Jeanette Lerman, still from *Enemy Alien* (1975). Courtesy of the National Film Board of Canada.

p. 284: Kagan McLeod, poster art for the Kung Fu Fridays screening of *The Eagle's Killer.*

pp. 298–299: Rosette, photograph of Mary Stephen, Jonathan, Julien, Julie and Eric Rohmer at Cergy-Pontoise, outside of Paris (1989).

p. 304: Philippe Bridgeman, Alec MacLeod and Mary Stephen, still from *Labyrinthe* (1973).

p. 311: Poster for Mary Stephen's *Vision from the Edge: Breyten Breytenbach Painting the Lines* (1998).

p. 313: Mary Stephen, self-portrait (2005).

pp. 314–315: Kevin Lim, photograph of audience members before a Reel Asian Festival screening (2006).

p. 323: Phany Lun, stills from *telefunk 8*, dir. Nicole Chung (1998).

p. 324: Maurizio Chen, stills from *Wilson Leaves Home*, dir. Nicole Chung (2007).

p. 325: Maurizio Chen, still from *Sweater People*, dir. Nicole Chung (2005).

p. 328: Wayne Yung, stills from *Field Guide to Western Wildflowers* (2000).

p. 329: Wayne Yung, stills from *The Queen's Cantonese* (1998).

p. 330: Michael Fukushima, still from *Minoru: Memory of Exile* (1992). Courtesy of the National Film Board of Canada.

p. 331: Linda Ohama, still from *Obachan's Garden* (2001). Courtesy of the National Film Board of Canada.

pp. 332–333: Julia Kwan, still from *Eve and the Fire Horse* (2005).

Set in Arno designed by Robert Slimbach
and Flama designed by Mário Feliciano

Printed and bound at
the Coach House on bpNichol Lane,
October 2007

Edited by Elaine Chang

Designed by The Office of Gilbert Li

Cover image: still from Midi Onodera,
I have no memory of my direction (2005)

Coach House Books
401 Huron Street on bpNichol Lane
Toronto, Ontario M5S 2G5

T: 416.979.2217 / 800.367.6360
F: 416.977.1158

mail@chbooks.com
www.chbooks.com

toronto
reel asian
international film festival

Toronto Reel Asian International Film Festival
401 Richmond Street West, Suite 309
Toronto, Ontario M5V 3A8

T: 416.703.9333
F: 416.703.9986

info@rafilms.ca
www.rafilms.ca